It started with a
Kiss
in the
magical land of
Cornwall

It started with a
Kiss
in the
magical land of
Cornwall

Judith Lea and Philip Elliott

A CIP catalogue record for this title is available from the British Library

First paperback edition 2022
Book design by Publishing Push

Paperback 978-1-80227-762-3
eBook 978-1-80227-763-0

www.judithleaphilipelliott.com

www.instagram.com/judithleaphilipelliott

CONTENTS

Destiny

by Judith Lea

The Puppet Master was at play,
on one very sunny Cornish day.
He'd worked so hard to cast his spell;
would they get it together? Time would tell.
Fate had decided it was meant to be,
but reality decreed that neither was free.
What happened next in this magical land
are the stories and tales in the palm of your hand.
Written by us with 'warts 'n' all,'
there's no holding back: 'We're in freefall.'
From Newquay to Truro, Marazion to Hayle,
we've researched the history to tell you this tale.
Stories of life, sadness and joy
of the northern girl and the southern boy.
For one, a new life in Cornwall was the dream,
but when meeting each other, did they form a team?
Only 'we' and Cornwall know the answer to that,
not forgetting, of course, the Mousehole cat!

Chapter 1

The Dream

Judith:

I didn't want an ordinary life; I wanted more. I wanted to live by the sea, somewhere beautiful and wild, so I chose Cornwall, or did Cornwall choose me? I had only been there once in my life, but I had felt an instant magical connection, the rugged coastline pulled at my heartstrings, and the sea soothed my restless soul. It was the start of a love affair that I could not or would not ignore; all I had to do now was make these dreams come true.

So what makes a northern lass with a young family take such a step? I think fate called me. 1980 was a very difficult period (understatement of the year). My youngest son Antony had been diagnosed with a hole in his heart, and that's when he had the operation to correct the defect. He was seven years old, and remembering that time still fills me with abject fear. The day prior to the operation, I discovered that the boy in the next bed (to Antony) had died overnight; I was terrified now. Next, a nurse turned up, carrying a teddy bear with a plaster on its chest. She explained to Antony that he would have his chest cut open, his heart mended, and a plaster would be stuck on him like the teddy bear. I don't know who was more mortified: me or Antony. I put on a brave face, told him I would see him tomorrow, then I kissed him goodbye and left. How I drove home, I will never know; I couldn't stop crying.

The operation took twice as long as expected, which was followed by days in intensive care until, eventually, he was well enough to be discharged. I could finally breathe. He climbed into the back seat of the car, threw his Parka coat over his face and never spoke a word the whole way home. I thought the operation had mentally scarred him for life, and I believe that was the moment fate intervened.

The tiny seed in my head began to germinate; I wanted my boys to live a better, healthier life, and the dream of living in Cornwall slowly began to grow.

Philip:

I hadn't had a dream, but I was living one, probably one similar to what Judy wished for. It was June 1976, six years before Judy took those momentous steps to realise her dream – I know I'm a shit, but I do like to remind her that I moved to Cornwall before she did. For those of a similar age to *moi*, you will remember that 1976 was one of the best summers ever, and here I was, living in this magical place called Cornwall. Every day I had wall-to-wall sunshine from sunrise to sunset, the most fantastic beaches close by, and double-shift stints on the buses. Whilst thousands of holidaymakers spent their days on the beaches, I was fighting the helicopter downdraught along Eastern Green (as it took off on its way to the Isles of Scilly), attempting to give change from notes on the open top deck of the St Ives bus. Oh, what fun we had!

What was I, a boy from Welwyn Garden City, Hertfordshire (that's just north of London for those of you whose geography is on the iffy side), doing, living in Cornwall? I had never been to Cornwall; my family holidays had always been taken on the East Coast of England, at places such as Great Yarmouth or Walton-on-the-Naze. If I am totally honest, I didn't even know much about the place. I can only apologise to the people of Cornwall for, as I will repeatedly state, it is a magical place, and like the many thousands of tourists who visit each year, it affected me deeply.

The answer to the question, 'How had I ended up in Cornwall?' is simple. It is because my girlfriend Sam (soon to be my wife), whom I had met at teacher training college at Plymouth, lived there. After we both dropped out of college (I blamed the fifth-form girls at Southway Comp, and Sam's dad blamed me), I moved into her family home.

Sam was not Cornish; she was an Essex girl, the family being from Romford. They had moved down to Cornwall to take over the shop in a village called Wall, three miles outside of Camborne (see Jethro's appearance on the Des O'Connor show to find out why the train only stops at Cam'bn Wednesdays, Fridays and Saturdays). Attached to the shop was a house called 'Michigan Villa,' a grand name for a grand house: at least from the outside. The story goes that many moons ago, a Cornishman went to the state of Michigan in America. He made his money in mining before returning to his native homeland, whereupon he became lord of the manor and built himself a big house. It was (and still is) an imposing property, but in 1976, it was in dire need of modernising.

Whilst Judith was playing 'Earth Mother' in Sandbach (Cheshire), Sam and I were yo-yo-ing between the 'Villa' and a rental home (in Camborne), then the 'Villa' and our first mortgaged home (Wimpy Estate, Camborne), then back to the 'Villa.' Finally, we moved into our second mortgaged home in Lower Pengegon (edge of Camborne). Having an empty 'Villa' to keep moving into meant avoiding 'chains,' which was very handy. We moved into 22 Lower Pengegon in February 1982, the first of many coincidences between Judith and me. Indeed, I sincerely believe that fate was moving our 'pieces' along converging routes on the 'board of life.'

Judith:

Were we (the husband and I) brave enough to change our lives? It turned out we were. Did we have a proper, thought-out plan? Definitely not. We sort of winged it. The husband got a job offer as a manager of a store in Camborne (I know it's not exactly St Ives or Newquay, but baby steps ...), starting at the end of June 1982. We put our house up for sale (a sensible decision), but then I got slightly distracted when I took out my first-ever credit card and maxed it to the limit on a two-week trip to Disneyland, America (maybe not such a good idea). It was our first-ever flight/holiday abroad. Could we afford it? No. Would I do it again? Yes, in a heartbeat. We flew back home the day of Prince William's birth, the 21st of June 1982 (free drinks, yippee), and the husband left for Cornwall the following week to start his new job. I was to follow with the boys a month later (July 1982) after they broke up for the summer holidays. So it was all quite simple, really: just put the house up for sale, give up two well-paid jobs, say goodbye to friends and family and 'Bob's your uncle,' as the saying goes. Was it hard to leave? For me, definitely not. I had no parental family home; my mum had walked out on me (with my younger sister) when I was fifteen, my dad had a new wife and son, and believe me, I was way down the pecking order. Did I care? Not one jot. I had a husband I loved and two beautiful sons; I was twenty-eight and escaping to Cornwall to live my best life. The dream had become a reality.

I had given up my job at the local primary school, so, come leaving day, there were speeches and presents galore. It was a bit like being at the Oscars, only there was no red carpet, and I couldn't act (I had no idea I was so well thought of): all very nice and civilised. This was followed by a monster party/booze up at the Foden Social Club, organised by my fellow lady footballers, to ensure that I had a send-off I would never forget (I was their superstar midfielder. Eat your heart out, David Beckham). It was fabulous. I loved those girls: we had spent years partying and playing competitive football together in the UK, and we had also done a European Tour (very messy). So with all the goodbyes done, it was time to pack up my racing green (clapped-out) Riley Elf and start my 'New Life in the Sun' (I mean Cornwall).

Philip:

Um mm, 'A green car. Another coincidence?' Bear with me: whenever someone says this to me whilst on the telephone, my standard reply is, 'Certainly, as long as it is on a hot naturist beach.' Bear and bare – get it? Never mind, earlier I told you that I had met my girlfriend whilst training to be a teacher at the College of St. Mark & St. John (Marjons) in Plymouth (now known as Plymouth Marjon University: how grand a title is that?). Well, I hadn't applied to go to Plymouth; I had applied to go to Marjons in fucking Chelsea – a forty-minute train and tube ride from home – so I was well pissed off when told they had sold up the Chelsea site and were moving to Devon. I seriously considered applying to go somewhere else, but in the end, I decided that I did like the seaside, so I would give it a go. Boy, am I glad I made that decision, but I digress.

Being mobile is very important for a student, and in my first year, I only had a 90cc Honda motorbike; it wasn't cool (but was very cold during the winter). During the first summer holiday, I started to take driving lessons. I was working full time at my dad's factory and earning good money, a third of which my mum took for upkeep. That was the rule. I believe I may have inadvertently opened a can of worms, though, because my mum saw my payslips. I often wonder if it made her think about how much dad actually earned, compared to what he gave her for housekeeping, as he always seemed to have a wad of notes in his wallet. Yes, it was a very old-fashioned world back then. Anyhow, I bought my first car during that holiday, a green Morris 1000 (green Riley anyone?) for £5 off a family friend. It had over 200,000 miles on the clock. Although I had only had a few lessons, the driving instructor believed I was ready to take the test, so I applied and luckily got a cancellation date before returning to Plymouth for the new term. I will just add here that I have a poor test/exam history: my school report was full of the phrase 'a disappointing exam result,' plus, I struggle and stutter in pressured situations. Well, I only made one mistake on that first test, but mounting the kerb on turning left out of the test centre is not the way to get a pass, and I didn't.

That was 'Plan A' down the drain. Kelvin, a friend from college, came to the rescue for 'Plan B.' He could drive but did not have a car. If we could get my car to Plymouth, he could sit in with me, enabling me to gain more confidence/experience and give us mobility whilst there. Kelvin had a generous father (but not generous enough to buy him a car), who agreed to drive him from Reading (his home) to WGC. Then Kelvin could co-pilot me to Plymouth, but his dad had insisted we go via his home at Reading just to make sure everything was okay. Good job we did, because we discovered the dear old Moggie was using almost as much oil as petrol. We got to Plymouth without mishap, and just before Christmas, I took and passed a re-test using dear old Moggie. I also learnt some car mechanics via a Haynes Manual. Moggie's oil problem had been diagnosed, and I had to replace the 'cylinder head' using parts bought from the local scrap yard. No YouTube in those days, just the Haynes Manual and some second-hand spanners.

Being mobile meant we could explore the area around Plymouth when not studying, especially at weekends. We made many trips into Cornwall, beaching, sightseeing or pubbing. Was there an unseeing hand that was guiding me towards this mystical land? I now believe there was.

Moggie eventually died and was replaced with Moggie 2, a Morris 1000 van before that also died and was replaced with an Austin Cambridge estate, complete with a new-fangled 8-Track tape player bought at a local pop-up auction house. Then followed a Fred Flintstone (it had holes in the rear passenger's floor) Triumph 2000. This car lasted until I moved to Cornwall and got replaced with a Triumph Spitfire; when the weather was this hot, you just had to have a soft top.

I was in my first 'proper job' (a phrase I discovered that is used by the Cornish a lot, especially when describing a task well done), and Sam had landed a good job at the Redruth tax office. Travelling top down to the Penzance bus depot via the back lanes was, especially in the sunshine, marvellous, and I was happy in my work: we had lots of fun on the buses. The job was meant to last just three months, but I was there for eighteen. My first day was interesting; no one had warned me that the Cornish speak a foreign language, even when speaking English! My first day as a conductor, working out of the Penzance depot, saw me on the Penzance to St Just run. To my surprise, a lot of people boarded at the bus station (by the harbour), and when I asked the first old lady where she wanted to go – I had my fare stage book open in my hand because I knew I would have to look everything up – I did not understand her answer. It was gobbledegook, but she put thirteen pence into my hand, so I gave her a ticket for thirteen pence, as I did for virtually everyone else too. They were only going one stop, up the very steep hill that is Penzance high street (Market Jew Street, to be precise) to a place called The Greenmarket, right at the top of town. It took a while, but eventually, I tuned into the Cornish accent, which I absolutely adore.

Of all the tales I have to draw on about my times 'on the buses,' what follows is my drunken after-dinner masterpiece, written more soberly here. It involves the very popular tourist route out to Lands' End. The return trip to Penance includes going down, and back up, the long steep hill to Sennen Cove. With a packed bus, we started back up the hill, but after about fifty metres, we came to a halt. After a discussion with the driver, I asked all the men if they would mind getting off and walking up the hill with me. They were happy to do so, but unfortunately, it did not solve the problem: the bus would not move. In the end, I had to ask everyone to get off the bus, children included. I believe there may have been one or two disabled people left on board. Empty, the bus started to creep up the hill whilst I walked up the hill taking fares from the passengers. They all thought it was hilarious, and in my defence, I have to say that the fare to Penzance was the same from the top of the hill as it was from the bottom.

Judith:

The journey down to Cornwall took about twelve torturous hours. Antony never shut up the whole journey, and Shaun, my eldest, who hated travelling, slept for most of the trip, only waking up to throw up. This was much to the amusement of Antony, who took great joy in offering him food at every opportunity (brotherly love, not! - evil child). We eventually drove into the campsite at a place called Four Lanes, where the husband had secured an old twelve-foot touring caravan (delightful) for us all to live in until our house was sold.

Philip:

Four Lanes! Fuck, you had done your homework – not! If you ever want to know what it's like to live in a house, new or old, full of mould, then buy one in Four Lanes. Natives told me to avoid the place when I was looking for a house (sorry, Jude). However, Four Lanes had one thing in its favour; it was close to the best pub in the area: The Countryman. It was a very popular and busy place with a great landlord, plus it served up great grub. I was introduced to it back in the summer of 1978 after starting work for the South Western Electricity Board (SWEB). It was tradition for the office staff to go there for an extended lunch on Fridays. It would be fair to say that not a lot of work was done on a Friday afternoon (in our defence, we would normally have one of The Countryman's infamous puddings to help soak up the alcohol). Oh, yes indeed, those were the days.

Judith:

Bizarrely, I actually loved that caravan. I had no job (for the first time ever in my life), practically no housework, I cooked one-pot meals, and there was an excellent local pub called The Countryman. The only real negative was the location. Four Lanes was at the top of a very large hill on the outskirts of Redruth, and subsequently, on most days, it had a Cornish mist/drizzle hanging over it. Fortunately, the campsite had a launderette (no hope of pegging out washing), and you only had to drive the six miles down the hill to Portreath beach to find the sun. The boys and I spent most days on this delightful, pretty, local family beach. It had a beach with soft, fine sand, a harbour wall (which was once a busy port importing coal and exporting copper), and it was very popular with surfers and body-boarders who loved the high tides and big swells which allowed them to surf the harbour wall, or 'the Vortex,' as it was known. At certain tide times, it also had a cluster of rocks that filled up with seawater to become a natural swimming pool. A glorious place to watch the world go by and just dream the day away. The boys swam, caught crabs, made sand castles (with Cornish flags), and ate ice creams. All the things children should do at their age: it was exactly the life I wanted for them and me. I feel I should perhaps mention that the hill down to Portreath is very steep, and if you have an old car with a dodgy handbrake, like me, parking on such a hill might be free, but it is not ideal. I have had some very sweaty moments attempting to manoeuvre in and out of tight parking spaces, but your driving might be better than mine.

The summer holidays, like all things in life, came to an end. We upgraded into one of the static eight-berth caravans and, after our northern house sold, we decided to buy a general store and off-licence at Lower Pengegon (convergence alert!); it seemed like a good idea at the time. This meant that once the contracts were exchanged, we needed to fetch the contents of our northern house down to Cornwall. This is where I need to fill in some background with regard to my sister, who is three years younger than me. When she was little, she had this amazing skill of being able to hold her breath until she passed out, which she regularly did whenever I upset her so that I would get into trouble big time. Needless to say, we didn't always get on that well. The passing out, plus the fact that she would lend me money and then charge me interest at the age of ten, didn't endear her to me.

When the parents divorced, we didn't see each other for a number of years and only reconnected in our early twenties. She was still a horror. She had a job at the vet's and lived in the flat above the premises. Once, she deliberately left a dead German Shepherd (dog) for me to fall over (in the dark) when I visited her after work; she laughed her head off when I screamed in horror. She had decided to come down on the train to visit us, and the plan was for her to return home with us in the 7.5-tonne lorry we had hired to collect our house contents. The husband was a man with a plan, and as he drove into the campsite and hit the air brakes, the lorry sort of jumped like a scalded cat sideways across the car park. My sister and I just looked at each other. Still, the deed had to be done, so the five of us piled into the vehicle like lambs to the slaughter (only 305 miles to go). The first hundred miles to Exeter, on the single carriageway road, were terrifying. He nearly killed four cyclists, and every time he braked, one of the boys cracked their head on the dashboard. When he overtook another vehicle, the sister and I just shut our eyes, too terrified to look. As he pulled into Exeter services to go for a pee, the rest of us just sat on the pavement in abject horror; we seriously discussed taking the train the rest of the way as we feared for our lives (sounds dramatic, but it was). However, lack of money and the need to show solidarity, plus the fact the next 200 miles were all motorways, meant we had probably done the worst part of the journey. Fingers crossed that would be the case, and credit to the husband in his new Tonka toy. He did get better at driving it, but we were ecstatic to arrive in one piece. It was 'job done' for my sister, but I still had to repeat the journey in reverse with all our worldly goods (God help me).

Philip:

Oh dear, what travails poor Judith endured to realise her dream. Meanwhile, winding the clock back five years, what a life I was leading (sorry, gorgeous). I loved everything about Cornwall (we won't talk about lunchtime and half-day closing, quaint though it was), the golden sands, the rugged cliffs, surrounded by sea, and of course, the laid-back population. Is this what paradise was like? It must have been close. Going down to Gwithian (the nearest beach, and what a beach) for an after-dinner swim before sitting watching the sunset was just indescribable. I will try to paint you a picture of Gwithian Towans beach, to give it its proper name.

Blasted by the breeze off the Atlantic, the magnificent beach at Gwithian Towans is always a colourful scene of windsurfers on the water, land yachts (called blokarts these days) on the beach and kites in the sky. Backed by sand dunes tufted with wild grass, at low tide, there is a vast amount of sand to enjoy and large areas of rock pools are uncovered, which are great for kids to explore. There is golden sand all the way from Godrevy Lighthouse to the River Hayle (which is far too treacherous to attempt to swim across – on the other side of the river are Lelant, Carbis Bay and St Ives). The beach is a favourite destination for surfers as the constant swell coming in from the ocean provides good all-year-round conditions. Common seals are a regular sight near the beach, and the area is a breeding ground for colonies of seabirds such as guillemots, razorbills and cormorants. As I said, it's magical.

Chapter 2

The Reality

Judith:

Well, God was on my side. A few prayers to the traffic angels must have done the trick because we arrived safe and sound at the doors of our first Cornish property. It was November 1982, and we were now the proud owners of Pengegon Stores (not the most original name) in a place called Lower Pengegon, which was a mile from Camborne town centre. We had never run our own business and knew nothing about the area, but we had youth and optimism on our side. It was a large shop with family accommodation: four bedrooms, a garage, an acre of land to the rear, and was a lot cheaper than the house we had sold 'Up North.' The words 'Location, Location, Location' should have permeated our brains, but they didn't. The shop overlooked some waste grassland, and there were a few private cottages and a large council estate nearby. I wouldn't say it was ugly, but compared to the likes of St Ives, it was. I was very naïve; I expected my customers to buy nice healthy food, but the reality was they predominantly bought bread, cakes, cigarettes and booze. Plus, as most of them bought on 'tick' until payday (benefit day), I couldn't see us buying a second home in Spain anytime soon. We had barely moved in when the bailiffs started to turn up chasing money from the previous owners, but we had rose-coloured specs on and never noticed the red flag. When we moved in, what we didn't know was that Pengegon was considered to be one of the most deprived areas in Cornwall. However, ignorance is bliss, and all I needed to do was learn how to play shop. At its basic level, it was just buy stuff, sell stuff, and repeat. What took me longer was learning the dialect; I really struggled to understand what the customers were asking for. Pointing and guessing – a bit like being in a foreign country – initially worked until I tuned in to the accent.

Philip:

You were lucky they bought anything at all from a 'foreigner,' i.e. non-Cornish.

Judith:

The shop initially needed a damn good clean, and that's coming from me with poor eye-sight and an aversion to housework. Thankfully, our first visitors were my mum and her husband. They rode in like the cavalry, rolled up their sleeves and shifted the grime, leaving me to focus on the shop. This was a major miracle as, historically, our 'mother and daughter' relationship was not good. I always felt second best once my petite compliant sister came along. I shouldn't have been surprised when my mother did a moonlight flit with most of the house contents (and my sister) when I was fifteen, but I was. The relationship plummeted even more when she found out I was pregnant. The words 'Money can buy abortions' have never left my head. Needless to say, she didn't attend my wedding and never saw her first grandchild until he was six months old, but a lot of water has passed under the bridge since then. Were we close? Perhaps not, but I was thankful for all her help. We were up and running; I just needed to make sure I didn't trip up.

Philip:

Writing this book has highlighted just how much fate and coincidence have played a part in our relationship. Sam and I moved into Lower Pengegon nine months before Judith and her family and I am nine months younger than Judith.

Let me pause the story for a moment whilst I give you a little background about my journey to Lower Pengegon and my roles at SWEB. I started in 1978 as a clerical assistant in the Engineering Planning Department, where my telephone extension was 343. Well, being a 'Southerner,' and combined with my stutter, I used to have the piss taken out of me when answering the telephone because of my problems in stating my name and extension number. After two years, I had the chance to escape Ext 343 and became the clerical assistant in the Transport Department (Pool was a big depot, and there were over two hundred and fifty vehicles and items of plant to be maintained). It was an intense role, but I loved it and the guys who worked there, except for Ken, the gofer. It was because of Ken that I learnt to drink tea and coffee without milk. When he made the drinks for the afternoon tea break (the canteen provided the morning tea and butties), he often used milk that was curdling, and I was not a fan of milk anyway.

Another two years passed, and then in 1982, my boss suggested I apply for the vacant clerical position in what was known as the Cornwall Control Room. It was shift work and paid substantially more than what I was on. It was an attractive proposition, but I was concerned about my stutter.

Ah, the stutter. I am not a confident person, and the cruelty of my peers at school, followed by the (often not deliberate) insensitive actions and words of adults, especially work colleagues, inevitably made the issue worse, not better. When asked the question 'How would I describe myself?' one word always came to mind: 'Wallflower.'

The online Cambridge Dictionary has two definitions for the term wallflower. The first is for a plant: 'a pleasant smelling garden plant that has yellow, orange or brown flowers which grow in groups.' The second is for a type of person: 'a shy person, especially a girl or woman, who is frightened to involve herself in social activities and does not attract much interest or attention.' Perhaps it should say, 'especially a girl or woman and Philip Elliott,' for the second definition is me to a tee, though friends and work colleagues will often dispute this fact. This may be because once I have got to know someone, in the right circumstances (generally under the influence) and with years of experience of coping with my shyness and stutter, I have been known to turn into a chattering, flirtatious, life-and-soul of the party type person. But, I hasten to add, it is not very often.

My stutter started in high school and is still with me today, but I have at least learnt how to manage it. As I grew older, I learnt a trick, especially in interviews: it was a bit like playing chess and looking several moves ahead. If I could see a word coming up that I knew I would have a problem with, e.g. any word beginning with 'm' or 'p' (yes, that's right, I have spent my whole life struggling to tell people my name), I would take a detour with my thought process, and answer questions avoiding the troublesome word. It worked most of the time.

And so back to 1982. The money for the vacant role was very tempting, but would I be able to cope? The job involved operating a radio (analogue in those days, so everyone tuned into the frequency being used could hear you: a daunting thought for a 'wallflower'). Plus, not only did one have to answer the telephone to engineers, but outside of office hours, when the switchboard staff went home, all the incoming calls from the public (all of Cornwall) came through to the Control Room. Crikey! All of those unpronounceable Cornish places and surnames. For once in my life, I went for it and got the job. Yes, I did have lots of pronunciation and stuttering moments, but at least it gave my colleagues and the customers plenty to laugh at, and I learnt to laugh along with them. At least with the phonetic alphabet (on the radio), 'M' and 'P' are 'Mike' and 'Papa' rather than Mmmmmmother and Phphphphilip.

Judith:

The husband went to work, the boys settled in school, made new friends, and I ran the shop. The words 'open all hours' still haunt me today. I went from being a goddess in the kitchen to Wendy Craig in the TV show Butterflies. The number of meals I burnt whilst serving customers ran into the hundreds; I could see the dread on the family's faces the minute I dished up a meal (utter nightmare). As if I hadn't got enough to do, the husband decided he wanted a German Shepherd Dog, and I am so glad I embraced that idea. If we were going to have one, I wanted the best we could find, so we did some research, bought one with a good pedigree (unlike Phil, who bought the runt of the litter) and called him Ross.

Philip:

Here's another coincidence. Whilst living in the Wimpey house, Sam and I decided to get a dog, and for me, there was only ever going to be one type: a German Shepherd (oh dear, I had the same taste as the husband!). It proved a harder task than anticipated because GSD (German Shepherd Dog) puppies were expensive, and we were poor. Then we spotted an ad from a farmer near Truro where the advertised price was just within our reach.

However, by the time we telephoned, there was only one left. Yes, Judith, she was the runt of the litter, the one nobody wanted. We fell in love with her on the spot, and, runt or not, she did have a decent pedigree, not that that meant anything to us. We had scraped together the asking price of £50 and exchanged it for a six-month-old Alsatian, not quite the cute young puppy we were hoping to get. We were Blake's 7 fans, so we named her Kali, after one of the show's female characters.

We had made a bed up for her in the dining room and left her shut in there for the first night. We were greeted in the morning with a room full of stinking cow pats and a sad-eyed dog that was hard to tell off. Sadly, this scenario repeated itself every night, and we were struggling to find an answer. She was getting lots of long walks and love, but every night was the same. In frustration one evening, I moved her bed into the shed and left her there for the night. In the morning, she was sitting outside the back door waiting to be let inside the house. She had chewed her way through the shed to escape. What to do? As a final resort, we put her bed on the landing outside our bedroom, and hey presto, she was happy, and there was no more mess.

Judith:

Ross was gorgeous. We enrolled him at a GSD class in Redruth that did obedience and show training, and we made a lot of new friends. We became part of the Cornish GSD showing fraternity, attended open shows in and out of the county, and did very well. I always thought I was better at showing lark than the husband, so twelve months later, I bought my own dog and named her Rega. We were now a family of six, travelling to dog shows whenever I could get cover for the shop. Beach, what's a beach? Never saw it: what had happened to the dream?

When the financial reality did set in, I knew I needed to make changes to the business. You don't need two brain cells to realise that 10p on a loaf or 15p on a packet of cigarettes wasn't going to work. The most expensive item we sold was a bottle of Calor gas, and that's what the poor people of Pengegon heated their houses with. My profit was £2 per bottle, so it made sense to start a delivery round (with a delivery charge), which took off big time. I took the orders, and the husband did the deliveries once he got home from work.

I had made friends with a couple up the road who ran a clothing store in Camborne, and they were also struggling financially. Jean and I decided to buy some antiques and collectables from the local auction room and resell them at local antique fairs. We did particularly well selling at Truro. The extra cash came in very handy as we both had families to feed.

Truro is the only city in Cornwall and is famous for its ancient, cobbled, narrow streets with stunning architecture featuring Gothic and Georgian styles. It has a magnificent cathedral with three spires (one of only three cathedrals with three spires in the UK). Construction started in 1880 and was completed in the late Victorian era. The name, Truro, is claimed to come from the Cornish word 'Tri-ver,' which means three rivers. The Kenwyn, the Allen and the Tinney rivers all come together to form the Truro river. Roger Taylor (drummer for the legendary rock band Queen), although born in Norfolk in 1949, actually grew up in Truro: what a lucky boy.

Whilst buying antiques, I noticed the household goods were cheap to buy. We already had a delivery round for Calor gas, and a very large shop, so why not move into selling furniture and electricals? Stroke of genius (even if I do say so myself). So that's what I did, and what fun it was going to auctions a few times a week. It got me out of the shop, it was exciting, and I made loads of money. It was around this change-over period when my dad and his new family called in to see me. We had always been close, but when my mum left, we were living together, but not living together. I had a new boyfriend, he had a new lady friend, and one Saturday morning whilst he was at work, it was left to me to show prospective buyers around our home. They loved it and bought it, so technically I made us homeless. I was sent to live with strangers whose house my dad was purchasing, and he lived with the new lady friend's grandad. It might have all worked out in the end, but I was pregnant and hormonal and fell out with the strangers, so one day, I walked out. I was then moved to live with new 'strangers' until the house purchase went through about a week before I got married. I'm sure if it were these days, social services would have had a field day.

My wedding day didn't quite go as planned because my dad's new lady friend (who, unbeknown to me, was also pregnant with my stepbrother) sliced her left hand as we were preparing food for the wedding. I have no idea why I was sent to A&E with her, but I was. When she needed to change gear in the car, she shouted 'Now' as she put her foot on the clutch pedal, whilst I manually moved the gear stick accordingly. Pretty impressive when I had never driven a car in my life. I had no time for pre-wedding nerves, even though I was having a full Catholic wedding ceremony (six weeks of training with a drunk priest: ghastly) in the church at the end of the road. As I walked up the aisle on my dad's arm, I noticed the church floor had a crack running the full length up to the altar: there had been subsidence overnight. Was it a sign, was I blessed or cursed? I never did live in the new house. The husband and I lived with his elder brother and then with his gran until we bought our first home. I was like a nomad. It had been a hectic seven months; I had lived in five houses, fallen head over heels in love, got pregnant, passed six O level examinations and married. Phew, what a rollercoaster!

Philip:

Speaking of weddings, some might say that there were also 'signs' at mine (that little shit pulling the strings was having some fun, I guess). Sam and I were married in Gwinear Parish Church on Saturday 26th, March 1977.

It was a small wedding with only immediate family and a few college friends, including Kelvin, who was my best man. The service was notable only for the fact that when kneeling down at the altar, everyone could see how much I paid for my shoes, as the sticker was still on the sole. And then there is the matter of our wedding car. Ahh, the wedding car: a shit-brown Morris Marina hire car. It was meant to have been my brother's white 264 Volvo: there are many tales to tell regarding David and cars, but this one goes like this. David and his wife had my mum and dad in the back and were travelling down to Cornwall the Thursday before the wedding. David is not a slow driver. After three hundred miles of driving on motorways and dual carriageways, the road after Bodmin Moor is a single carriageway, but if clear, it is still fast. Then one has to slow down for the Chiverton roundabout (a few miles outside of Truro and just before the Camborne/Redruth bypass starts). The car in front of David slowed down, but David did not. The vehicle he rear-ended was shunted across the roundabout and into the garden of a house, stopping just short of the house itself. Luckily only minor injuries and shock were suffered, but of course, and more importantly, we now had no wedding car. This is the reason why the colour of the hire car matched my suit.

If the shoe label and wedding car episode were not signs regarding our future married life, then the honeymoon added several more. Thanks to my brothers (trying to jack up the car before we left), the rear exhaust box fell off before we had gone five miles (of a nine-hour drive to Norwich). Suffering from carbon monoxide poisoning and sleeping on a boat on a tidal river, I spent my first night of married life spewing my guts up. Official consummation of the marriage would have to wait. In our week on the Norfolk Broads, we built a snowman on Great Yarmouth beach, sunbathed, and on our final night, whilst tied up alongside Norwich City's football ground, were set drift in the middle of the night by yobbish Man United fans. Did they not know we were also fans? Was this marriage doomed?

Judith:

Everything was going pretty well. I had made a good friend called Debbie; she had a Rottweiler (called Kissy) and a Great Dane. She also had a red Reliant Robin three-wheeler to drive them round in because she only had a motorcycle driving licence.

'The dogs wouldn't wear a motorbike helmet,' she said.

She looked like Dell Boy, bombing about everywhere. She also had a son of Antony's age and an alcoholic husband for good measure, so there was never a dull moment. Her dog, Kissy, and my dog, Rega, both hated other dogs, so we stupidly decided to attend dog training sessions at Redruth with a guy called Roger. The first night we threw both dogs in the back of my car, praying they wouldn't kill each other. On arrival at the hall, we sat three seats away from everyone else, as the sight of any other dogs set ours off into a snarling frenzy. I spent most of the time on the floor trying to stop Rega from attacking the other dogs, and Debbie was doing no better. Roger assured us he could fix any issue, so we persevered for a number of weeks. We watched grown women cry as he lambasted them; I found it very entertaining. Debbie got more stressed as the weeks went by, and one night she gave Kissy a tranquilliser to calm her down. Roger proudly demonstrated the 'Sit, stay and come' procedure with Kissy, stating any dog could change its behaviour with training and what a shining example Kissy was. I was shaking with laughter as Kissy sat with a spaced-out look in her eye, and it took all her concentration even to stand up. That was it; we weren't going again. Debbie couldn't handle it, and I couldn't be bothered.

Philip:

In 1983 a work colleague of Sam's mentioned to her that her daughter's dog had just given birth to a litter of (GSD) puppies and did we want one. This time around, we had the first choice. When you hold a six-week-old puppy in your hand, you will never want to let it go, but we had to wait until it was twelve weeks old before taking Deyna home. Oh yes, you Blake's 7 fans will be aware that Deyna was another female character from the show. Deyna's first night with us was a little different to Kali's. I know one is supposed to show tough love and ignore the puppy's whimpering on the first night, but I gave in. I made a bed up on the floor in the dining room and slept with her cuddled up to me.

That hand of fate is definitely playing with the Judith and Philip pieces, moving us closer together, but keeping us apart at this stage. Sam's work colleague's daughter used to take her dogs to the Redruth GSD class (yes, the very same one that Judith and the husband attended) and recommended it to us. As I wanted to do a 'proper job' with Deyna, we went, but to me, it was too orientated towards showing. So, in the end, I took Deyna to another Redruth class, this one recommended by a colleague at my work. Of course, I do not need to tell you that this class was run by Roger who was good but very scary. Like Judith, I have witnessed him reduce grown adults to tears; he would probably be called a bully these days, but he was effective. He was ex-military and shouted like a parade ground sergeant major. He would always say his job was not to train your dog – that was the owner's job. His job was to train the owner how to train the dog, and he expected to see improvements each week. This meant you had to do homework, i.e. work with your dog during the week. Eventually, my shifts got in the way of homework once too often, and, being fearful of another balling, I missed a session. Then two, and, like Judith, I never went back, though I did keep working Deyna myself whenever I could. Neither Jude nor I can remember seeing each other at Roger's class, but that doesn't mean to say we weren't there at the same time, especially as we both recall seeing him reduce a woman to tears.

Judith:

My old friend Linda rocked up to visit, complete with her two children and the kitchen sink. She had been my best friend when I lived 'Up North'; like me, she had one sick child and a son called Shaun but spelt Sean. We had worked at the factory where my husband was the manager, and the CEO was dating my sister (I had introduced them). He eventually became my brother-in-law. Our job was to pack weed killer into bags, and we looked like Homepride flour monsters after every shift. She remembers her dad using the weed killer in his garden, and nothing grew there ever again. We joke to this day that working in this factory is why we are both bonkers.

She was having marriage issues, not really surprising as she used to leave him notes to say, 'Your tea is in the oven.' It would be a loaf and a tin of beans. By the time she rocked up, I had a few rescue GSDs that I retrained and re-homed as and when I could. We still laugh today when we talk about her visit; she went to get some liquorice allsorts out of the jar on the shop shelf and found it full of ants (gross). When her daughter sliced her finger cut/stick pasting, one of the rescue dogs took great pleasure in licking up all the blood. Maybe she might have stayed in Cornwall had those two incidents not happened, but after a few weeks, she decided to go home and face the music. She arrived to find that her husband had thrown all her belongings out of the marital home, so she ended up moving back in with her parents. Unfortunately, we lost touch with each other. Living at opposite ends of the country, life just got in the way. It would be twenty years before fate intervened, and we reconnected.

Philip:

Cor blimey O'Reilly! Ants in the liquorice allsorts; in my case, it was ants in the Sugar Puffs! My college friend Jonathan was visiting us at the Wimpey house and loved his cereal; only this particular morning, there were more ants than puffs in the packet. As Judy stated, gross!

Judith:

Oh, happy days, then the bubble burst. The husband lost his job when the shop he worked at closed, and he started playing out with the wrong people. Drugs and other women also came into play. It was a recipe for disaster, but I never saw the writing on the wall: I was too busy trying to pay the bills and keep a roof over our heads. I had taken my eye off the ball, both regarding my husband and my children: a big mistake.

Chapter 3

First Contact

The Puppet Master:

It is time to up the ante. I shall allow both horses to visit the same water hole but not allow them to drink.

Judith:

You don't always see what's staring you in the face. On the surface, life just keeps rotating: work, eat, sleep and repeat. I was certainly unaware I was a 'salmon swimming upstream;' I was far too busy juggling family and business demands. Of course, it wasn't all work and no play (I still didn't see the sea, mind), and as a family, we were all still very sporty. Having played football and volleyball 'Up North,' I joined the local Illogan ladies team (boring), whilst the husband and boys joined local football teams, and we all joined the local volleyball team, which suited us fine. We were like expats: we had moved to the seaside for a better life, but still did in Cornwall what we had done 'Up North.'

Philip:

I played football, but Cornwall played rugby. Sam's dad had been a sporty person, claiming that he had once been a coach of the Olympian athlete, Mary Rand (who I seem to remember was also living in Cornwall at the time, but don't quote me on that). He had a few contacts in the area, so when I looked to join a football team, he put me in touch with Helston FC, with whom I had a trial. Helston were supposedly one of the better football sides in the area; however, everything is relative. It became apparent after a few games that the standard of football was way below what I was looking for and was used to. I was not enjoying my time with Helston and eventually left them. Instead, I ended up being a big fish in a small pond (well, I was several years older than most of them) after accepting an invitation from a work colleague to come and join Trevu FC. They played in a league several tiers below Helston, but it was fun.

Judith:

Having joined the (dog) showing scene, the next step was to breed our own superstar dog; so, from our first litter of puppies, we kept the best and called him Bill. Well, if he was going to be the next Cornish Champion, we needed to feed him the best food. Apparently, in the dog show world, that meant raw tripe, and that's how my third money-making business accidentally started. Tripe is the stomach of a cow. I found a local abattoir that was happy to sell me one, and I returned home triumphantly with a smelly black bin bag. It was gross; it needed to be washed clean, hand minced, and then packed into a plastic bag and frozen. It was simple, cheap and nutritious dog food. You know the expression, 'Where there's muck, there's brass,' well that applies to tripe. Before I could blink, due to my doggy connections, I was collecting up to twenty stomachs a week; everyone wanted it: demand sometimes outstripped supply. I spent bloody hours washing, mincing and bagging up the horrible stuff; I hated that tripe, but each stomach made me around £15 net profit. We needed the cash now that the husband had lost his job and couldn't, or didn't want to, get another. He preferred to play 'car repair man' with a dodgy guy across the road. So, when this stranger came into the shop one day and asked for tripe, my first thought was, '*Bloody hell, another stomach a week to process.*'

But, smiling nicely, I said, 'Just a minute,' went into the back to get a crowbar, returned, opened the large chest freezer, hacked out twenty bags, took his money and waved him on his merry way.

Later, I learned his name was Phil: the Puppet Master had engineered 'First Contact.'

Philip:

Tripe; what a thing to have in common, but yes, Sam and I fed Kali on tripe as recommended by the farmer's wife from whom we had bought her, and she thrived on it. The only issue was sourcing the tripe. There was only one place we found locally that supplied it, a farmer's supply shop up the hill on Falmouth Road in Redruth. All was hunky dory until the day I arrived to find it closed. The business had gone bust. Now what to do?

Riding to the rescue came Sam's elder sister when she told us, 'There's a lady up the road from you who sells tripe.'

How on earth she knew that fact is a mystery to me, was the Puppet Master at play? Whatever, I will forever be grateful to her for sharing that information.

So, bag in hand, off I trot the four hundred yards up the road to find the shop and the lady. I found the shop, but it was closed. The sign on the door said it was open! Looking around, I could not find any sign with opening times on it. All very frustrating indeed for a Sagittarian.

After several more failed attempts, I arrived one day to find the shop door open. At last! Entering, I was greeted by a shop full of second-hand furniture, and then this bouncy, smiling woman with a ponytail appeared from out the back to ask if she could help me.

Establishing that she did indeed sell tripe in pound-weight bags, she said, 'How much would you like?'

I asked her to fill my bag up. Then I watched, bewildered, as she picked up a three-foot-long crowbar and walked over to a large chest freezer. Opening it up, she climbed onto it, stood precariously with a foot on the front side edge and started to whack the crowbar into the innards of the freezer. WTF!? After a short while, she jumped down, asked for my bag, and proceeded to fill it up. I paid and left bemused, wondering who this crazy smiling woman I had just met was.

Judith:

Despite all my money-making schemes, money was very tight. The Calor gas was obviously a winter earner, the furniture was predominately spring and autumn (holiday let turnover time), but summer was a disaster. We were struggling and decided to get out before the bailiffs started to come after us. We sold the business, and friends offered us a vacant shop with tiny living accommodation in Camborne as an interim solution until we got back on our feet. So, in the autumn of 1986, we moved in lock, stock, barrel and broke. Changes were needed if we were going to get back on the housing ladder. The husband had to get a job (which he did), and my job was to keep the furniture business going to tick us over. The shop gave me breathing space; no more tripe, Calor gas, food or booze to worry about. For once, I could be a salmon floating on my back going downstream. My energy levels were low; I was in recovery mode. Christmas was looming, we were sort of homeless, and my marriage was on the ropes. It was a good job that I had friends.

Philip:

Thanks to Sam's sister and the mad lady in the shop, I had a source for tripe. This meant Kali and Deyna were happy, but my marriage was less so. I struggle to remember the exact reason we decided to move from Pengegon, but I think Sam and I both recognised we were moving apart; the love and lust had waned. As the cliché goes, we were sharing the same house but living separate lives. There was no animosity, but neither of us had the strength to state the obvious nor take action about the situation. With hindsight, we should have gone our separate ways when we sold the Pengegon house. Instead, we moved into 'the shed' that Sam's elder brother had vacated in the garden of his (and Sam's) parent's property in St Hilary (he had extended and converted the garage into living accommodation for himself). It was during our time living in the shed that we finally accepted the inevitable: our marriage was over. We had grown apart, and neither of us could see a future together; therefore, I made arrangements to move out. Luckily for me, a colleague at work owned a chalet at Hayle Towans that he and his wife kindly allowed me to move into until I could find somewhere permanent to live. So in September 1986, I moved into the chalet and stayed there for three months. The weather was glorious, and I had a fabulous time. I could have lived there permanently, but a) I did not own it, and b) local bye-laws restricted occupancy to ten months of the year.

I had to find somewhere to live that was both cheap and close to work. There was only one choice, really: the Tolvaddon Estate in a Dean 'kit house.' So-called, at least by me, because in my first role at SWEB, I used to sit at a desk next to a window and watch lorry after lorry, loaded with prefabricated wooden bits of houses, go past, heading towards the new Tolvaddon Estate being built by a developer called Dean. I used to think that it was one estate I would never want to live on, but life and fate had dealt me this hand.

Judith:

Ah, the stranger, 'Phil.' Well, I remember him being a returning tripe customer, chatting about dogs and volleyball, and him fetching his football team to learn to play the sport. We played in a hall at Ludgvan (two and a half miles north-east of Penzance) on a Sunday evening and at the Carn Brea Leisure Centre on a Thursday night. I had previously played when I lived 'Up North' and was quite happy to teach Phil and his band of merry-men how to do it. When living at Four Lanes, The Countryman pub had become our local. The landlord was very supportive of community sports, and he kindly agreed to sponsor our volleyball team, so we competed under the name of The Countryman.

One of my favourite fixtures was against the women's team from Royal Navy Air Station Culdrose. The base is located just outside Helston on the Lizard Peninsula and is one of the largest helicopter bases in Europe, with 3000 personnel. It generates £100m into the local community every year.

If you are ever lucky enough to be in this area, then a visit to Kynance Cove, which is owned by the National Trust, is a must. The contrast between the cove's white sand and the dark red and green serpentine rock is a breath-taking sight.

Back to volleyball and visiting RNAS Culdrose. Just getting into the airbase to play was exciting, with its layers of high security, and once inside, the facilities were second to none. We were even allowed to have a swim in their pool after the fixture, and occasionally we won the game (icing on the cake). 'For me, the Sunday and Thursday night training sessions were just a bit of fun, and Phil and his gang added to that. He was the blond guy with twinkling blue eyes who taunted me under the net. I liked the banter, he made me laugh, and he had great thighs (but I kept that thought to myself).

Philip:

When the football team that I played for, Trevu, decided to enter a Superstars-type (the 1970s and 80s TV programme) multi-sport team competition at the local leisure centre, one of the sports was volleyball. A game none of us knew anything about, but I knew a lady who did. Yes, that's right, the tripe lady! During a conversation with the tripe lady - (Fuck! Did I, Mr Wallflower, actually make small talk with someone? Must've done, 'else how would I have known she played volleyball? Amazing!). Anyhow, I now knew her name was Judy. Not only did she play volleyball for a local team, but she actually helped run it, and yes, we were welcome to come along to learn how to play. About nine of us did, and most of us stayed long-term as we loved the game so much.

Had the Puppet Master started to mix chemistry into his or her little game? I ask because I have vivid memories from those early volleyball training nights. Memories of looking under the (volleyball) net at this vivacious, sparkling, smiley-faced, bright-eyed vision of female sensuality dressed in her vest top and short shorts. I could not take my eyes off her, and my memory says she smiled at me every time she caught me looking at her. Was I flirting? If I was, it was not knowingly: I do not have the confidence to do that. Judy will tell you that, as far as she was concerned, I was definitely flirting with her. Was this the water hole?

Judith:

Christmas was looming, I was still technically homeless, and my marriage was hanging on by a thread: I needed something to look forward to. Out of the blue, the 'nice' man Phil with the sexy thighs invited the husband and me to a birthday/housewarming party: happy days. On arrival, the place was bouncing. Loads of people were there, the house looked amazing, Phil was beaming from ear to ear, and I'm sure he made a pass at me as he took my coat. I hadn't been to a party since my Foden Ladies' footballing days. I felt like I had been let out of jail. I had forgotten how much fun it was to let your hair down, so for one night only, I forgot all my problems, danced, drank and socialised as if my life depended on it. The party was huge fun, but the house was a wreck by the end of the night. If you are ever the last to leave a house party, trust me, do not say, 'If you need a hand to clean up in the morning, give me a call.' Bad idea! You are drunk, likely to have a hangover from hell, and besides, who in their right mind would ever take you up on such an offer?

Imagine my shock when the phone rang at stupid

o'clock the next morning, and it was Phil asking if I was up to giving him a hand to clear up. Why does the word 'Yes' come out of my mouth? I seriously need to learn 'No.' I am such an idiot.

Philip:

In my days back at Welwyn Garden City, and then at college in Plymouth, I had been used to attending house parties. This was something that did not seem to occur in Cornwall, at least not in our circle of friends and work colleagues. Therefore, Sam and I held parties in our home, and even if I do say so myself, they were very successful events. So when I separated from Sam, it did not stop me from putting on a party at my two up, two down, end-terrace Tolvaddon house, where I was now living on my own. It was to be a joint birthday (18th December) and housewarming party. As my new house was basically a shit hole, it meant I could go overboard with decorations.

I filled the bath with water and put in red food colouring along with a blow-up shark. The living room was cleared of all furniture - there wasn't a lot. I parked my car, a BMW 5 Series, in the backyard and made it comfortable for the dogs as they would be in it for the duration of the party. The TV and Hi-Fi remained. I used the sails from my newly purchased sailing dinghy to hang on the walls, together with various blow-up animals and birds, combined with Christmas decorations hung from the ceiling and walls. The kitchen decoration was minimal; hey, it's the store room for the booze, right?

My memory fails me with regard to my bedroom. Was it decorated or not? I don't think so, as it was used as the cloakroom.

Once people started arriving, I never had a drink for the rest of the night. This had nothing to do with trying to be a (sober) host in control. I was already pissed as a newt because I had been drinking vodka all day long, in effect having my own private party, i.e. loud music playing whilst preparing the house.

I do remember Judy arriving as she asked me, 'Do you have an ashtray?'

I replied, 'Yes, it's the rear garden!'

In those days, I was a very anti-smoking person. She also claims that when I offered to put her coat on my bed (with all the others), I stated that 'I would rather put her on it!' I have no memory of this. Uncontrollable flirting? One for the psychologists. Invites had gone out to Trevu Football Club, the Countryman Volleyball Team, colleagues at work (SWEB) and West Cornwall Athletic Club, and the party was a roaring success.

During the party's final stages, two things happened. First, and I have no memory of this, I apparently drop-kicked a large box of loose crisps, scattering them all over the living room. Second, as Judy was leaving, she uttered the immortal words that I am sure that she regrets to this day.

'If you need any help to clear up in the morning, call me.'

The Puppet Master:

Move the pieces together, move them apart. Move the pieces together, move them apart.

Philip:

At first light, on the morning after the party, I'm loading the dogs into the car to take them for a long walk on the beach. Normally I would do that and, upon returning, tackle the mess. I am quite happy clearing up myself; I just put the music on and have a drink to hand, no problem. On this morning, and do not ask me why, for I do not know the answer (unconscious attraction or fate again, or that fucking Puppet Master pulling more strings?), I telephoned (landline) Judy, a married woman, to take her up on her offer to help me clean up. What was I thinking? Anyhow, only she can tell you what she thought about being woken up (what to her, I now know she would consider as the middle of the night) to be asked to come and clean. Had I put her in a position she could not get out of? Probably. Was there some unknown force working on her as there was on me? Almost definitely. Whatever, she agreed I could pick her up on my way back from the beach.

Judith:

Having stupidly agreed to help with the cleaning, I was up, dressed and very hungover when Phil arrived to pick me up. He was his usual chirpy smiley self, with no sign of a hangover. My head was banging, and I felt sick every time I bent down. I must have hidden it pretty well as either he didn't notice or was too polite to say how awful I looked. I still, to this day, have no idea why I offered to help, and I am still gobsmacked that he picked me up. Did I fancy him? Well, that morning, I definitely did not. My main priority was not throwing up.

The Puppet Master.

If only they would open their eyes. Three hours alone in the house, and not one advance made. Jesus! Move the pieces apart again.

Judith:

Whilst living at the shop, out of the blue, I got a call from my friend Ellie, asking if she could come and stay for a while. She had been my best football friend from 'Up North' and had worked for years for the Ministry of Defence. Her department had been disbanded, and she was at a crossroads in her life. She was a blast from my past and a breath of fresh air: a very direct northerner who didn't mince her words. We had the odd fallout on the football field, usually because I had 'dropped' (tackled) one of the opposition who she fancied, and once, we actually came to blows. We had done the Foden ladies' week away on the European tour, playing in Belgium, France and Austria. What a wild time, but as they say, 'What happens on tour, stays on tour,' and that is still our mantra. We (the husband and I) were desperately trying to get a house deposit together, and he had persuaded me to do some topless modelling. Ellie was horrified. She did try to talk some sense into me, but it was easy money, and I couldn't turn it down. We both (husband and I) knew our marriage was on the rocks, but I was still of the belief it could survive.

Philip:

It was now 1987, and I was playing volleyball on a regular basis. It was to my new (volleyball) friends that I turned when faced with a dog care problem. When Sam and I separated, we didn't share the kids (we didn't have any) as most separated/divorced couples may do: we shared custody of the dogs. Sam had them on weekends because she worked a normal Monday to Friday 9 to 5 job, and I had them during the week because I worked shifts, so it was easier for me.

I would give them a good walk before starting a morning shift (8-2). For nights (11-8), they would get an extra-long walk in the afternoon, normally on the beach, and then they would sleep overnight until I returned in the morning to give them another long walk (along the clifftops) before I went to bed. It was afternoon shifts (2-11) that caused the issue, but then I had a thought and put it to Judy and her husband. Their youngest son, Antony, attended Pool School, close to Tolvaddon, which was virtually (only a very slight detour) on his walk home. I asked if he would like to earn some pocket money by calling into mine on his way home from school to feed and let my dogs out in the garden.

Being a Sagittarian with a bit of OCD thrown into the mix, this arrangement was not without its anxieties. I didn't possess much, but I did have a half-decent Hi-Fi system with an expensive stylus on the tonearm, plus a decent TV with a reasonable (vinyl) record and tape cassette collection. My problem was that I was rather anal, i.e. I treated all my belongings with extreme care. I like to think I have mellowed in this regard, but that is up to others to say. Antony accepted my offer, and I was extremely grateful for that, but when I showed him around, it was with great reluctance that I said he could use the TV and Hi-Fi.

All went well for a few months until I came home one night and discovered that Antony had used one of my new blank cassettes. I was not happy. In my world, one did not take something that was not yours. In my mind, it was stealing. I approached Judy about it, and basically, Antony told me to feed my own fucking dogs.

To this day, I regret my actions. In my defence, I blame my makeup. This would be one of only a few instances during my time with Judy where my dogmatism caused a problem between us and/or her boys. Please also bear in mind that I am not a father; I am an introvert and have poor interpersonal social skills. I overreacted to the actions of a fourteen-year-old boy who was doing me a big favour and paid the price for it.

Chapter 4

Collision Course

Judith:

Early in the New Year 1987, we moved into the cheapest house in Camborne we could find. I was thirty-two, and the Cornish dream was over. Life had knocked the stuffing out of me, but I needed to dust myself down and 'girl up.' It was probably the first house I didn't turn into a home. The husband became more withdrawn the more weed he smoked: the lovely man I had married seventeen years ago disappeared before my eyes. Nothing I tried improved the situation, so I stopped trying. I hid the problem from everyone, put on a smile and carried on regardless. Then suddenly, the sun came out, and that nice man Phil asked me if I fancied racing a dingy.

I had no idea what that involved, but at least I would see the sea, so I said, 'Great. Count me in.' I was no longer processing tripe, I smelled better, and I really needed an outlet from my home life problems, of which Phil had no idea.

Wasn't sailing a glamorous sport? Looking sexy in a figure-hugging wetsuit, drinks at the sailing club with the G&T brigade: what's not to like? The wetsuit looked good, the boat looked impressive, and the sea was sparkling and inviting; what could possibly go wrong? Well, with no experience, obviously everything. I quickly learned the words 'ready about' meant capsize. 'Ready to gybe' meant a more spectacular capsize with the rescue boat waiting with great glee to 'save you – at the cost of a round of drinks in the bar,' and 'spinnaker up' was the start of the biggest roller coaster ride of your life. But it was exhilarating, exciting, adrenaline-fuelled, and totally bonkers, and I fell head over heels in love.

Philip:

Not long after moving into Tolvaddon, I saw an advert in the Camborne Packet (a local rag) for an Osprey Sailing Dinghy. An Osprey is (although by modern-day standards very old-fashioned) a 17' 6" long, powerful two-person trapeze racing dinghy. In a two-person dinghy, one person is the 'helm,' i.e. they steer the boat and control the rope for the larger sail (mainsail), whilst the second person 'crews,' i.e. controls the smaller front sail (jib) and also the spinnaker if the boat has one. The Osprey does – a very big one. The Osprey also has a trapeze wire for the crew. This is a wire attached to the top of the mast that at the bottom end has a hoop that 'hooks' onto a hook on a harness worn by the crew. It allows the crew to place their feet on the side of the boat and lean out over the water providing more leverage to keep the boat upright. For an Osprey, the average crew member is 6'5" tall and weighs 14-18 stone (one needs to remember this fact).

To this day, I have no idea why I bought this boat

(from a local building developer who owned a Ferrari Daytona and would make a re-appearance in our lives a little bit later on). I suspect the term 'impulse buy' would be used today. I had no tow bar on my car (more cost) and nobody to sail the boat with me, but I quite happily emptied my bank account to pay the £925 demanded for Osprey Sail Number 1075 (sail numbers are like car registration numbers). Was it my destiny, another piece being added to the board of fate?

I had learnt to sail whilst at school, at Cheshunt Water in Hertfordshire, and had been with the school on several holidays at the Hertfordshire schools base at Barton Broad. I loved it. I wasn't particularly good at it, but I loved it.

My ex had been a member of the Mount's Bay Sailing Club (with a clubhouse situated at Marazion facing St Michaels Mount). Mount's Bay must be one of the most fabulous places in the world to sail from, and I often wonder if the tourists ever felt jealous of those of us using these fantastic facilities.

Marazion has always attracted visitors, many of whom came as pilgrims to the Benedictine Monastery on St Michael's Mount and stayed in the town. John Wesley, the founder of the Wesleyan church, preached here in 1789. For centuries, tin and copper were exported from both Marazion and St. Michael's Mount by traders and shippers. The town was surrounded by mines, such as Wheal Prosper, Wheal Crab, Wheal Rodney, Tolvaddon and South Neptune. These mines remained active until a depression struck the industry in the late 19th century.

The coming of the railway in Victorian times saw the first true holidaymakers arrive in Cornwall. The mild climate and bathing were seen as a respite from city life. Artists were attracted to the clear light and beautiful scenery.

Today, Marazion is one of Cornwall's most popular tourist destinations. Nearly 300,000 paying visitors climb up to St Michael's Mount every year, with thousands more just taking a stroll to the tidal island. The town itself remains one of Cornwall's hidden gems, waiting to be discovered.

And here was I, in Cornish terms, 'a foreigner,' enjoying life without a care in the world, being able to sail in such a beautiful place. As previously stated, I didn't have a dream, but I was very fortunate to, in effect, be living 'Judy's Dream.'

When we returned to Cornwall from College at Plymouth, Sam took up sailing again, this time in a Laser. For many years, she had sailed a Mirror dinghy with her younger sister. A Laser is a single-handed boat, which resulted in me only getting to use it when the wind was strong, and she wimped out. I spent a lot of time upside down whilst learning how to control that dinghy, an orange-hulled boat we had named 'A Clockwork Orange.' On odd occasions, when his normal crew was not available, I got the chance to crew for Sam's older brother in his Osprey, but other than that, I knew very little about racing techniques or setting boats up.

For now, I stored the boat in my garage, having first knocked a hole in the end wall (the garage was only 16' long, and the dinghy, remember was 17'6") and rigged up an orange tarp over the nose that everybody reckoned looked like a condom. Who on earth was I going to get to crew the boat with me?

The Puppet Master:

Who indeed? Time to take the horses to another water hole.

Judith:

Since moving into the house that wasn't a home, I had got a job in a shoe shop in Truro. One Sunday evening, whilst playing volleyball, that 'nice' man Phil, who had turned up tanned and glowing, had tormented me about being off work the next day and said he was planning to spend it sunbathing. The next day was a glorious summer morning, and when I got to the station to catch my train to work, I just thought, '*Fuck it.*' I rang up to say I was sick, then rang Phil to ask if he wanted company for the day, and he said the immortal word, 'Yes.' So there I was, sitting on a seat (in my work uniform) at the station, waiting for him to pick me up. No swimming costume, towel, drink or sun cream (all that Girl Guide training down the pan). What possessed me?

He rocked up, I jumped in the car, and off we went. I thought we were going to the beach, but twenty minutes later, we turned into this lane. He opened a gate which was padlocked, drove through woodland, and eventually parked on a neatly cut grassed area. I think he must have been a boy scout in a previous life because the boot contained sunbeds, towels, magazines, food, drink, and god knows what else. Once he had loaded me up like a donkey, I followed him down a path and 'Wow!' I felt like we had walked into a set from a Tarzan and Jane film. Steep cliffs were surrounded by foliage which reflected into a bottomless lake. It was stunning, and it completely took my breath away. Phil set up camp, then promptly stripped naked, said he needed to get a couple of hours sleep as he had been on nights, and asked me if I could rub some sun cream on his back. So I did! Well, what would you have done? So, there I was in paradise. I never gave it a second thought; I whipped off my uniform and joined the sun fest. It felt amazing. The sun's rays caressing my naked body for the very first time was like experiencing your first kiss with a new lover. It was so relaxing I must have dozed off, and when I woke up, Phil passed me a glass of wine and cooked me a steak. All too soon, the time ticked away, and it became time to return home. What a strange, wonderful day – had I dreamt it?

Philip:

Flirting? Maybe, but Judy considers 'stalking' to be a more appropriate word! I was unknowingly out of control. First, there was tripe, followed by volleyball, the party, sailing (yes, all 5'6" and nine stone of her was now crewing for me), and now 'naturism.' Wikipedia defines naturism as 'a lifestyle of practising non-sexual social nudity in private and in public; the word also refers to the cultural movement which advocates and defends that lifestyle. Both may alternatively be called nudism.' For me, it was not a chosen lifestyle; I had discovered the pleasure and well-being gained from swimming and sunbathing naked, and that's what I enjoyed doing. Simples (to borrow a phrase).

After the Spitfire died, I bought an old Triumph 2.5pi from a SWEB engineer and promptly drove it down to the south of France. For Sam and me, this was our first foreign holiday. It was a self-drive Eurocamp holiday to Marseillan Plage. Finding the campsite, we were shown to our pre-erected tent. The campsite was situated right behind the beach, lovely. In hindsight, I now wonder whether this next bit was an unknowing prediction of how our marriage would work out. Whilst shopping for supplies, we decided to buy some beach toys, including two blow-up rowing boats (rather than one double). Because the bed was very uncomfortable, I slept a lot of nights in mine, on my own!

Towards the end of this holiday, whilst sunbathing one morning on the beach, there was a commotion about two hundred yards to the right of where we were. A big crowd was gathering at the water's edge. We went to investigate. It turned out to be some local fishermen who had beached their boats and were selling their catch. What caught our eye was the fact that the people joining the crowd from the right-hand side of the beach were all naked. They did not have a care in the world that those coming from 'our' side of the beach, or indeed the fisherman, were clothed or at least in costumes. It transpired that Marseillan Plage is situated next door to Le Cap d'Agde Quarter Naturiste, a renowned worldwide naturist holiday resort.

However, it would be a couple of years before I got to try swimming and sunbathing naked. It was September 1980. We had booked a last-minute holiday at a place called Sérignan Plage. It was in a mobile home. The mobile home was, well, a bog-standard mobile home, but better than the pre-erected tent. The campsite was barely a quarter full (it was due to close at the end of September), and many of the facilities were closed. There was only one sanitary and shower block open, and it was shared by both sexes; so French, but a bit intimidating for us Brits. Then one day, whilst on the beach, a young couple with a toddler set up camp next to us and proceeded to strip naked before settling down. They were not in the least bit concerned that other beach users, including Sam and I, were wearing costumes. I wanted to know what it was like, so, gathering up my courage, I slipped my trunks off. It felt good, really good. Fears of getting aroused? It didn't happen and never has. A little later, I plucked up the courage to have a dip in the sea. Swimming naked is glorious, and from that day on, I never wanted to wear a costume again. However, there have been times in my life, especially during my marriage, when the situation has dictated that I must. On that holiday, Sam did agree to walk further along the beach – deep amongst the nudists – to allow me to participate in my newfound love, though she, at that stage, declined to try it.

During my near ten years of marriage, we did enjoy several naturist holidays, with Sam (somewhat reluctantly) joining in. Nevertheless, in the end, it probably played a part in us falling out of love and separating.

Judith:

So the summer was spent working, sailing and playing volleyball, and I didn't get another invite to go sunbathing. Did I look at Phil differently after the 'dream day?' Was that when he became more attractive to me? Who knows? I did spend a lot of time on the boat sailing with him that summer, and despite numerous capsizes and subsequent bruises, I had a lot of excitement and fun. The more time I spent with him, the happier I felt; he was easy to get on with. He didn't put any pressure on me, and we had a lot in common, even though we were very different people. One day he rang to see if I fancied taking the dogs for a walk on Perranporth beach. As far as I was concerned, it was a no-brainer; I hadn't been there before. It was (is) majestic; miles of golden sands, huge surf and sand dunes as far as the eye could see, glorious. He picked me and my dog Billy Bonkers up, and off we went. It was another beautiful day, and my first thought was, '*He smells nice.*' There was a moment as we were walking back across the dunes when I thought we were going to kiss. I think that was the moment I realised I fancied him. My heart had fluttered, and there were a few butterflies buzzing around inside me.

Philip:

Add dog walking to the stalking list. Writing this book has made me realise why so many of our friends and acquaintances thought we were having an affair. I can see now that I was acting, even if I didn't think so at the time, as if we were indeed a couple. With volleyball and sailing, we were spending a lot of time together, and like Judy, I too thought we were going to kiss that day whilst walking back over the dunes at Perranporth. For a moment, there was an uncontrollable urge to hold and kiss her, but then there was hesitation too. Then, the moment had passed.

The Puppet Master:

They can drink if they want to; it seems they do not.

Philip:

Summer 1987 finds me playing regular volleyball (training and matches), sailing the Osprey with Judy, and driving minibuses for the athletic club. I think I have yet to point out that I was secretary for the West Cornwall Athletic Club and Team Manager for the Cornish AAA Women's Team. Plus, I coordinated and was secretary for the annual Cornish AAA Championships and drove minibuses all over the country for the various teams. The Trevu football team also arranged friendly cricket matches (arranged by members who played serious cricket for local teams) during the summer (football) break.

One such game took place on the evening of an England football match; I believe it was a World Cup qualifier. Someone had brought along a portable TV and, to be honest, most people were more interested in football than cricket. The team we were playing with were rubbish. They won the toss and elected to bat first. As they were all out for some miserly total, our captain decided to reverse our batting order, i.e. the worst at batting, who would normally go in last, went in first to give the opposition a chance. Our normal opening batsmen would soon have got the score required to win the match on their own. It was a good plan and allowed those of us who could bat to watch as much of the game as possible. However, the bad batters did not last very long before they were out, and soon I got a call to say it was my turn to bat. Grudgingly leaving the TV screen, I made my way to the crease and proceeded to attack the bowling: we only needed a few more runs to win. I hit the first and second balls to the boundary – four runs each; the third was a full toss that I hit clear over the boundary for six runs, and my batting partner and I ran between the wickets for two runs from the fourth. Only four runs needed to win now, but getting overconfident, cocky even, I stepped down the crease intending to hit the fifth ball for a boundary (four runs), oh the glory of getting the match-winning shot. Well, that was the intention, but I mistimed the stroke and bullseye – a direct hit to the crown jewels and pain, lots of pain. It was at that point that I realised I had forgotten to put my (cricket) box on. I retired from batting; the next man in got the winning runs, the England game finished, and I made my way home. I was due in at work at 11 pm as I was on nights. Fortunately, I had a competent trainee working with me, and I left him to do the job whilst I slept under the counter, to be woken when required.

Getting home the following morning, I was amazed to see how large my right testicle had become. It was the size of a Florida orange, i.e. huge. Time to go to the doctor. After examination, he gave me some painkillers and a sick note, saying that the swelling would go down of its own accord, but there may be an issue with me having children in the future. He was not amused by my reply.

'You mean I wasted £50 on a vasectomy!'

The Countryman Volleyball Team had been entered into an annual competition held at Weston-super-Mare, to be held on a September Sunday. (Though my swollen testicle had subsided, it was not fully shrunken and was still sore; therefore, I would not be able to play.) The West Cornwall Athletic Club Ladies Team had a Southern League match in Greater London on the same weekend, but on the Saturday. Having already got a minibus booked for the athletic team, it seemed a sensible idea to book it for an extra day to take the volleyball team to Weston-super-Mare.

So once again, we (the women's athletic team) were crossing Bodmin Moor, in thick fog, on our way home (around 1 am) with everyone in the minibus, bar me, the driver, asleep. On this particular trip, I arrived home with the minibus just after 2 am. Being very tired, I set the clock for 4 am and went to bed. Waking, I cleaned the minibus and prepared it and myself for the trip to Weston with the volleyball team. A couple who lived on my estate were due round to mine at 5 am, and we were due at Judy and her husband's at 5.30 am. I was knackered, but it would be all right as Judy and the husband were the other named drivers. I could let them take over the driving, sleep on the trip up to Weston, and be the main driver on the way back.

The Puppet Master:

Or so you thought.

Philip:

I arrived at Treswithian dead on time (this is me, the Sagittarian, remember) to be told by Judy that the husband had a migraine and was unable to drive, and she had been up all night delivering puppies and had not slept a wink all night. Wonderful. Being young is wonderful too; hey, a two-hour drive on two hours of sleep: no problem. I am pleased to say that we made it there and back without any issues. Perhaps my years of driving up and back to the 'smoke' had given me some sort of inbuilt auto-pilot.

Judith:

Ah, yes, the volleyball tournament. Never again. Great fun, but exhausting.

I had been living in a bubble of summer sunshine, I adored sailing on the sea, and for once in my life, I felt like the green pea that birds-eye hadn't rejected. This was where I belonged; the sea was my happy place. How would I get through autumn and winter without it? I didn't want the storms and winter weather to come. I prefer calm waters, but sometimes you have to ride the wave and see where it takes you.

The Puppet Master:

Just a little nudge, and now the pieces on the board are touching.

Philip:

It was the evening of Thursday 8th October 1987, and whilst giving Judy a lift home following volleyball training, she mentioned that she had spotted an advert in the West Briton (a local newspaper) for an end-of-season sale of second-hand wetsuits: she knew I was in need of a new one. As I was working over the weekend, I said it would be Monday before I could go to have a look. Judy, who was also off work on Monday, offered to go along to keep me company if I wanted.

Oh yes indeed, I wanted, and replied to her, 'That would be nice.'

Chapter 5

Kisses are Dangerous

The Puppet Master:

Time for the superglue.

Philip:

Monday 12th October 1987. The dawn gave way to a beautiful sunny day with clear blue Cornish skies: an omen, perhaps? It was just another day, or so I thought. I had just finished a run of night shifts, and upon getting home, I first took the dogs for a walk (I have them full-time now), then had a bath and some breakfast. I had no need for shut-eye because, with the imminent closure of the Cornish Control Room, all the administration work that we, as Control Room assistants (as opposed to the Control Room engineers) used to do, had already been moved to the Exeter Control Room. Therefore, there was no option but to have a kip. After dressing, I drove over to Judy's to pick her up and make our way to Newquay to see what the Newquay Surfing Centre had to offer. I am feeling good, excited, in fact. Why am I so excited? Is it because Judy is accompanying me? Almost certainly, but am I stalking/flirting again? No, definitely not; after all, it was her idea; she was the one who spotted the advert.

Judith:

I caught the wave accidentally. It was 12th October 1987. I had just got a new job at (the soon-to-be-open) local petrol station, and that evening I was to attend an induction, training and welcome event at a very posh hotel in Redruth. It was also the day I was going to Newquay with Phil; he was after a new wetsuit, so off we trotted to do the business. Ah, Newquay, I had never been there before. I knew it was a surfing paradise and a magnet for holidaymakers looking for a good time, but on this sunny, tourist-free day, it was quiet, and the sea was sparkling like a sapphire. I really hoped we might be able to have a look around once the shopping had been done.

Philip:

Finding the surf shop, I proceeded to try on several wetsuits; I was feeling good and, yes, still excited. There I was, struggling in and out of various wetsuits that Judy was passing to me and taking from me in this minuscule cubicle and, in-between wetsuits, I was standing in just my kecks (underpants). It all seemed so normal. Who was I kidding? This woman, although very beautiful, was married. What was I doing? What were we doing?

The Puppet Master: You cannot resist your destiny.

Philip:

I settled on a Long John and, with Judy's approval that

it looked better than the others, I duly parted with the £39.99 demanded. Well, that had not taken very long. In fact, it was and still is typical of me when shopping that I go to get what I want, get it, and return home. Except, in this case, I didn't return home. Well, not straight away.

Judith:

It was such a nice day, so when Phil suggested we drop the wetsuit into the boot of the car, grab an ice cream, and go for a walk around the Towsan Headland, I jumped at the opportunity. I was curious to see what Newquay had to offer, and it seemed a shame not to make the most of the glorious weather and just head home. Clubbing at Tall Trees or cabaret at The Talk of the West was off the agenda, but a walk to explore the headland – that was right up my street. So that's what we did. Now, was that a good or bad idea?

Philip:

We often say that our relationship 'started with a kiss' (and we have a gold disc on the living room wall above a copy of the wetsuit receipt to prove it), but in reality, our relationship status changed on that walk. 'That' kiss came later in the day.

Judith:

We walked for a bit, finished off the ice creams, and then sat on a bench high above the headland, watching the surfers catch the waves. They looked like dots on the ocean; the sea gently ebbed and flowed in the warm sunshine. Large gulls and tiny birds pecked at the scrub near the rocks close to where we sat, and I wondered how many people had touched or sat on them, what their stories were, and how their lives had turned out: it was truly magical. Reluctantly, we decided to move and continued our walk around the headland. I felt the urge to touch one of the large rocks as we left the seat. I think it cast a Cornish spell on me because somewhere along that headland, our hands became entwined, and it felt like the most natural thing in the world. Neither of us mentioned it, but I think we both knew something had dramatically changed between us.

The Puppet Master:

Nearly there, the glue just needs to set.

Judith:

Back at his house, 'for a coffee' – I never thought of 'for a coffee' being a euphemism – the first kiss happened (note to everyone, 'kisses are dangerous'). It was a tender, gentle kiss. There were no words, just eye contact, and my eyes said 'Yes.' Well, one gentle kiss led to another, then another, and as the intensity grew, I knew I wanted to make love with this man; it was my destiny, the perfect end to a perfect day. No words were spoken, they weren't needed; our bodies spoke for us. Yes, we had sex, but it was more than that; there was a deeper connection. It was only when I fell off the cloud and came back down to earth that reality struck: I had an hour to get to my induction training, '*Help!*' So off I went, no time to even think, let alone process what had just happened, or what it meant, if anything. That would have to wait until tomorrow.

The Puppet Master:

My job is done.

Philip:

How did 'coming in for a coffee' turn into a first kiss, followed by the most passionate sex I had ever experienced? It was euphoric, but then we came down to earth with a bump. Judy had to rush off to attend her training and was due to start her first day in her new job in the morning. I was home alone, pondering what on earth had happened. I was on such a high, but sleep was not forthcoming when I went to bed. I slept not one wink.

By six in the morning, I was still just lying there listening to Radio One – it had been on all night – and wondering what to do. My head is a mess, my eyes red from crying. I should be ecstatic, but I am not. In fact, I do not know what I am feeling. I have never felt this way in my life, and my emotions are all over the place. A cloud of melancholy hangs over me.

Yesterday had been such a beautiful day, but it had taken an unexpected path; I think it shocked both of us. Thirteen hours ago, I was on cloud nine, feeling like the luckiest man in the world, but now all that I can think is:

'*What have you done, you stupid fool?*'

'*Have I destroyed what was probably the best friendship I have ever had?*'

'*I am a stupid, stupid fool!*'

I desperately needed to speak with Judy, but she was at work that morning. No mobiles back then, so there were no secret texts or calls; I just had to wait until Judy got a chance to ring me. When she did, we made arrangements for her to come over to mine on Wednesday morning. I think she was as confused as I was. It was another rest day for me, so I was left alone to fret: it was indeed a torturous day. One minute I felt totally elated, in heaven, high in love (or lust); the next, I was in deep depression, confused as to what had happened and wondering what to do about it.

Judith:

I have to say, when you are a wife, a mother and work full time, in all honesty, there is not much time to think about anything, but after yesterday's happenings, I now had to face up to my actions. I had committed adultery with one of my best friends. I still had no regrets; I felt guilty about cheating on the husband, but my main worry was that I would lose Phil as a friend. Yes, we had crossed a line, but we both wanted it. Why was I so stressed that I had fucked it up? Of course, the sensible thing to do would have been to nip it in the bud straight away; my life was complicated enough. I had no idea what Phil was thinking. We would just have to be honest and open with each other the next time we met and discuss how we were going to carry on. His friendship was more important to me than sex.

Philip:

Wednesday 14th October. The plan had been to talk over what had happened; however, the chemistry between us was too great, and we ended up in bed again. The discussion happened post-sex, over vodka and a dish of dolly mixtures, and included (a bit late now) her concern over protection. A pregnancy was all we needed, but my mid-twenties vasectomy meant we were okay on that front.

Judith:

We obviously had an overwhelming physical attraction, and now it had been let out of the box, we were unable to put it back in, so we carried on. There were no barriers between us now, so we embraced the change in our relationship. Was it love or lust? Time would tell; we were too busy enjoying ourselves to worry.

Philip:

It was out of our hands. We got together whenever we could, sometimes walking the dogs before or after sex, but always with vodka and dolly mixtures! Judy had assured me that her marriage had been over a long time before the 12th, but she was still married and living in the marital home with the husband and her boys. She had to work out how to deal with that.

Judith:

There comes a time when you need to decide what you do want and don't want in life. Was my decision to ditch the 'husband' down to my relationship with Phil? Was he the catalyst? No, definitely not. Actually, it was a random man who made me realise I was at a crossroads in life. I was on my way home from work on the train when the man got chatting with me. He tried to persuade me to stay on the train and go home with him (he was on leave from the armed forces), and I wanted to remain on that train and never ever go home. It was a lightbulb moment in my life; I realised that I had to change my life before I ran away or did something stupid. He will never know that it was him who made me realise that, to survive, I needed to extract myself from my current situation. So, extract myself I did. Having told the 'husband' that evening we were over, I grabbed Billy Bonkers and left the house to avoid further confrontation and give us both time to think things over. I felt a huge sense of relief, having brought the issue to a head, but an enormous amount of anxiety about how things would pan out. I had never ended a relationship before. I didn't have a manual, I was out of my depth, and I had no idea what would happen next. I was scared and worried about how the boys would react once they were told, and at this stage, I had no idea whether I would leave, or if the 'husband' would be the one to go. It was a very difficult time. The 'husband' opted to go, I was not really sure what the boys thought, and I hadn't told Phil the situation, although he did find out, but not from me. I was 33; it was November 1987; I had been married for 17 years, and now it was well and truly over.

Philip:

One day in November, Judy tackled the husband and told him it was over between them; I was not mentioned. That same evening, there was a knock on my front door. It was the husband. I invited him in; he stood by the stairs (it was an open plan room) whilst I sat down on the sofa. He was very angry and spouted on about how he was not going to stand by and let nearly seventeen years of marriage go down the pan. All the time, I was just pleading silently to him, 'Please hit me and not my car' (in my defence, it was because I was broke and had no money for car repairs, not because it was a nice metallic blue 5 Series BMW). I dislike confrontations and try to avoid them at all costs, but when they do happen, as in the situation I now found myself in, I tend not to say anything. It is not a planned response; it is just how I am. In this case, I think the husband could not cope with my silence, and he left with both me and the car intact (phew).

Judith:

I would like to say all's well that ends well, but obviously,

I had never gone through a split before, and it's a steep learning curve. Eventually, I told family and friends. I would like to say I had their support, but believe me, I didn't. My mother told me I was an 'impulsive bitch,' and as the 'husband' had a very nice manner about him when not in the home, most people felt I had treated him badly. Needless to say, it was my own fault, as I had never disclosed his adultery and drug use or his nasty behaviour towards me for the two years leading up to the split. I couldn't see there was anything to gain by telling them after the split, as no one would have believed me. Fortunately, I think the only person who had seen the 'husband' in his true form before and particularly after the split was Phil. So I had one friend on my side who was non-judgemental: thank god for small mercies. Did the separation affect our relationship? Yes, I think it did, but not in a 'let's move in together' way: in my head, that was never on the cards. He did, however, not back away from my situation; if anything, he was always there, quietly in the background, helping out where he could, and I was very grateful for his non-interference.

Philip:

We could now be more open about our relationship, attending sports and social events as a couple. Several friends and acquaintances told us they knew we had been having an affair, and nothing we could say would persuade them otherwise. One couple, close friends of Jude and the husband, were very off with her and downright hostile to me. They clearly blamed me for the breakdown of Jude's marriage. Judy was livid but could see it was because she had not talked to anyone about the problems in her marriage, so she decided to open up about the husband because she believed it was unfair that I was taking so much flack.

My life had taken an unexpected turn; I had a girlfriend and was very happy. When I separated and moved into Tolvaddon, I fully expected to be alone for a long while, if not forever. I had no illusions with regard to my makeup, shyness, and lack of self-belief when it came to relationships. As it turned out, my time alone lasted less than a year; how lucky was I? Extremely, is the answer.

Our relationship continued to grow, and life was good. Judy sometimes stayed over; her boys were more than capable of looking after themselves for a night. I also sometimes stayed over at hers, though that was more of a struggle for me; it was, after all, the marital home, the home of her two teenage boys, plus she had GSDs as well. It tested my interpersonal skills, and I think Judy recognised this, choosing to stay more at mine than I at hers.

Then it was December, my birthday month: time for another party. A date was set, and the organising began. On late and night shifts at work, I started a storyboard using A3 sheets of paper, first detailing my cricket accident and then the weekend athletic club and volleyball trip. There were enough of these to paste on three walls of the box room – the fourth wall was a window. As this was to be the food room, my plan was to give people something amusing to read whilst filling their plates. As well as the usual cold food, I also planned to serve hot food, including BBQ stuff, using an electric BBQ borrowed from the works cookery demonstrator – it seemed like a good idea at the time. I positioned this in front of the window to allow the smoke to escape through it. Makeshift tables filled the rest of the room, loaded with food.

Again, furniture was removed (including having to dismantle my large Scalextric setup in the box room), the house decorated, and loads of booze bought. All was going well until the first person put some food onto the BBQ. I might have a Physics O Level, but I hadn't thought this one through very well. The upstairs quickly filled with smoke. Rather than go out of the window as planned, the breeze actually blew the smoke back into the house. Help! What to do? Fortunately, opening the front bedroom windows allowed a through-draught that ensured most of the smoke did go out of the window. It gave the guests something else to laugh about.

Judith:

Money once again became my main priority, and I hated how much this subject controlled my life. I now had only one part-time job, and there was no way the 'husband' could, or would, help towards the household bills, so picking daffodils became the obvious way to supplement my income.

Things you need to know if you ever choose this line of work:

1. Chat up the gang leaders as they decide who is chosen to work each day. Know your limits, and don't promise what you won't deliver.

2. Always say you have more bunches than you actually have, as you are paid per bunch. Lying is very necessary in this case.

3. Be aware if it is very muddy, spot a tree early in the day to climb up and eat your lunch in. It stops arguments with others later on.

4. Pick with friends who have a sense of humour as this makes the day go much quicker. One of my friends once told the guy picking in the next row that she was a witch. When he asked her why she was telling him that, she replied, 'The daffodils know.'

5. Do not turn up in the new boyfriend's BMW. It looks like you are a rich bitch, so why are you picking daffodils?

6. Know when to call it a day and spend your earnings in the local pub on an afternoon bender. It's good for the soul.

7. Do not let your youngest son persuade you to take him picking on your birthday, as he will only last an hour, then bugger off home.

8. Do not be surprised if the boyfriend turns up

with a bucket of batter mix on the front seat of his immaculate car, as it's likely to be pancakes for your tea.

9. If you are OCD or a Sagittarian, it's not the job for you; it's impossible to pick every flower exactly 12 inches long.

10. If you are on benefits, never give your true name or address, and have a quick exit plan if the DSS raid the farm.

So there you have it: the 'dos and don'ts' of daffodil picking in the 1980s. I have to say that without the three months of picking, I would have really struggled financially. Coupled with my part-time evening garage job, I managed to pay the mortgage, put food on the table and keep up with the bills. Plus, I was as fit as a butcher's dog. On the negative side, yet again my focus was on earning money as opposed to ensuring the boys were okay. I think I probably did more harm than good because I didn't take the time to talk to the boys about the split properly. I had more conversations with Shaun as he was older and more aware of the situation; however, with Antony being younger, I chose not to really tell him the 'whys or wherefores.' Probably, in his eyes, I just left him to deal with it on his own. Nowadays, I think you would probably go down the 'and how do you feel about this' route, but at the time, I didn't. Later on in my life, that mistake definitely came back to bite me on the bum.

Philip:

January in Cornwall is daffodil month, and for many years, the saviour of low-paid workers, i.e. almost everyone in Cornwall. It was a means of earning money and not declaring it, especially for those receiving benefits. When the DSS raided farms, and some poor souls got caught, charged and fined in court, their only option to pay the fine was to return to the daffodil fields! Shaun, Judy's eldest lad, was an expert picker. He knew all the tricks and could earn a lot of money from it. Judy was almost as good and, in her present circumstances, needed as much money as possible, so she returned to the field in '88.

For me, three daffodil memories spring to the fore, though I am sure Judy will have many more stories to tell; after all, it was she, not me, who did the picking. The first involved me insisting that she took my car, as I had no plans for the day and didn't need it. She was reluctant but agreed in the end.

On returning home, she said, 'Never again.'

Apparently, turning up to pick daffodils in a shiny BMW portrayed the wrong image!

I had covered the rear of the BMW in blankets and used green garden plastic fencing to create a barrier between the rear and front of the car. Without this, the dogs would always come into the front, which is not good when they are soaking wet and muddy or sandy. However, now that we had three, sometimes four, dogs to take out, the BMW was not suitable. The answer was a very cheap small van, in this case, a two-cylinder Daihatsu panel van. It was what they called in Japan, a 'Kei' class (basically meaning 'mini'), and as usual for me, it was a rust bucket, but it could easily accommodate four dogs in the back. Perfect for taking them to the beach or North Cliffs.

So, back to the daffodils. On one occasion, I picked up Judy, Shaun (I think Antony may have picked this day as well), plus Judy's friend Doreen and one of her sons, another Antony. As we pulled up outside Doreen's, the boys, having arranged to pretend to be a military black operations unit, jumped out and took up covering positions. In taking up his position, Shaun caught the driver's door mirror, pulling it right off. I know it was an accident, but it was still a 'count to ten and keep calm moment.' It was the first of many incidents that challenged the differences in our upbringings and lifestyles.

My third daffodil tale involves picking Judy and Shaun up with a big bucket full of pancake batter that was sitting on the passenger seat and tied up to the ceiling in an attempt to stop it from spilling. I had admitted to being a bit of a 'pancake king' and had offered to make tea that night. The only issue was that we were going to Judy's house to have it, and I had made the batter at mine. They may have laughed, but they did scoff down all my pancakes.

Judith:

So the money side was sort of sorted, the new relationship

was very definitely blossoming, and with the 'husband' out of the house, I finally felt I could breathe again. I was also falling in love with both Phil and life. We spent time walking the dogs and getting to know each other. We were actually very different people; I was very touchy-feely and open, but Phil appeared to be more cool and detached. There was the odd time when I wondered if it would work long-term. I think the initial physical attraction, coupled with the fact we enjoyed similar things, was probably how we got over any differences and why by March, we both hated not being able to spend all our time together. Phil had talked about us moving in together on various occasions, but I was very doubtful about it working out. If it was just him and me, I would have had no hesitation, but I had major doubts he would cope with me and two teenage boys. Was he mad? This was a man who never wanted children and had actually had the chop in his twenties: why risk spoiling what we had?

Well, to cut a long story short, in a moment of sheer madness, after having a serious talk to myself, I rang him and said, 'Yes, let's do it.' I told myself, 'If it works for a week, a month, a year or forever, what have I got to lose? Be brave.'

I decided he probably stood more chance of surviving the shock to his perfectly organised life if we moved into his house. So, the decision was made, and we agreed that he would ring back once he was ready for us to move in. I thought that might be the next day or the day after, but, bloody hell, he rang back within a few hours to say that he and the house were ready for us all to move in, so we did.

Philip:

As January moved into February, I can remember that I often put on an album from my collection whilst we had our vodka and dolly mixtures. I believe Sting's 'An Englishman In New York' was a favourite, but I would also subject Judy to Barclay James Harvest and Pink Floyd. During several of these sessions, I would raise the subject of moving in together as, being forever the practical one, it seemed to make more sense to only have to pay for one home, not two. The ever-practical Sagittarian in me also suggested that we sell both houses and buy a new one that belonged to all of us. Each time, Judy deferred on a decision, preferring to keep going as we were. I think she thought I would struggle to share my space not just with her, but with her boys as well. As ever, she would be proved right.

Then, in March, she rang me one morning to say she had come to a momentous decision: she and the boys were going to move into my house. Although my house was smaller than hers, she thought it would give me a fighting chance. I was ecstatic; all I wanted at that time of my life was to spend every hour of every day with Judy. She made me feel so happy; I used to get all tingly inside just thinking about her. An unexpected dream was about to become a reality. However, there was an elephant in the room – the boys – and neither of us, especially me, had any idea how it would pan out. I believed our feelings for each other were so strong that we could overcome any obstacles put in our way. This would be the start of a new, exciting chapter in our lives.

Anyhow, the 'love-smitten wonder boy' charged around his house, preparing it for its new occupants. Within a few hours, I rang Judy back to say that the house was ready for her and the boys to move into. Keen, or what?

Phil, always grinning

The mischievous Judith, age 9

My Gorgeous boys,
Antony & Shaun

Phil, still grinning, nearing the end of his first,
and only, marathon (from Lands End to Redruth)

It Started With A Kiss –
October 12th 1987

Chapter 6

All Together Now

Judith:

Initially, we thought Shaun might be a problem, but bless him, he was totally up for it; Antony, however, was not. Phil tried very hard to make it work with the boys; he wanted us all to start a nice new life together. Not in an 'I'm your new father/stepfather way,' but in a quiet, 'let's all rub along well together and have some quality time,' kind of way. Antony turned fifteen a month after we all moved in together, and Phil made him a fabulous birthday cake. We took him sailing, got him a regular ride crewing on a dinghy, had his friends over, and Phil set up a Subbuteo table in the garage where many tournaments were held. Could we have done any more? Who knows? I certainly don't.

I was so happy; I was actually living with someone who both loved, looked after and respected me. Naturally, there were a few teething problems. On day one, I broke the washing machine door, and on night one, a burn mark appeared on Phil's posh TV. Empty cereal packets drove Phil mad, and, of course, being on the nightclub route meant Shaun's friends often sofa surfed at ours on a Saturday night. God knows how Phil survived this baptism of life with the Lea family, but he did. Had the tables been turned, I know for a fact I would have failed miserably.

I might be easy-going, but I have got a feisty side to me, especially if you push my buttons, which Antony had down to a fine art. Needless to say, one morning, Phil, open-mouthed, watched me arguing with Antony. I think he was horrified to watch me put him up against the wall and inform him that 'Your dad doesn't want you, but I love you and do want you. Regardless of what you want, you are staying with me.' Not one of my finer moments in life. I should have explained in a better way that I had offered his dad the 'home that wasn't a home' so that the boys could visit whenever they wanted. However, he had turned that down and wanted the house sold instead. I also should have told Antony that, at fifteen, I had been separated from my sister, and that there was no way I was going to let that happen to my family, but I didn't. The house did get sold, and like an idiot, I split the money fifty-fifty; I even paid the husband's half into his bank account.

Philip:

Sometimes I am just stunned by the coincidences between us. Would you believe that when I separated from Sam, I withdrew £2,000 from my bank account, half the small profit we had made when selling the Pengegon house, and paid it into hers?

Judith:

The house gods had been kind the short while we had lived at Treswithian, and we came out with £5K each. 'The husband' had taken up with a new girl and her two children. He blew the lot on a trip to America and, of course, took Antony away with them. I think that was probably the moment 'the husband' became the hero. Needless to say, 'the husband' never contributed a penny towards child maintenance to Antony. Was I bitter about that? You bet I was. There was no plan when the boys and I moved into Phil's, and Phil and I never really discussed finances/roles we just went with the flow. However, there was no way I was going to let him take over the role of stepfather or finance me or the boys. Although we were living together, I was very independent; I kept my own bank account, bought all the food, and contributed to the household bills. I had picked up more work at a second-hand furniture shop and local auction rooms; we were doing just fine.

Philip:

Ah, yes, on the day Judy and the boys moved in, Judy did indeed break the door handle on my washing machine. I admit the design was not the best, but I had never had an issue with it, and I am supposed to be the clutz! No turning to google or YouTube for help back then, so it was out with the tool kit to take the top off and have a look-see. Fortunately, one could reach down inside to release the door catch to rescue the washing. This was just as well because it took a few weeks to get a replacement part. In the meantime, the top had to come off after every wash to get at the door release. What Judy did not mention is that a few days after fitting the new part, Shaun did what his mother had done, i.e. broke the bloody door handle again!

Poor old Shaun's first denial of any wrongdoing occurred on the first morning following them moving in. I came downstairs and immediately noticed that there was a cigarette burn (a nice melted U shape) on the top of my (pride and joy) TV. This was the first of many disturbances that had to have been caused by a poltergeist as none of the humans would ever take responsibility. It is fair to say that life as I had known it was no more.

I had a lot to learn, especially about material possessions, and sharing space with two teenagers. My quarterly telephone bill went from £4 to £40, and putting a telephone lock didn't even stop them. (It was a telephone with a round dial with finger holes in it. The lock fitted in a hole and supposedly stopped you from dialling out.) I eventually learnt that you can still make a call by tapping the required number of times on prongs that stick out from the cradle rest i.e. for the number two, tap the prongs down twice.

Also, the 'What's mine is yours' ethos didn't last long either, especially where cereal packets were concerned. The problem, in this case, was that when they, i.e. the boys, and even Judy, emptied a packet, they did not throw it away but put it back on the shelf. This meant I thought there was lots of cereal to choose from when often there was none – so annoying. In a short time, a lock was put on our bedroom door, and stuff, including 'my' cereals, were kept in there. So no: 'What's mine is not necessarily yours!'

And then it was the turn of poor old Antony; I remember this incident a little differently to Judy. I had been on nights and was in bed when, if I remember correctly, Antony was playing a record at too loud a volume. Communication not being my thing, I screamed down the stairs at him to turn it down; I was trying to sleep, for fuck's sake. A polite request and explanation may have received a different result, but he back-chatted me, and Judith stepped in to sort him out. I was left open-mouthed at the top of the stairs watching the love of my life put her six-foot son against the wall whilst reading him the riot act. I sheepishly went back to bed.

Judith:

The first three months were probably the benchmark for our relationship. Looking back, I think we survived because there was massive chemistry between us. He made my insides flutter, he made me laugh, and he let me be me. Of course, the fact that he worked shifts helped, as it gave me and the boy's normal family time, but I think, more importantly, it also gave Phil his alone-at-home time. Probably the only person not to get alone time was me. I was either mother or lover, and that set the pattern of our life together, even though, at the time, I didn't realise that was the case. We had no plan and no priorities; I just lived in the moment and dealt with whatever came up.

The sailing became our quality time together, and we trotted off to the sailing club, racing the boat two/three times a week. I had a lot to learn on the water, but fortunately, off the water and in the sailing club bar, I was a professional, even though I didn't drink gin and tonic. Our array of capsizes on the water were joyfully enjoyed by the club members. One day, upon entering the bar, they held up cards like ice skating results, and I felt quite proud to receive 5.8 for artistic impression. I think it was because that day, I had catapulted off the trapeze wire and completed a double somersault before I crashed, obviously very elegantly, into the water. My personal guide to racing a dinghy is as follows:

- Make sure the bung is inserted in the transom (back of the boat) before leaving the shore, or the boat fills up with water and sinks.
- Preferably, only sail with someone who knows what they are doing.
- If the sails are flapping like demented demons prior to launching, it's probably best not to even enter the water as it's 'far too windy.'
- If there is an 'offshore' wind, i.e. blowing from the beach out to sea, the minute you launch the boat, jump in quickly. If you don't, you will be left like a

drowning rat in the surf or dragged along out to sea if you haven't let go.

- Once afloat and aboard, if told to 'hook on and get out,' do so immediately; otherwise, it is instant capsize when windy, and you will not have even made it to the start line.
- Do not panic when coming up to the start line with all the other boats. Screaming does not help anyone in this instance.
- Once you start the race, you are on 'a beat,' i.e. wind in front of you. If it's windy, it means you have to get on that trapeze wire pretty darn quick, or the captain will have a panic attack.
- Instant decision-making is imperative. If the captain asks, 'Are we clear?' i.e. we are on port and have to give way to the starboard boat, it means if you get it wrong, either a collision happens, or a late tack (turning the boat) means it's capsize time again.
- The 'ready to gybe instruction' is the most dangerous time: capsizing is a high probability.
- This is followed by the 'reaching' leg, i.e. the wind is on the side of the boat. In an Osprey, this involves putting up the spinnaker, often called by me, 'the bastard kite.' This includes hooking an enormous sail onto a pole and attaching the pole to the mast. This is followed by me, the crew, hooking onto the trapeze wire, hiking out onto the side of the boat, pulling the sail until it fills (with wind), all the while edging my way to the back of the boat. I call it the suicide leg:

one wrong move, and you are in the drink again. Very exciting, though, when you get it right.

- The final leg of the race is a 'run,' i.e. the wind is blowing from behind the boat. It's time to catch your breath, actually sit in the boat, still flying the 'bastard kite', look out for dolphins and admire the view.

- Assuming you have completed all of the above, repeat again and again until the race is complete.

- The crew must accept that the captain is always right, and instructions must be followed. However, if he shouts at you too much, the best way to get your own back is to let go of the 'bastard kite', as this usually results in a spectacular capsize, especially on a 'close reach' (very fast point of sailing).

So there you have it, 'how to race', courtesy of Judy Lea, sailor extraordinaire, not! All I can say is, 'it must have been love.' Who in their right mind would even consider taking up this sport just to get it on with a bloke? Only joking, of course. I bloody loved it; it was exhilarating, exciting, scary and at times surreal. Sailing at Marazion was magical. The castle in the sea was stunning, the sun and rainbows across the water were mesmerising, and when the dolphins came to play alongside the boat, you felt you had hit the jackpot. Where else in the world could be better? I felt I had come home; it was where I should be forever. This lucky Pisces woman had landed in her natural habitat.

Talking of natural habitat, I was invited back to the

'Tarzan and Jane' paradise setting. By now, I had learned it was a private naturist club, and I turned out to be an '*au naturel* sun goddess.' No bruises, capsizes or stress there: just Phil, sunshine, beauty and quiet. We escaped there whenever we could; it became my place to align my physical and mental health. It gave me space and time to relax and daydream. There is nothing better for your soul than to lie naked under the warm sun, with a gentle breeze caressing you, whilst listening to the birds sing to each other. I loved everything; although the water in the lake was icy cold, a quick dip to cool off made you tingle from head to toe. The beauty of the setting took your breath away - a tiny piece of paradise; known and visited by very few people.

Phil had been a member of the club for a while, and the people I did meet were very welcoming and lovely to me. On one of my early visits, I met James: not exactly a vision of loveliness in his calf-length boots, cowboy-type hat, and his unbuttoned white shirt that didn't cover his penis or arse. I must confess, as a newbie to this lark, it was a bit of a shock, but I think the actress in me stopped my face from projecting my thoughts. As it turned out, we became really good friends; he was living there, in a tent, whilst writing a book. It transpired that James lived with his (German) wife (they were both in their sixties) and a younger (Dutch) woman (who was in her thirties), with whom he had had a son. How very avant-garde; another first for me, having had a rather naïve life so far. I found him a very knowledgeable, articulate and interesting man, and we chatted a lot in those early days, but more about James later.

Philip:

The Tarzan & Jane paradise was Rajel Sun Club, a small naturist club situated near Sithney, a couple of miles outside of Helston (Cornwall), and regrettably, now defunct. One had to know the landmarks on the back lane to find the correct five-bar gate and, thus, the entrance to the club. From the gate, a narrow grass track led up a steep hill to a grassed car park area. From here, a path led to the badminton court field, where there was a choice of two paths. One went past a chemical toilet shed to a small open camping field, whilst the other led to the quarry itself, now a very deep, very cold lake. The lake was surrounded on three-quarters of its circumference by high rock walls, and where the rock wall finished was a grass, multi-layered, sunbathing area, including a built-in BBQ and the path to the car park.

Once separated from my ex and living on my own, I had looked for opportunities to pursue my new hobby of naturism, but they were limited. There were a couple of clubs in Cornwall, but single men were regarded as pariahs: the Devil reincarnate. However, through research via magazines and the library (no google in those days), I discovered that a part of Perranporth Beach, known as Perran Sands, was regarded and used as an 'unofficial' naturist beach. The dogs were about to get lots of long walks along Perranporth Beach as I tried to discover where the nudists went.

The area they used was at the far end of the beach, a nearly two-mile walk from the main Perranporth town beach, but eventually, I learnt of the other places one could park, rather than in the town centre, with shorter walks/runs across the dunes to the beach. One involved trespassing on MOD property, and another took one past the ruins of Saint Piran's Oratory (see below). I spent many happy days there, sometimes with the dogs (taking a homemade shade and obviously taking plenty of water for them) and sometimes not.

It was during my research (to find the nudist beach) that I first came across the story of Saint Piran. The ruins of his oratory were used as a landmark to ensure one was on the correct path to the nudist part of the beach. According to Historic UK, 'Saint Piran,' or 'Perran' as he is also known, is famed for his discovery of the precious metal tin. Saint Piran is the patron saint of tin miners, and Saint Piran's Day was originally observed as a 'tinner's holiday' by the numerous tin miners of Cornwall. Saint Piran's Day is celebrated each year on 5th March as the national day of Cornwall.

Whilst other Cornish saints have been feted as the patron saint of Cornwall, Saint Piran is most commonly associated with this accolade, and the flag of Saint Piran is now also recognised as the Cornish flag. The flag shows a white cross on a black background and is said to depict the saint's discovery of tin, 'the white metal' flowing from the black Cornish rocks.

Scholars argue as to the origins of Saint Piran, and no definitive history has been agreed upon. However, many believe he was a bishop who travelled to Cornwall from Ireland in the early 6th century when he was exiled from the Green Isle by those who envied his healing ability. Legend suggested that he was thrown into the sea, attached to a millstone. Yet somehow, he managed to sail safely to Cornwall, landing on a small beach near Newquay, which was named Perran Beach in his honour. It was here that Saint Piran built his oratory – a small chapel – its remains can still be seen today, submerged in sand.

Following a revival of Celtic traditions towards the end of the 19th century, Saint Piran's day has remained popular throughout Cornwall. It is celebrated with marches, festivals and Cornish-themed events, such as the annual Lowender Peran festival in the village of Perranporth, with attendees resplendent in the Cornish colours of black, white and gold. Whilst traditional Saint Piran's Day events are not well documented, the week running up to 5th March, known as 'Perrantide,' is said to involve the spirited consumption of both food and alcohol. The 19th-century Cornish expression 'drunk as a perraner' certainly suggests that a good time was had by all!

Having established a beach where I could enjoy the pleasures of my new pastime, I continued to search for other opportunities. I discovered that the BN (British Naturism) South West swimming gala was coming up, taking place at the Polkyth Leisure Centre in St Austell, but I doubted I would be allowed to go, being a dreaded 'single male.' The local paper came to my rescue again. There was an advert in it for the naturist swimming gala. Included was a telephone number, so I rang it and spoke to a very nice lady called Janet. I was informed that one entered events on the day, and more importantly, if I had any trouble getting in, to ask for her. I did indeed have trouble getting in; marshalling the door were members of one of the local naturist clubs who had a 'thing' about single men. To be fair to them, virtually every naturist club in the UK shared the same fear about single men. As good as her word, Janet came to my rescue and told me to seek her out at the end of the day. Having gained entry, my natural Wallflower instincts took over, i.e. I spoke to no one and kept myself to myself, but being able to swim sans costume in a swimming pool for the first time was just heavenly. For the record, I came second in my heat for the men's fifty-metre front crawl, but nowhere in the next round, or indeed in the back and breaststroke events either. Another first for me was the experience of changing and showering in a mixed sex environment. It just seemed so bloody normal, natural even.

Being the good boy that I am, after the swimming had finished, I sought out Janet in the bar, who introduced me to her husband, Dale, daughter Jackie and her six-year-old daughter. I was asked if I wanted to become a member of their club. Wow! To these people, being a single man was not a deterrent. In hindsight, Judy and

I often wonder if Dale and Janet thought I might have been a suitable new partner for Jackie! And that, folks, is how I became a member of Rajel Sun Club.

As for James, he was one of life's characters and as Judy stated, he and his family became very good friends. Mind, I am convinced he would have liked Judy to join his 'harem,' which, at the time we first met, included another Dutch girl, this one being just twenty years old, as well as the two mentioned by Judy earlier. James was a fascinating person and had been the first person to sail across the Atlantic Ocean in a catamaran. It was in the early fifties, but he did not receive the recognition such a feat deserved because his crew were two single German girls (one of whom would later become his wife), 'just not cricket, old boy!' Please, when you have finished our book, you must seek out James's book about his Atlantic adventure. It's called 'Two Girls Two Catamarans' and is written by James Wharram.

Judith:

So in the first few months of living together, we cemented our relationship. We unknowingly built our foundation for our future, even though I think we were blissfully unaware at the time. Surprisingly, we had never actually been out on a date, and here we were, now happily living in sin together. For the first time in my life, probably since the age of fifteen, someone was actually putting me first and looking after me: that was a beautiful and very novel experience.

He wanted to take me away on holiday to France. Was I dreaming? 'The ex-husband' had never taken me away on holiday ever; it had always been me who suggested/ organised any outing. Of course, I said 'yes,' and before I could blink, it was all arranged: wonderful. So all I had to do was pack a bag and look amazing. I have to confess, as it got closer to the departure date, a few niggling doubts crept in. '*What if we got fed up with each other?*' We had never been together twenty-four hours a day on our own; work, boys and general life had always interrupted our time together. Ever practical, I decided to take out a credit card: my 'get out of jail' card, in case it all went tits up. At least I could get myself back to good old Blighty. Shaun had assured me he would look after Antony for the two weeks we were away. Was it really a good idea to leave two teenagers home alone? I had my doubts, but food shopped for them as if I was never coming back. That just left the dogs to worry about; I think I forgot to mention we had four between us. I had Ross the Boss and Billy Bonkers, Phil had Kali Kripple and Deyna Dunce; all very large German Shepherds. Well, one thing I could be sure of was that they wouldn't get a walk while we were away, and there would be a mountain of dog poo to pick up when we got back. I think Phil went slightly over the top with his yellow Post-it notes all over the house. Things like 'Remember to give me water' on the dog bowls and 'Please put bleach down me' on the loo. I had to remind myself he had never had children. He had no idea he was wasting his time, and I hadn't got the heart to tell him it was all in vain.

Well, that was the household worries sort of addressed; now, I only had myself to consider. What do you pack for a naturist holiday in a naturist village (apparently the size of a town)? Yes, my second trip on an aeroplane and my first naturist holiday. Phil had told me people even shopped naked in the shops (that didn't sound very hygienic to me), but I have always been open-minded. Obviously, I wouldn't need a bikini. Did I need knickers, and did anyone actually wear any clothes whilst they were there? Apparently, the most important piece of kit was a towel to sit on; well, that was easy enough. Just to be on the safe side, I opted to take the normal items of clothing for holidaying; I like to have all avenues covered. Boy, this was a giant step up from the Tarzan and Jane setup I was used to. I'd be fine; I had my gorgeous lover with me, and he had been on naturist holidays in the past. All I had to do was enjoy myself for fourteen days.

Once we left home, I found it all very exciting; car to London, plane to France, then a coach transfer to the holiday town, all a first for me. Thereafter followed a lot of firsts; we met some lovely oldies at the rep's meet and greet pool party, drank copious amounts of alcohol naked, danced naked, sunbathed naked, swam in the sea naked and had a jolly good time. I took to it like a duck to water – there was no going back now, and the freedom had transformed me forever. More importantly, Phil and I had the time to take our romance to a different level.

I suppose, in a way, it was our honeymoon, and I didn't need my 'get out of jail card.' What a relief.

When I look at the photos of us from that time, the memories seem timeless, and although I didn't realise it then, we were actually in the prime of our lives. We were thirty-three and thirty-four, young and beautiful; surely life couldn't get any better than this. The holiday was a breath of fresh air and a huge success; not only had I cast off my clothes, but I had also cast off the chains of responsibility and regained my love of life. Something that had been missing for a very long time. I felt very blessed.

Philip:

Is it not normal to invite your new live-in girlfriend to go on holiday with you? Perhaps not to 'Le Cap d'Adge Quarter Naturiste,' a large holiday resort, often referred to as the 'Naked City,' situated in the Languedoc-Roussillon area of Southern France.

Although Judy had only been joining in with my naturist activities for a few months, she was loving the experience, and it seemed totally natural to me to invite her to a naturist resort for our first holiday together. It was many years later before she admitted (to me) that she had taken out a credit card to ensure she could get back to the UK should the holiday not work out. Oh, she of little faith! For my part, I had no such worries. I was just looking forward to a nice holiday in the Med.

Judith:

Having fallen in love with this wonderful holiday place, I was keen to learn more about it, and this is what I discovered.

The naturist resort sits at the eastern edge of the town of Cap d'Agde, which is a seaside resort on France's Mediterranean coast. It is located in the commune of Agde, in the Hérault department within the region of Occitanie. Cap d'Agde was planned by architect Jean Le Couteur as part of one of the largest state-run development schemes in French history. In the 1960s, the only buildings at the Cap were small houses that were typically used by locals over the weekends. It is now one of the largest leisure ports in the French Mediterranean.

The land adjoining the long sandy beach at Cap d'Agde was owned for many years by the Oltra family, who farmed the olive groves behind the sand dunes adjoining the beach. After the Second World War, the Oltra brothers noticed that people were coming in increasing numbers to camp on their land and that many of these people liked to bathe and sunbathe nude.

The Oltra brothers began to formalise arrangements for campers on their land. This subsequently led to the creation of the Oltra Club, which is a caravanning and camping resort. The camp grew increasingly popular, especially with young families. German and Dutch tourists were particularly numerous.

In the early 1970s, the government of Georges

Pompidou drew up plans for the development of the Languedoc-Roussillon coastline. Naturism initially had no part in these proposals, but Paul René Oltra, one of the brothers, persuaded the authorities to include plans for a naturist resort at Cap d'Agde. In 1973 the 2km long beach was officially designated as a naturist beach, and the 'Quarter Naturiste' was born. In the height of summer, there will be over 40,000 naked holidaymakers there! Amongst naturist circles, Le Cap d'Agde is very much regarded as a Marmite place, and we fall into the 'love it' camp.

Philip:

A lovely place that Le Cap is, we first had to get there. One of the disadvantages of living in Cornwall, especially back then, was the need to travel 330 miles to Gatwick to catch an aeroplane. For this holiday, it meant Judy got another chance to drive my BMW, this time on a longer trip than just to the local farm to pick daffodils. It would also be her last time driving any distance in it, as upon our return, it failed its MOT, so we decided to be sensible and buy a little economical hatch. Ha! But more of that later.

In my mind, it was with some trepidation that we were leaving the two boys at home with four dogs to look after – with good reason, as it turned out. The OCD Sagittarian in me put a Post-it note on anything I believed they needed reminding to do. Judy said I was wasting my time, and she was right. However, several years later, when visiting Antony in his university lodgings house for Christmas, I had to smile when we found the house covered in Post-it notes written by him because his fellow students were not doing agreed chores. But I digress. We were packed, all the paperwork was in a folder, and I was due to start my leave following a night shift on Saturday night. Our flight was early Tuesday morning, so we would be leaving Cornwall at midnight on Monday.

Sunday morning was a sailing time (we raced Tuesday and Friday evenings and Sunday mornings, with an occasional race on a Saturday afternoon). It was quite normal for me to sail after a night shift; sailing was fun, and I could sleep in the afternoon. Normally, at any rate. On this day, I had finished my night shift at 8.30 am, came home (5 minutes) to change, have a cuppa (having already had breakfast at work) and pick up our sailing gear. We then set off to Marazion, home of the Mount's Bay Sailing Club (situated directly opposite St Michel's Mount if you are familiar with the area), where our Osprey dinghy was stored.

It was a beautiful sunny day; we had a lovely sail, and after showering, we were upstairs in the bar enjoying an après sail drink. Then my name was being called. Apparently, my work was on the telephone (landline situated downstairs): very strange. Had I forgotten to do something; was there a major incident, and I was required back at work? Picking up the handset, John, a colleague from work who had taken over from me earlier that morning, informed me that the police had been in contact and were currently sitting outside our house. The house was insecure, and the dogs were running loose in the street. John did not know what had happened, but he did know that a neighbour had told the police that I worked for SWEB. When they called, John knew I would be sailing in the morning.

On returning home, there was indeed a police car parked outside the house. That would have the neighbours' net curtains twitching. We could see that the bottom window to the small front porch was smashed. The officer had been told by my neighbours that a small dog, being walked off lead by some old codger past our front door, had run up to the porch window and had been exchanging barks with Ross the Boss. We guess that Ross, in an attempt to get at the little dog, had charged the window, smashing it. We have no idea what happened to the little dog and its owner, but Ross, Bill and Deyna had all come out through the smashed window and started circling our little Daihatsu van (that we used to take the dogs to the dunes and beach in). One neighbour, braver than the others, attempted to shoo the dogs back into the house. Ross, not liking humans, went back in, but the two young dogs ran off.

The officer explained that he had gone round to the back to try the back door, but Ross had charged it, so he retired to the safety of the car! Another police car was out searching for the dogs. We entered the house to discover the door from the porch to the living room was open. The boys (well, it transpired to be Shaun) had failed to shut this door when they went out, allowing the dogs access to the porch. Kali Kripple was in her bed, and Ross greeted us as normal. Leaving Judy to clear up, I took the BMW and went looking for Bill and Deyna. Our problem and big fear was that our estate was surrounded by fields full of sheep, and the farmers would not hesitate to shoot a dog if they caught it worrying their flock.

A short drive later, along the back lanes, I spotted a police car parked up. It was in the entrance to a farm lane with a large five-bar wooden gate across it. As I drew up alongside the panda, the officer pointed to the gate. Behind it, sat side by side with lopping tongues and smiling teeth, were Bill and Deyna. I got out, opened the rear door (of the car), went over to the gate and opened it. Both dogs dutifully trotted over to the car and jumped in. Shutting the car door, I went over to thank the officer. He had spotted them down the lane and judged he had enough time to shut the gate before they could get to him. These officers were frightened of GSDs.

So, half asleep and in blazing sunshine, I spent two hours doing a temporary repair job on the broken window before I was able to get some sleep. At least I had all day Monday (day one of our holiday) to replace the glass and recover before making the trip to Gatwick.

Landing at Montpelier, we disembarked to glorious sunshine. Quickly ushered onto a coach by our holiday rep, we were soon heading for Le Cap. The bus took a scenic route, meaning Judy was able to get her first views of the Med and its golden sand beaches and soon we were there. Rooms were allocated, cases were slung on the bed, clothes cast onto the floor, and grabbing a towel, off we went to the beach. Oh, what bliss.

That first night was party time; two of them, actually. Firstly, there was our holiday firm's welcome gathering with free wine, to be followed by one hosted by one of the swimming pool operators, complete with an entertainer. I was not keen; I am not a wine drinker and abhor the British abroad singing silly songs. I don't normally go on package holidays either, preferring to make my own arrangements, but it was cheaper to use one to go to Le Cap. So what went wrong? I will always blame the wine, but by 10 pm, I was stark bollock naked in the middle of the swimming pool singing along to the 'Birdy' song, complete with actions. How embarrassing! Judy, being a naturally outgoing person (some might say mad), needed no encouragement.

Friends were quickly made, and for once, back in the UK, we all kept in touch. We even visited some of them, but, as became the norm for us, it was always us who made the effort to travel.

The holiday pattern was set; early breakfast, mornings on the beach swimming, sunbathing, reading and playing bat and ball – something everyone did. Lunch was had back at the apartment, followed by a siesta – nothing like a good bonk and a couple of hours sleep to set you up for more swimming and sunbathing etc.

With me being a fussy eater, we were self-catering, and early in the first week, I sent Judy down to the shops to buy some steak. At this stage, she was not comfortable about buying food naked, so she put on her (Frankie Goes To Hollywood) 'Relax' vest combined with a pair of minuscule cut-off jeans. A hunk (her words) of a French butcher gave her an enormous lump of quality fillet steak for a silly price. So guess what? I made her wear the same outfit every time we needed to buy meat.

All too soon, it was time to return home. Would the house still be there, would the dogs still be alive, and what sort of mess had they created? We were amazed. The boys had done us proud, and the damage was minimal. Phew!

Chapter 7

Highs & Lows

Philip:

As mentioned earlier, when my poor beloved BMW went for its MOT following our holiday, it failed. There was some rust in the sills, and new brake discs, pads and pipes were required. The mechanic did the normal mechanic thing, sucking in through pursed lips and estimating it would be at least £200 to put right. Was it worth it, and was it likely to cost us more in the future? If it is something we have managed to do during our years together, it is to make decisions: choosing a path with no regrets, even if it turned out to be the wrong one. In this case, we decided to be sensible; sell the Beemer and buy a practical little hatch. A man bought it for spares; the wheels alone were worth what he paid us for it, so, money in hand, we went looking for a practical hatchback. A Ford Fiesta seemed the best bet: cheap to buy and run, but fuck me, how boring it was going to be. I knew we had to be practical: financial circumstances dictated the compromise, but still, it was going to be a bit of a comedown.

My car history was not littered with classics, but most had character. My motoring life had started with the family friend's Morris Minor 1000 saloon, followed by a Morris Minor 1000 van, an Austin Cambridge estate, a Triumph 2000, an Austin 1100 and a Fiat 128. (This was a great car to drive, but the driver's door fell off at work. Cornwall's damp rusted away what little metal there was.) Then I had a Mini Clubman, a Renault 8, the VW Camper, the Triumph 2.5pi, a Mk3 Spitfire, a Reliant Regal three-wheeler van, a green BMW 528, a minibus (which belonged to the athletic club, but I looked after it and used it as a run-around), a Mk4 Spitfire, and finally, the blue BMW. Now, to go with the very rusty Daihatsu van, we were going to buy a Fiesta. My motoring life was over; I must have been seriously in love: why else would I be doing this?

We searched all the local papers for garage and private ads, and eventually found what seemed to be what we were looking for at a garage near Helston. So off we went for a test drive. After parting with slightly more than our agreed budget, we came home with a white Daihatsu Charade 5-door GT-ti! The Fiesta was very clean but was brown and only had three doors; not that practical with two strapping teenagers. Parking it back in its spot after the test drive, we asked the salesman what the car next to it was. It was white with black bumpers and red stripe trimming, a bit like a VW GTI, but I didn't know what it was (and I'm pretty good with my cars). As I've just stated, it was a Charade. We asked to take it for a test drive; it had five doors, a turbocharged three-cylinder engine, a high roof with a large sunroof, and it went like shit off a shovel. It was unanimous; we were having it. We were now a two-Daihatsu family.

Before Judy moves our story forward, I will just mention one final tale involving the BM. Trevu FC organised a fundraising car Treasure Trail (they were all the rage back then). We were not fans, mainly because we were useless at quizzes and crossword puzzles, but hey ho, it was for my team, so we joined in. Filling the car up en route (it had a large tank, but one was lucky to get more than 20MPG from it), we duly arrived at the council office car park, in Redruth, at our allotted time on a Sunday morning. We were given our clues. We read the first one and did not understand it; we did not know whether to go left or right out of the car park, so we pulled over, waited for the next competitors to arrive and then followed them.

The route took us out to Radnor and Scorrier, where the clue seemed to be instructing us to go inside and have a pint at a pub. So we did and got talking to the punters, explaining why we were there. We were told that the answer to the question was outside on the swinging pub sign; we hadn't needed to go inside at all. Then it was out to the coast to Porthtowan, Portreath and onto Gwithian, and then inland to Connor Downs. There, I had to leave Judy at the crossroads to try and figure out the current clue whilst I nipped down the road to refill the car. We had used a whole tank of petrol and were barely halfway through the clues. It was not going well. As we were well past the allotted time allowance, we decided to give up and head to the Countryman Pub in Carn Brea, the finishing point, hoping to get there before everyone left. We failed. Only the organisers had remained to check us in, and there was not even time for a quick pint as the pub was shutting.

Judith:

Life at the new Elliott/Lea household was working pretty well; we all somehow managed to rub along okay. We had a roof over our heads, food on the table, a decent social life and Phil and I were very much in love. A lot of my old friends had dissed me because I had ditched the 'husband.' I found that quite hurtful, but there was no way I was going to tell anyone the ins and outs as to what had transpired. Although in my eyes, the marriage had broken down because of the 'husbands' behaviour, there was a large part of me that felt very guilty about breaking up the family home. I had always believed marriage was forever. My parents' divorce had left a huge scar on me, and now history was repeating itself on my sons; something I had promised would never happen, but it had. All I could do was keep the boys together, there was no way I was going to let them be split up, as I was from my sister, and at least I managed to do that.

Philip:

My work colleagues may have taken the piss out of my 'instant family' – knowing about my vasectomy and decision not to have any children whilst married – but

I was exceedingly happy with my new situation. I think it was a surprise to both of us that there were fewer obstacles to overcome than we had expected. Sharing space is not something I am good at, but as Judy stated, working shifts helped provide home alone time, at least for me, if not for her. Having to walk the dogs also gave us the excuse, if that is the right word, to enjoy time alone together, or indeed, just alone, whilst enjoying the beauty of our surroundings. This is where the location of Tolvaddon earned itself a big tick because we had Tehidy Country Park and the North Cliffs on our doorstep. Both were places where we could walk the dogs, and whilst Tehidy was walkable from the house because there were no paths along the lanes, it was safer to transport the dogs there by car. I also used to go for long runs on a circular route, including paths through the woods and the coast path along the North Cliffs, a place that Judy called 'our back garden.'

Judith:

We had the best 'back garden' in the world; it was called the North Cliffs - a stretch of coast between Gwithian and Portreath. The tall cliffs look pretty foreboding, and over the centuries, they have struck fear into the hearts of many a sailor. There are spots along here known as Deadman's Cove and Hell's Mouth, where numerous vessels have succumbed to the sea. Below the towering cliffs, the waters are a sparkling azure blue with tantalising small sandy coves, but you really need to be a mountain goat to access them. On a beautiful summer's day, this was the place to be if you wanted to avoid the tourist crowds. The coastal heathlands blaze with gorse and heather, the grass is sprinkled with wildflowers, and the rocky ledges are home to nesting seabirds. Think Poldark (Ross and Demelza) on horses, stealing a kiss with not a soul in sight. Well, we were Phil and Judy (with a rusty Daihatsu van), but we also stole lots of kisses hidden in the grasses where the only onlookers were the butterflies, birds and bees. How lucky were we to be able to spend quality time together in the best place in the world? The answer is 'very lucky.' I think I would have liked to have lived there years ago and been a smuggler, off-loading illicit cargo from one of the secret coves, pitting my wits against the Revenue men. How bizarre that all those years ago, if caught, the punishment was to be transported to colonies such as Australia, now such a desirable place to live.

The cliffs were also our favourite place to walk the dogs. I remember one morning we had taken the dogs for a leisurely stroll along the coastal path.

We held hands and chatted, and I said to Phil, 'How lucky are we doing this when others are at work?'

We both felt quite smug. That was until when we reached the van and realised, to our horror, that we had locked the keys inside it. Our smugness quickly turned to panic as we were both due at work in a couple of hours. We had to jog home at double pace, which the dogs thought was great fun; not for us, though. Once home, sweat beading off us, Phil headed back on his bike with the spare set of keys to rescue the van. We got to work on time by the skin of our teeth, and we made damn sure we never committed that mistake again.

Philip:

All dogs require exercise, but large dogs demand lots of it, and I was happy as a sandboy taking them, even in inclement weather. We had lots of places to walk the dogs, but Basset Cove, on the North Cliffs, was the best place to take them where they could run off lead. Early morning walks before morning shifts, Sunday sailing or planned days out to the beach generally entails having the area to myself. However, taking them after a night shift meant one had to be more careful (of letting them off lead) as there were often more people around, and generally speaking, people tend to be afraid of German Shepherds.

There are a few doggy stories that form part of our socialising anecdotes, and I shall begin here with the sheep story. It was the morning after a night shift, and it was raining stair-rods. Our dogs went for a walk regardless of the weather, so, donning waterproofs, I loaded the three of them into the back of the Daihatsu GT-ti and off to the North Cliffs we went, to Basset's Cove, to be precise.

At Basset's Cove, an unmade lane ran down towards the cliff-top car park, which was out of sight from the little car park by the main road. Alongside this lane was a strip of dune-type grass about 15m wide. From the car park at the cliff top, one could walk along the cliff-top coastal path to Deadman's Cove, back up another footpath to the main road, crossing it into the woods (Tehidy Country Park) and back to the car.

On this particular morning, I parked up, turned off the engine, pulled the hood of my waterproof over my head and tightened it around my face; it was evil outside.

'Right,' I told myself, 'the sooner you do this, the sooner you get to bed.'

Getting out, I walked to the back of the car and pulled up the hatch. As usual, Bill and Deyna jumped out, taking chunks out of each other in their excitement, whilst Kali, being older and not brilliant on her hind legs, took her time. Locking the car, I made to follow the dogs, but then I looked up.

'Oh Fuck!'

A flock of sheep were not in their field, but were huddled up under the Cornish hedge that was the boundary between the field and the lane. The boundary fence alongside the lane consisted of barbed wire strands. The flock now had two German Shepherd dogs in amongst them, with the third about to join them. Bill and Deyna had realised they had some playmates. I grabbed Kali and screamed at Deyna to 'Stay.' Deyna obeyed – all the hours spent dog training had paid off – and I got her on a lead. Bill was not my dog and had not been living with me for that long, so today, he was ignoring me as he chased sheep down the lane towards the cliff top. I had visions of seeing him and several sheep on the rocks 60 feet below the cliffs. How was I going to explain that to

Judy?

I had never seen sheep jump, but I can confirm that they can jump about six feet vertically. The flock dispersed in all directions: some over the Cornish hedge, some over the barbed wire, some went over the road and into the woods, and others followed Bill and the sheep he was chasing down towards the cliff top, with me following up behind. As I crested the brow, giving me a view of the cliff-top car park and coastal path, I was relieved to see Bill chasing a sheep along the left-hand path. At least he was going in the direction of our intended walk. Eventually, he got tired of the chase and came back to me. Finally, I had three dogs back on the lead, and a flock of sheep scattered to all points of the compass. Bed and sleep could not come soon enough.

Then there is the tale of the Camper Van. So, here we are, back at the North Cliffs, at six thirty on a Sunday morning, giving the dogs a walk before we go sailing. Parking up at the top car park at Basset's Cove, I let Bill and Deyna off lead (there were just two dogs now as Kali had died) and headed towards the cliffs. At these early times, there were often cars and/or camper vans parked up overnight in the lower car park. Local bye-laws prohibited this, but as stated earlier, the bottom car park could not be seen from the coastal road, and it was very rarely policed.

Bill, as was his wont, was running ahead, and as we approached the car park, I could see that on this morning, there were two cars and a VW camper van parked up.

Bill went up to the first car and cocked his leg against a tyre. Then he trotted over to the second car and repeated the process. As Deyna and I closed the gap to him, he trotted over towards the camper which was between us and the coastal path we were taking. He sniffed the rear tyre and then moved forwards; suddenly, all hell broke loose. I could hear a woman screaming and dogs barking; a right old commotion! I ran across to the camper to find the sliding door open, and, looking inside, I saw Bill standing on top of the bed, tail wagging, drooling, and with lovely white teeth on show. Sat up in the bed was an ashen-faced woman hanging on for dear life to her little pooch whilst screaming her head off. Her husband was speechless. I stepped inside, grabbed Bill's collar, and shooed him outside.

As I retreated, I said, 'It's not a good idea to leave the door open, as you have found out.' I closed the sliding door, and the three of us proceeded along the path to finish our walk, with me having a little chuckle to myself.

My final doggy story involves a black rubbish bag, and Judy was with me on this occasion. This time, after cocking his leg on a couple of cars, Bill trotted over to some black rubbish bags that someone had left behind the low wall separating the car park from the cliff-top coastal path; Deyna had followed him. Judging from how both dogs had wagging tails and seemed excited, we assumed there was food in the bags, and they had found an opening to one of them as they were licking something.

'Jesus!'

All four of us jumped back in surprise as a man jumped up from the ground attempting to shoo the dogs away. We called them back to us and put them on their leads. The guy was walking the Cornwall Coastal path and was sleeping overnight in a sleeping bag, using large black bin bags to keep the damp and rain out. The dogs, licking his face, had awoken him (from sweet dreams or nightmares? Who knows?).

There is one more North Cliffs story, and while it does involve walking the dogs, it is not a doggy story as such, but hey, we thought it worthy of a mention as it brought yet another North Cliff smile to our faces.

It occurred on a midweek lunchtime North Cliff dog walk; Judy and I were both on days off. As usual, we parked in the top car park of Basset's Cove and started to walk down the path towards the cliff top.

As the bottom car park came into view, I said to Judy, 'I think I recognise that car.'

It belonged to a SWEB Electrical Engineer, one with a reputation of being a bit of a ladies' man (and one who pops up again later in our story).

Sure enough, as we got closer, I confirmed it definitely was his car. The windows were steamed up, and the car was gently rocking. He was obviously having some extra curriculum lunchtime activity with another office girl conquest.

We gave it a wide berth and continued on our walk. If he did see us, he never mentioned it in the rest of my years at SWEB, including when he attended our house parties. Like my brother David, he was a fun person to be around.

In hindsight, we realise that we only had ourselves to blame for our dog walking incidents (there are many more, other than those I have mentioned). When we took our dogs for a walk, during the drive to wherever we were going, they got very excited and expectant, and, on being released from the car or van, they went 'mental' (to use some modern parlance). Once, we parked up behind an estate car at Gwithian Towans. Four German Shepherds gently jumped out the back of it, all off lead, and they trotted off quietly with their owner across the dunes. Meanwhile, our three were doing loop-the-loop in the back of our van.

We looked at each other and said, 'Why aren't ours like that?'

Of course, we knew the answer; it was our fault.

Our dogs were our playmates. We would rough and tumble with them in the house and garden, and when out walking, especially with Bill and Deyna, we encouraged them to play silly games. For example, when the time was short, we used to give them a quick walk on a hill with a small copse on it at Tolvaddon, on a roundabout under the A30 dual carriageway, would you believe? Towards the top of the hill was a large shrub about twenty feet in diameter. We taught them to chase each other around it. We would hold them at opposite sides of the shrub and then let them go, and boy did they go. Around and around, until one of them would realise they were not catching the other up, so they would turn around to chase the other way, and so it went on. It was a great way to wear them out quickly, and to boot, the hill was three minutes from the house. I believe they do say, 'Dogs take after their owners.'

Judith:

As you have probably gathered, I am a more fair-weather sort of dog walker, which is why all the interesting dog stories belong to Phil. Who in their right mind walks dogs at silly o'clock in the morning or when it's teeming with rain? Certainly not this girl. What we did have in common was our love for sunbathing, preferably naked sunbathing, and when we couldn't get to Perranporth, the North Cliffs once again ticked the box. I didn't need a lot of persuading to put my mountain goat hat on; we managed to find a precarious route down to one of the tiny sandy coves, perfect for indulging in a bit of sun, sea and sex. If I ever won a lot of money, a private, secluded beach would be at the top of my wish list, but for now, I had one for free; we just had to risk life and limb to reach it.

Our cove had a rocky overhang (nature's natural shady area for when it got too hot), fine white sand, and easy access into the sea to cool down. There were large rocks you could just sit on and dangle your toes into the crystal clear waters below; I felt like an exotic mermaid surveying my terrain. I had everything I wanted in the world there, and that was Phil. I loved everything about him, and in this place, nothing else existed, well, normally. One day, the sound of a helicopter could be heard getting closer. We were having an after-lunch kiss and cuddle in the sunshine when suddenly, all our possessions started to take off in all directions. The bloody helicopter was hovering immediately above us, and the noise was unbelievable. After what seemed like a lifetime, it moved towards a large rocky outcrop in the sea and then began a practice rescue operation no more than one hundred yards from 'our' cove. How dare they invade our private space? We had managed to rescue and secure most of our scattered belongings and were now standing, stark-bollock-naked, to watch the show. As they lifted the last person from the rocks, we clapped our hands to show our appreciation, then made hand signals politely asking them to 'fuck off.' That was a pretty special day: helicopters and Phil, two of my favourite things.

Philip:

Had that helicopter planned to visit 'our cove,' or had the pilot just spotted two naked homo sapiens having some fun on the beach (that definitely is a euphemism for having sex)? Regardless, the use of a Sea King Helicopter to dampen, or rather totally kill, one's ardour seemed a bit extreme. Were those pilots aware, I wonder, of the effort it took to reach those secluded beaches along the

North Cliffs? It had taken a while to discover the goat paths leading down to Deadman's Cove, and one had to tread carefully the whole way down. On one of the early descents, having reached the bottom of the cliff path, Judy stepped onto a relatively large flat-topped rock. She was being just a little too overconfident as she walked across the rock and made to step onto the next smaller rock towards the actual beach. The rocks were wet as the tide was on its way out, and she slipped. Fortunately, she has amazing reactions and managed to grab a handhold to stop herself from falling into the water. I was out of reach, so I could not grab her, and I was very relieved to see her get that handhold. To fall into the water amongst the rocks at that point could have had very serious consequences. One big lesson was learnt from that day onwards: both of us always made sure we had good trainers on, and we took extreme care clambering over the rocks. However, the effort and risk were definitely worth it as there were actually three coves one could use (the first and second for sunbathing and the third for hanky-panky). These coves were also used to take photographs that accompanied a story we sent for publication to H&E Magazine; that would be another holiday paid for.

Judith:

So you can be Ross and Demelza Poldark on the cliffs, Tarzan and Jane in the cove below, and Robin Hood and Maid Marian across the road in Tehidy Country Park.

The latter has over 250 acres of peaceful woods and lakes to explore. It was formerly owned by the Bassets, one of the four most powerful families in Cornwall with extensive lands and mineral rights. Inland at Carn Brea, you can find the Basset memorial, built in 1836 to honour Sir Francis Basset (1757 – 1835). The settlement and manor of Tehidy were first recorded as 'Tedintone' in the Doomsday Survey of 1086. Now it is owned and managed by Cornwall County Council and is an enchanting place to visit all year round. I loved it in the autumn when all the leaves on the trees changed colour and dropped to the floor, creating a cushion of softness underfoot. It was far nicer to walk the dogs there when we had Cornish drizzle. The trees protected you from the wind and rain, as opposed to the North Cliffs, where you were unable to escape the weather's fury. So there you have it, what a wonderful back garden we had, all on our doorstep and free. My Cornish dream had come true. I was in the right place with the right person at the right time. All my stars had aligned, and I felt true happiness.

Time and weather permitting, Perranporth was our default place where we went to sunbathe and swim nude. In fact, because we were there so often, we left BBQ coals and assorted beach paraphernalia in a small cave above the high water mark. They never got stolen, and it was far easier to take that chance than to keep lugging everything across the beach/dunes.

Visiting this beach also gave me the opportunity to meet new and interesting people. I enjoy chatting to people from a broad spectrum of backgrounds, and at Perranporth, there was always an eclectic mix. There were your regulars, now and again people, and just on holiday people, all seeking a safe place to practice nudism.

One set of regulars were not naturists; they were soldiers from the Penhale Camp, an army training camp located on top of the cliffs, on the other side of the headland to Perran Sands beach.

The camp has history: it was established in 1939 as a World War II emergency measure to train anti-aircraft gunners. In 1943 it was occupied by the United States Army Corps of Engineers as part of the build-up to Operation Overlord, i.e. the D-Day landings. The engineers built the fourteen Nissen huts on the camp, which were still being used as accommodation for training unit's right up until the camp was closed by the Ministry of Defence in 2010.

Do you remember that earlier in our story, Phil mentioned trespassing on MOD land to take a shorter route to the nudist part of the beach? Well, the land that he, then we, crossed (ignoring the MOD warning notices!) was part of what is known as Penhale Sands, or 'Peran Treth' in Cornish (meaning St Piran's sands, or Penhale Dunes). It is a complex of sand dunes and a protected area for its wildlife. It was designated as a 'Site of Special Scientific Interest (SSS) in 1953 and became a 'Special Area of Conservation' (SAC) in 2004. It is the most extensive system of sand dunes in Cornwall.

Philip:

On more than one occasion, whilst running over these dunes with Kali (my first dog), I encountered soldiers in camouflage, complete with weapons, on a training exercise. The first time it had been a case of, '*Oh fuck, what do I do?*' and without any real thought, I just ran a bit faster and hoped Kali would follow (she did). 'Flight, rather than fight', as the saying goes. A local businessman, who was part of the regular naturist crowd, informed me that he believed 'they were only cadets.' That may well have been true because I did find it strange that I was never challenged. Or was facing up to a slobbering German Shepherd too much for them: who knows?

Judith:

The soldiers Phil encountered may have been cadets, but the ones involved in my next tale were definitely proper soldiers: I know because we chatted with them. It was yet another glorious hot summer's day, and whilst we were laid out worshipping the sun, there were two teams of soldiers carrying a telegraph pole (one each) up and down the sandy path that led from the top of the cliff to the beach. They did this several times before stopping at the bottom to have a rest and take on water. Lots of fit, sweating, testosterone-fuelled hunks of masculinity; it makes me shiver just thinking about them (sorry Phil – oh, I forgot, he was at work this day, poor sod).

Whilst they were resting, one of the instructor

sergeants approached Jackie and me.

He said, 'The soldiers' next task is to run the two miles along the beach to Perranporth Town and back. It would be a great incentive for them to have the two most beautiful girls on the beach start the race for them.'

What a flatterer; it was probably more to do with the fact that Jackie and I were naked. Nevertheless, we replied, 'Of course we will,' and there is a picture to prove that we did.

There was another time when Jackie picked me up to go to the beach. Yet again, poor Phil was on a morning shift; he would join us in the afternoon. However, all the excitement of the day was over before he reached us. A group of us had been having a chat when there was suddenly lots of shouting and screaming near the water's edge, so we all went to investigate. A woman was hysterical; her husband had gone into the water, and now she could not see him.

The sea on this beach can be very dangerous, and there are treacherous rip currents; this is a specific kind of water current that can occur near beaches with breaking waves. A rip is a strong, localised, and narrow current of water which moves directly away from the shore, cutting through the lines of breaking waves like a river running out to sea. A rip current is at its strongest and fastest nearest the surface of the water. If they do not understand what is happening or don't have the necessary water skills, swimmers who are caught in a rip current often panic. They may exhaust themselves by trying to swim

Judith Lea & Philip Elliott

directly against the flow of water. Over the years, people, including soldiers, have regrettably drowned whilst swimming in the waters of Perran Sands.

NB: It may save your life one day if you take the time to understand and respect water and learn what to do should you get into trouble. My advice would be to visit the 'RespectTheWater.com'website and/or, on social media, search for #FloatToLive and #RespectTheWater. Always only swim between the flags if the beach you are visiting is patrolled by lifeguards.

Apologies for the detour, but I am passionate about water safety. However, let's get back to our hysterical lady. The naturist part of the beach is not lifeguarded, but the town end of the beach is. Occasionally, one of the lifeguards would scoot up the whole beach on a quad bike. Fortunately for the guy in the water, one could be seen heading our way, so a young lad ran towards them, trying to attract their attention, whilst the rest of us all tried to spot the man in the water.

'There he is!' shouted one of our group, pointing several hundred yards out to sea; he had quite definitely been caught in a rip.

When the lifeguard reached us, he took his surfboard, paddled out to the man, and brought him back to shore. The man was unconscious and now not breathing. The lifeguard commenced first aid whilst using his radio to contact his colleagues to update them and request an Air & Sea Rescue helicopter. It's the quickest way to get an injured person to hospital from such a remote beach. By the time the chopper arrived, the man was conscious but in a poor way. He was put on board and flown to the hospital, and then we left the lifeguard to deal with the family.

What is it about naked me and helicopters? It's never happened again, but I do have one more helicopter story to tell.

It was another day in paradise, well, Perranporth Beach, and I got talking to this very tanned single guy who had just returned from a holiday in Florida. He was very articulate and good looking, but could not catch a frisbee to save his life. He had no coordination for beach games whatsoever. That evening there was a naturist session booked at the St Ives Hydro, and I invited him to join us. I sort of befriended Adrian, and he became a close friend of mine. For all the hours we spent talking, I had no idea what he did for work. Somehow it's a subject that never gets raised in the naturist world, perhaps because 'who you are' is more important than 'what you are.' Imagine my surprise when one afternoon, whilst sunbathing on the beach, he asked me if Phil and I would like a go in the Culdrose helicopter simulator.

At that time, there was a TV show called the Krypton Factor, and on this show, one round consisted of the contestants attempting to fly a plane/jet/helicopter in a simulator. For the helicopter, they used the simulator at RNAS Culdrose. Of course, we said 'YES' and arranged to meet Adrian at his house in Helston the following week.

I gave careful consideration to my wardrobe and decided on a red jumpsuit. I thought it would make me look a bit like Anneka Rice from the TV show Treasure Hunt. Being the programme's 'skyrunner ', Anneka used a helicopter to take her to different locations to hunt for treasure. She became famous for shots of her bottom, either getting into or running away from the helicopter. I'm not sure to this day if it was a good choice or not, but when we found Adrian's house, I knocked on the door. To my surprise, this guy looking like Richard Gere (from the film An Officer and a Gentleman), opened the door. Bloody hell, it was Adrian! I had never seen him with clothes on before; boy, was he hot. It turned out he was a helicopter pilot, and his current role was as an instructor at RNAS Culdrose. He also told us that he had been part of the Krypton Factor game show, both training and marking the contestants. You could have knocked me down with a feather. This was my naked mate from the beach, who couldn't catch a ball to save his life, flying bloody helicopters. When we got to Culdrose and went through security, everyone we passed saluted him and said, 'Sir.' I was more than impressed. I might have been a superstar at beach games, but flying a helicopter was going to be a tad more difficult, especially with 'Sir' watching on.

Philip:
'Did I want to play on a multi-million-pound helicopter simulator?'

Come on, who the fuck is going to say no? Certainly not me. I believe it was Adrian's way of thanking us, especially Judy, for befriending him and allowing him to get involved in the naturist lifestyle in Cornwall. I have mentioned previously how difficult it can be for a single male to pursue such a lifestyle: I have been there. I was very excited when the day arrived to go and play on this 'big boy's toy,' and I think I was even more stunned than Judy when Adrian opened the door in his Naval Flight Lieutenant uniform. It was also a bit surreal having all these ratings, who looked about thirteen to us (and we were only in our mid-thirties), saluting him and calling him 'Sir.' It made me recall my Boys' Brigade days, and I made an effort to straighten my back and 'walk tall.'

Entering the simulator building, we were met with a group of trainee pilots, who again saluted Adrian before we entered the simulator control room; then, it was out into the simulator itself. Oh wow! Here I was, helmet on, strapping myself into the co-pilot's seat whilst Adrian got into the pilot's seat and Judith in the jump seat behind; she had let me have first go. Looking out through the cockpit, all one could see was a semi-circle of huge cinema screens; not that impressive, to be honest. Then Adrian started playing with this control box on the end of a cable; this apparently was the 'remote' as normally everything he was about to do from this remote would usually be carried out from the control room.

'Right, here we go,' he said as he started the engines and simultaneously, the outside screens were now showing us outside on the Culdrose airfield.

Christ, the noise was deafening. Adrian taxied the helicopter onto the runway and lifted off, flying along the Cornish coast for a while before turning out to sea.

'Hold on a sec,' he said, hitting a button on his remote and low, and behold, we were now flying over the North Sea.

We approached an oil rig, which he proceeded to land on, and then he talked me through how to take off, getting me to hold the controls and feel what he was doing. Once in the air, he started to circle the rig and gave control of the aircraft to me; I was flying a helicopter. Hallelujah.

'I just need to alter something on the remote,' he said.

This was my chance, I thought.

If Adrian, who seemed to have no hand-ball coordination whilst playing games, can fly this thing, then surely I could 'rub my tummy and pat my head at the same time.' There are only four controls to master to fly a helicopter: collective pitch control, throttle control, anti-torque control and cyclic pitch control. Simples. Ha!

I concentrated with all my might as I attempted to fly towards the oil rig's landing pad, trying to hover alongside it and then inch my way across, towards, and above it. I was actually sweating, and I was realising that one needed to be able to tickle one's feet and stand on one leg as well as rub one's tummy and pat one's head, but I was getting there. Then all I could hear was Judy and Adrian laughing their heads off in my helmet. I turned my head to see what was happening and was met with a cockpit full of smoke, red lights flashing all over the place and alarms going off. I had not noticed anything! Adrian had started an engine fire, the bugger. Before we finished our session, following a question by me about 'What do you do when an engine fails?' he took back control from Judy. On approaching the airfield, he turned the engines off and carried out a successful 'autorotation' landing. However, he was not happy, and so repeated the exercise, this time making a better landing, then that was it: game over.

On the way out, the trainees waiting to have their lessons all said words to the effect of 'That was an impressive autorotation landing, Sir.'

Adrian had a big grin on his face, as did we. What a fantastic evening it had been, one never to be forgotten.

Chapter 8

We Are Family

Judith:

During our first summer living together, my family decided to come down on holiday to give Phil the 'once over.' He must have passed the test, as, over the next few years, my sister, her two young daughters and my uncle came down on their 'annual jolly' every summer after that, sometimes bringing additional friends with them. The word had spread. We were a bit like (the TV show) 'Shameless', but without the drugs: we knew how to throw a party. Trips to the beach, outings on the boat and visits to the Minack Theatre were guaranteed to give all a good time. They were very happy, albeit very tiring, days. We would spend hours making sand castle villages, and every child from miles around would want to help. We would go home with blisters on our hands: that's serious construction. We built in all weathers: sun, rain and sea fog; it didn't matter what the climate was doing.

One year we had a 'save Willy' construction ongoing at Marazion beach, and it took most of the day. We had a blow-up whale that we were trying to prevent from being washed out to sea (God knows why - aren't you supposed to release whales from captivity?) and had built lots of sea walls topped with sandcastles to keep the tide out and the whale in. We were all so engrossed in our work we hadn't noticed we were being watched and filmed by about fifty Japanese tourists until they all cheered when the whale escaped into the sea.

I also remember one hot sunny day when Shaun turned up, looking like a rock star in a leather jacket, with a stunning blonde (also in a leather jacket) on his arm. The temperature was in the 80s, and how they didn't melt that day, I will never know. Having said that, they were far too 'cool' to make sandcastles; having a beer and looking good was much more important to them. Also, sunbathing was never on their agenda; snogging and sleeping were more their thing.

Shaun was stunningly good-looking, charming, and had a very easy-going nature. Needless to say, girls swooned at the sight of him and practically fell at his feet. Everything he wore looked amazing on him. He didn't follow fashion; he had his own style. Being a 'clothes horse,' even a sack would have looked good on him, which Phil and Antony much envied. My usual parting shot as he left the house was 'be sensible and use a condom.' I was actually thinking, '*Lock up your daughters, Camborne.*' He was working as a manager at a factory that made footballs, which was very appropriate, as he was the leading goal scorer for the local football team. He somehow persuaded Phil and Antony to join the football team, so it became a bit of a family outing now and again. His approach to life was very simple; earn money throughout the week, and spend every penny at the nightclub over the weekend. He was very popular as he was very generous, and he was well-liked by both boys and girls.

Once we were all living together, Shaun just went about life in his own merry way, and he would rock up for his tea now and again. Sometimes, during the week, he would spend nights at his mate's house, and more than likely, he would stay with some girl over the weekend. With him being away from the house more and more, it often just left the three of us.

Antony looked up to his brother, and Shaun was very protective of him. They had a very different outlook on life; Antony was less easy-going and less 'cool,' but much funnier than Shaun. I can remember Phil and I were planning to go to the local nightclub one night, and Antony informed us that he would blank us if we turned up: which he did. On the other hand, Shaun got the DJ to play a record for 'his mum,' introduced me to all his friends, and danced the night away with us.

Philip:

Blimey; first, Judy moved in with her two boys and two dogs, and then it seemed like all her family and relatives were queuing up to give me the once over. I had never known anything like it, but to be truthful, I enjoyed all the madness. It was all a welcome new experience for me, and I loved it. At this stage, we were not to know that we were experiencing a honeymoon period with all this family bonhomie.

As well as Judy's sister (with her two young daughters and uncle), her mother and stepfather visited (her mother is very nosey), and then her (adopted) cousin also came one year with her Dan Air pilot boyfriend, at the same time as her sister. This meant three adults, two nieces, plus Judy, me, the boys and three dogs all in a small two-up-two-down, end terrace house. One evening during this visit, all the adults were downstairs when we could hear giggling coming from the master bedroom above us. Upon investigation, we discovered that the girls had locked themselves in our bedroom (remember, the lock had been put on to keep my cereals safe from the boys). Unfortunately for them, we had a key and discovered them standing on the bed, merrily crayoning on the wall and laughing their heads off.

Judith:

Phil had now been introduced to my family and friends from 'Up North,' either by them visiting us in Cornwall, or us making the journey north. I got to meet his family from 'Down South' during trips to visit his dad in Hertfordshire. He had two older brothers, a younger sister and a father; his mother had died when he was twenty-two.

I got on best with his flamboyant brother, David, who was a larger-than-life personality and always turned out to be the life and soul of the party. His other brother and his family were very quiet and reserved, whilst I found his sister and her family very odd. However, his dad was absolutely lovely, and I loved him straight away. He didn't say much, but he had the kindest eyes.

I learnt that David held a fancy dress party 'Down South' in a very posh hotel every Xmas for his employees, friends and families, and we got an invite to the 1988 party. He apparently was very wealthy, a member of some millionaire's club. He had the trophy wife and two children, but he had separated from her and left the family several months before the party took place.

As the 'Pisco' party approached (Phil will explain the name shortly), David telephoned and asked us if we would stay an extra night. He invited us to stay at his house, saying that there was something he needed to talk to us about. My imagination ran wild about what the issue might be, as, from the tone of his voice, even Phil could tell something was amiss. He said he couldn't tell us over the phone; he could only speak face to face. We spent a lot of time surmising what was wrong. My suggestion was that he had made all his money from drug dealing, and the mob was after him.

The day finally came, off we set, and the party was incredible. The next day we had a late brunch at the hotel with everyone and left late afternoon to stay the night with David at his home. He hadn't mentioned anything untoward during the event, and Phil being Phil, hadn't fetched up the subject. Had it been my family, I would have more than likely locked them in a room until they spilt the beans, patience not being one of my strengths. We followed him back to his new home, which was quite difficult because he set off like an F1 driver, and there were no sat navs in those days. At this stage, I was unaware of his back catalogue of driving catastrophes, thank god, which I'm sure Phil will no doubt write about.

On arrival at his house, he showed us into the living room. He told us to help ourselves to food and drink, as he was just going to change into something more comfortable. Being a modern house, i.e. it had thin walls, it was a bit difficult to have a private conversation with Phil. I'm sort of pulling my face and using hand gestures at him, and I'm thinking, '*What the fuck am I doing here?*' I'm tired, hungover and really just want to go home. Phil made us coffee, put on the TV – his default setting for uncomfortable moments, and we just sat there forever, and forever. After what felt like a lifetime, David eventually came into the lounge. Bloody hell, he was dressed in a dress! He had on full make-up, a wig and high-heeled shoes; he was even wearing nail polish: no wonder he'd been missing for over two hours. I thought he'd gone for a cheeky cat nap; how wrong was I? He told us he had been cross-dressing for years and was intending to go the whole way: to become a proper woman. Well, that certainly woke me up! I couldn't even look at Phil, and I quickly put on my councillor hat and engaged in the 'How do you feel, and how can we help?' conversation.

He obviously liked talking about himself and said he was going to change his name to Dawn. No! No! No!

'That's not going to work,' I told him. 'David to Dawn would be a struggle for people - far too similar.'

So between us, we came up with the name Rebecca. So there you have it, he wasn't a drug dealer; he was a 'he' who was going to become a 'she.' In a bizarre way, it made me feel a bit better about myself. Phil had grown up in a 'normal' family; now, suddenly, he had joined the 'not normal' family, much more like me. Needless to say, this was only the start of the Rebecca saga, a source of many after-dinner anecdotes.

Philip:

'Ahh, Pisco (rather than Bisto)!' My two brothers are four and six years older than me. As a consequence, when they were growing up, they often socialised together (brotherly love would not last, but that is a different story), including playing football, especially for The Ludwick Boys Club and Lincoln Electric (my eldest brother's place of work). There was a close-knit group of lads (including one Billy Byrne, he of 'DIY SOS' fame, who – back in the day – used to sometimes come round for one of our mother's Sunday lunches) who continued to socialise together as they married and started families. Each Christmas, they would take over a hotel in Rushton, Northants (note for Judy, whose geography, as well as her sense of direction, is not great; Northamptonshire is in the Midlands, not 'Down South') from a Saturday afternoon until Sunday lunchtime. It was a fancy dress party (Jude and I hate fancy dress) with a sit-down meal followed by a disco. We only ever went twice – it had been taking place for several years, but my ex would never go. On our first occasion, as 'the entertainment' started, we were advised to cover our meal as it was put on the table and eat it as quickly as possible. One group had gone as the 'Ghostbusters' and had working ghost guns that fired foam. They fired it everywhere: over us, over the food and over any and everything that moved. It was manic, but good fun. Because everyone got pissed, and there was a disco, it became known as 'The Annual Pisco.'

The Pisco was a party for the adults; for New Year's Eve, they held a children's party (at one of the group's houses – alternating each year) where the kids were allowed to stay up until they dropped, whatever time that was. On the one occasion (pre-Jude) that I attended, some of the kids literally stayed up all night, which meant some adults had to stay awake with them, but not me. I managed a few hours of kip on the living room floor.

Returning to our first Pisco, the theme for the fancy dress was 'Films', and we went as 'Summer Holiday,' each of us wearing half of a London bus! David was dressed as Shirley Bassey (I can't remember what the connection to a film was), which in hindsight, was a clue as to what he wanted to talk to us about. By the way, he was not a monetary millionaire. He worked as a Financial Advisor, and because he had sold a million dollars (US) worth of insurance in a year, qualified for membership of the parent company's 'Millionaires Club.' This had many benefits, including all expenses paid trips to annual gatherings all over the world.

David, to Dawn, to Rebecca; basically, I didn't give a fuck. It was his life, and who was I to say what he should or shouldn't do? If it made him happy, then fine. However, I always thought that although the outward appearance had changed, the mind was still the same, and to me, Rebecca was no happier than David. His decision also cost him access to his children. Whilst the majority of his friends (and our dad) just accepted the change, the person closest to him, his wife, could not. She found his desires and wish to have a sex change abominable, and I think she was quite shocked at how accepting so many people were.

Judith:

Back at the ranch (Tolvaddon), so to speak, recovering from the trials of Pisco and the sex-changing brother, Shaun was looking for a new job as the factory where he had worked had been closed. He found a position in a jeweller's shop in Truro, but I will leave Phil to enlighten you as to the fun and games that job entailed. Phil tells me I am a tolerant but impatient person. It is a good job that he is patient, as his tolerance was to be tested soon enough.

Philip:

Shaun should have been born into the Instagram/TikTok/

Look at Me era; he had the looks to be whatever he wanted and loved being the centre of attention. From my point of view, back in those early days of living together, I just envied him and was, perhaps, maybe even jealous of him. This was because I was (even at his age, had been) a short dumpy person with man boobs, whilst he was tall, lean, dark and extremely handsome (or 'ansome as the Cornish would say). Whatever he wore, he looked stunning. He never had to worry about somewhere to put his head down for a night, as there was always a girl willing to share her bed with him. He had the world at his feet, and as they say, 'the world was his oyster.'

However, at this time, he was just irritating. When the job at the football factory finished, he got a temporary Christmas job at a jeweller's shop in Truro. However, this meant he had to get to Truro each morning as opposed to walking up the road to the factory. We would ensure he got up in time to catch the bus. The bus stop was forty metres away from our front door. Unfortunately, it was not in his makeup to go out and wait at the bus stop like normal people, oh no. He would stand at the back door, smoking, watching for the bus as it came around the estate and past the back door. Then he would try to run out the front door and get to the bus stop before the bus. He nearly always failed. This meant that either Judy or I had to drive him to Redruth rail station to catch a train. Very frustrating, and it would never get any better.

The one thing Shaun did exceedingly well was score goals. It is an overused cliché, but in football parlance, 'he knew where the goal was.' As Judy has said, there were occasions (normally, when Camborne Town were short of a goalkeeper) when all three of us (Shaun, Antony and I) played. There is a funny tale to tell about this involving Rebecca/David, but that is for later. Also, when the Trevu (my team) 5-a-side team were short, Shaun would turn out for us and score lots of goals. However, I do remember once, when Shaun had gone walkabout, that Antony stepped in his place. He scored half a dozen goals, then went home boasting, 'Shaun Lea! Who needs Shaun Lea?'

Judith:

Antony was now sixteen and was seriously thinking about a career. He decided he wanted to join the met police when he was eighteen. Having attended a police careers event, he made the decision to leave school, not attend college, and leave home to get 'life experience,' as recommended by the chap giving the talk. So he did a life-saving course in order to get a job as a lifeguard, and once qualified, he found a job 'up country' at a holiday camp. Unlike Shaun, he did not have a lot of confidence with girls, and although he was outstandingly funny, verbal communication somewhat failed him if a girl approached him (Phil says he knows the feeling). He did an outstanding rendition of his jabbering nonsensical language when he was put in this position, and friends used to beg us to take him with us when we visited, as he made them laugh so much. He also had lots of other stories that he told, which had you bent double, plus he could mimic anyone and anything. A girlfriend did, however, eventually appear; I think she stalked him until he agreed to go out with her. Unlike Shaun, whose girlfriends you never met, he fetched her home, but I think that was because she was a sex maniac. One day he told me to tell her he was out if she knocked on, as his willy was so sore it needed a rest and had I got any Savlon?

The day came for him to leave home for his first life-saving job. I drove him to the station with all his worldly goods, said my goodbyes, waved him off and cried all the way home. The nest was empty. Shaun had recently moved in with his friend, whose mother was a social worker, and Antony was on a train on his own, off on an adventure. I had asked him to ring and let me know he had arrived okay, which he did later that night. In his usual funny style, he said it was awful, that the shared room was filthy, and they were probably robbing him right now whilst he was on the phone, and that he was coming home. I persuaded him to give it a few days to see how he got on, then just leave if it wasn't for him, and come home. It looked like Phil and mine's 'home alone' freedom was down the pan already. Fortunately, two days later, he rang to say he'd 'got laid the night before,' so he was staying. Perhaps he had the Shaun magic but just didn't know it.

So, at last, Phil and I were home alone; I have to say life was much easier, not to mention cheaper. Apart from work commitments, we could actually do whatever we wanted, when we wanted. We joined in with everything on offer; we sought out live music events, sailed, beached and partied with friends and families. I was, for once, free of the day-to-day young adult responsibilities; they had become grown-ups. But boomerangs have a way of coming back.

Philip:

It was Rebecca (who used to be my brother) who would be the first from my side of the family to visit us at Tolvaddon (in 1989). On a couple of occasions, she fetched down my other brother's two boys with her, and on another, brought my dad as well. My younger sister also came down with her new-born child, her first. We had a lovely time 'playing tourist' and visiting several beaches, including Perranporth: she was the only one in either of our families to join in with our naturism. My uncle on my dad's side visited us for afternoon tea several times whilst holidaying in the area, but my eldest brother never made it down to us. However, we did meet up with him, his wife and boys when they were staying at Minehead Butlins (Somerset), where my youngest nephew, Ronnie, caused mayhem. He encouraged me not only to go down the black swimming pool fume but also to go down forwards, like him. He went first, and then I followed. As I went round the first bend, with my arms stretched out in front of me as directed, I slid up the side of the fume, and my forehead banged on a seam. As I catapulted out of the fume into the pool, I was hauled up by a lifeguard and taken to the poolside. I had a cut just above my right eye that was bleeding profusely; I still have the scar today. Minehead Butlins will be revisited later in the book for fun of a different kind.

Ronnie will also be remembered for the first time Rebecca brought him and his elder brother down to visit us at the Tolvaddon house. We had been out for the evening, and on the return journey home, we said to Ronnie, who was about ten, not to go upstairs to the bedroom until we had checked it (because there was a good chance Antony would be up there with his nymphomaniac girlfriend). But Ronnie being Ronnie, i.e. a little bugger, totally ignored our warning, and upon entering the house, he ran straight up the stairs and into the bedroom, only to encounter two bare bodies in his bed; he hadn't knocked on the bedroom door. This is the only time I have ever known Ronnie to be lost for words.

On the occasion that Rebecca brought my dad down with the boys, we decided to try go karting at Hayle. Rebecca and the boys were keen as mustard, me less so, and my dad, who was 75, didn't drive, but that did not stop Rebecca from persuading him to have a go. Judy, wisely, spectated. Rebecca and the boys, plus a stranger and his lad, had a fierce battle to be at the front whilst I brought up the rear. Well, not quite, because my dad was barely moving as he went around the track. Eventually, this mobile chicane caused an incident, and the stranger collided with my dad. This meant he lost the race, and he was mad. Afterwards, the stranger had a huge argument with Rebecca about my dad and eventually stormed off to his van. We all breathed a big sigh of relief because, at one stage, it looked like it was going to come to blows, but we sighed too soon. The irate man drove his van straight into the side of Rebecca's new Nissan sports car, causing a lot of damage; he had blown a fuse. The police were called, and the man was dealt with, but the pleasant evening out had turned into a bit of a nightmare.

Judith:

Another busy summer gave way to a pleasantly warm autumn, then one evening, returning from sailing and in need of a hot bath, there was no hot water. Typically, the one time we had chosen not to have a shower at the sailing club, we now couldn't have a bath at home (we didn't have a shower). Phil borrowed a test-meter from work and confirmed the problem – the bottom immersion heater in the tank had failed – and said he could fix it. I will let him regale the tale.

Philip:

Yes, indeed, the bottom immersion heating element in our Economy 7 hot water tank had failed. Well, working for the electricity board, I was able to buy a replacement at a discounted price, and one of the engineers I worked with lent me his special tool that is required to undo the element. He also talked me through the process, so I was ready to go. The water was turned off, the hot water tap was run to empty the tank, and a towel was placed under the element as I had been told to expect some water to leak out when I extracted it. As I eased it out, there was indeed a small trickle of water, followed by a great big flood. My scream of exclamation had Judy sending Antony up the stairs to investigate. He reported back down to his mother that he might need to use his lifeguarding skills to rescue me. I was panicking a bit because Tolvaddon houses had electric ceiling heating, and there was water pouring through the ceiling and dripping into the living room where Judy was trying to watch 'Corrie.' Although we did not use the ceiling heating, the elements were still in situ and connected (to the mains), and parts of it were now thoroughly soaked.

A few weeks before, we had bought this wonderful new Hoover wet and dry vacuum cleaner; it could suck up water: what a revelation that was. The problem was that so much water was held in the landing carpet that it took only a few seconds to fill it up, but it was much easier than trying to sponge it up. It took me over an hour to suck up what water I could. Did I mention that I was down to my underpants by this stage? The clothes I had been wearing were totally soaked. Buckets had to be left in the living room to catch drips for several weeks. It turns out my friendly engineer had forgotten to tell me about a second stopcock that also needed turning off.

Judith:

One of Rebecca's visits coincided with Phil being asked

to play in goal for Camborne Town, Shaun's team. Camborne Town was typical of teams made up of 'mates,' and I think they often looked forward to the after-match piss-up more than the match itself. Shaun and Antony would often regale the antics of one particular lad, 'Kinger,' who was always up to tricks, e.g. pissing over everyone whilst in the showers (was he an early version of Gazza?). When Kinger was told that Phil's brother/sister was coming to watch the game, he couldn't handle it and said he was not going to talk to "it."

Rebecca and I arrived just after the match had started and stood on the touchline to watch. At one point, a ball was kicked out, and it was heading straight towards Rebecca, who caught it.

'I nearly headed that,' she told me, 'but stopped just in time. I can't afford to mess up my hair or make-up.'

I just burst out laughing.

In the changing rooms after the match, Kinger came over to Phil and said, 'I thought your brother/sister was coming to watch?'

Perhaps he was expecting to see some sort of monster on the touchline, but he was flabbergasted when Phil told him that Rebecca had been standing next to me for the whole game. Rebecca would accept that she is not the prettiest of women, but obviously, she looks feminine enough to have fooled Kinger.

Chapter 9

Fun in the Sun

Judith:

In 1989 we returned to Le Cap in France, but in 1990, having watched 'Shirley Valentine' in the pictures, I suggested we go to Greece. I had this romantic notion of sailing on a boat, anchoring off a beautiful island, and indulging in sun, sea and lots of sex. I must have sold the idea well, as Phil leapt aboard with it, and 'Project Greece' began. I realised then that Phil loves the planning as much as the end product, whereas I, on the other hand, am useless in the details. If it were left to me, I would just do the bare necessity and hope for the best.

It turned out we were limited as to where we could sail, having had no experience in a yacht. Nevertheless, we were apparently allowed to sail in the Greek Ionian Islands, on a flotilla holiday, in a twenty-five-foot Beneteau. I was a bit concerned as that was only seven feet longer than our dinghy, and it apparently had a cooker, sink, loo and a bed. I had been thinking more of a super yacht with a large sunbathing deck, but as that was not an option, the twenty-five-footer it was: so that was what we booked.

Our adventure started with an overnight drive from

Cornwall to Gatwick, and Phil had me practising tying
bowlines and clove hitches at the airport. Who do you
know who takes a piece of string on holiday with them?
Upon arrival in Greece, a bus took us to the flotilla base
in Sivota. We had arrived, two very tired people with
two squashy bags and a piece of string: let the adventure
begin.

On the first morning, Phil was taken out for
instruction on how to operate the boat, whilst I just sat
at the beach bar chatting to the other 'plus ones.' A girl
called Annie was there with her boyfriend, and we had
an instant connection. By the time the boys got back, we
were quite sozzled, and believe me, it's not easy climbing
onto a yacht when intoxicated. Her knowledge, like
mine, was very sketchy; the only difference was that I had
been instructed how to tie knots, and she hadn't. Also,
her boyfriend was there to sail every minute of every
day whilst Phil and I intended to drop anchor, sunbathe
naked and have sex whenever possible.

Every day, the skipper gave the group instructions on
where to sail and what the weather forecast was. That
was it; we were all on our own until we met up later that
evening at some unknown harbour. My sense of direction
in a car was appalling, so I was useless in a boat. Phil
seemed to know where to go, so I just went with the flow;
I could pull up an anchor, set and trim sails, and cast off:
the dream team was in action.

I had decided to keep a diary of our trip, and on
day three, I wrote, 'Phil tried to kill me.' It sounds a bit

dramatic, but it actually was. On leaving the harbour that day, we sailed up a channel towards the open sea. The sun was shining as we cast off our clothes, and the sails were fluttering in the gentle wind: utter bliss. Being dinghy sailors, we should have registered the fact that the 'white caps' we could see on the water out to sea meant it was very windy, but we didn't. As we hit the open sea, everything not fastened down in the boat decided to throw itself onto the floor. The boat was at an angle which in a dinghy meant capsize was imminent. I wanted to hook on and hike out, but there was no such gear on a yacht. We eased the sails to level up the boat, but we were still overpowered. I left Phil to it and dived below to find the life jackets; we quickly put them on and used safety lines to tie ourselves to the boat. Phil decided we needed to reef the mainsail, i.e. make it smaller. He sent me out of the relative safety of the cockpit, forwards to the mast, to do the job. Have I ever done this in my life? No. Did I know what to do? No. He screamed instructions to me, and I did my best to pull down the sail and reef it in. I managed to clamber back to him eventually, and when we looked around us, there wasn't a boat in sight, only sea and the horizon.

I spotted what looked like an inlet along the shoreline, and we decided to try to sail into it, hoping to find shelter from the worst of the wind. Stroke of genius; we got our breath back, reefed even more of the sail in, and set off again. Much better now, the boat was flatter, and we began to make headway to the night's designated harbour. After a couple of hours of sailing, Phil decided the wind had eased enough to let out the reef, but I had my doubts. I thought we were being protected by a rocky outcrop. However, 'the captain knows best,' so I made my way along the boat, letting out the sail hook by hook. As I let out the last hook at the front of the boat, the wind hit us, the sail filled, and I catapulted around the front of the mast like a rag doll. It was a bloody good job that I was still tied onto the boat; otherwise, it would have been goodbye Judith. The hope of doing a girl overboard rescue was zero – I have never been so scared in all my life. By the time I worked my way back to Phil in the cockpit, my legs were like jelly. It had obviously scared him as well because he asked me to take over steering the boat as he desperately needed a wee. Not a bloody chance: at that moment, he wasn't my favourite person.

The wind did ease, and we completed the sail across the open water without further mishap, being the last of our group to enter the harbour. It turned out that most of them had dropped their sails and motored across the twelve miles of open sea, believing it to be too windy to sail! I had never been so pleased to see a harbour entrance looming into sight in all my life. In reality, it was only a short trip, but any dreams I might have had of ocean crossings were very definitely now off my agenda.

The days just floated by; morning swims, breakfast, briefings, lunch wherever we decided to drop anchor, shower and dress before sailing into the next harbour to 'park' the boat. I never did have to tie up the boat after all the knot-tying practice, as someone always caught my line for me. We had drinks aboard whilst people-watching, followed by an evening meal at the local bar and more drinks with interesting, articulate people. Absolutely a perfect way to live; I learnt how to sail a proper boat, how to windsurf, how to just 'be.' I wanted to live on a boat for the rest of my life. It was probably the happiest I have ever been, and when recently looking at photo albums, I discovered a photo of me sitting on the boat, writing my diary. I have since had it blown up, as out of all the photos we own, this is the one I look the happiest in. It now sits on my wall to remind me what true happiness is and what I should try to aspire to every day, no matter what shit life throws at me. Believe me; I've had a lot over the years. It was the first time in my life I felt free of responsibility, and it had the adventure element of not knowing where you were going next. Plus, the Greek people, who appeared to have very little, were so lovely and happy: it was infectious. I would have sold my soul to the devil to have lived that life forever. Why don't dreams ever come true?

Philip:

Watching Shirley Valentine on a cold, wet November evening certainly planted a seed: a holiday to Greece it was going to be, but the problem was which island to choose. A flotilla holiday seemed to solve the problem (great idea, Jude) because it would allow us to visit several islands, but there were issues. First and foremost, neither of us had ever been aboard a yacht, let alone sailed one. Would we be allowed to hire one? Secondly, flotilla holidays had a bit of a reputation back then. I certainly perceived it as being a 'ducklings following their mother' type of sailing; not sure how much fun that would be. Research was required.

Was it that fate thing again, or just luck? In September 1988, I enrolled on an RYA (Royal Yachting Association) 'Competent Crew' course at the local college. Not only did I learn about all things boating, including the weather, but it gave me something to do during downtime at work. (The Cornish Control Room was in the process of being closed down and centralised at Exeter. This meant work we used to do on late and night shifts disappeared.) In September 1989, I enrolled for the next course 'up the ladder,' i.e. 'Day Skipper,' which included learning how to navigate.

The research proved positive, and a two-week holiday with Sunsail was booked for May 1990 (any later in the year was just too expensive; May was already pushing us to our [budget] limit). Our lack of 'big boat' experience restricted us to the Ionian Islands, with the exception of Corfu, which was too far out to sea. For the first week, the flotilla would remain together (quack, quack), but we were promised 'free sailing' for the second week; it sounded like a good compromise. As well as completing my course, I also found a video (Betamax!) tutorial on how to moor (park) a yacht alongside a quay. Apparently, in the Med, the protocol was to park the bow (front, pointy end) first. It all seemed easy enough.

The leader for our holiday was a Brit called Paul (the vast majority of people running flotillas were antipodean), and we were his guinea pigs, i.e. it was his first time in charge. Paul had a New Zealand girl as his assistant hostess, Sya, and Richard, an Aussie mechanic, to help him keep us under control. Good luck on that front! Paul won us over at his first briefing when he tried to explain that to get on board, 'you have to get your leg over (the pulpit).' Well, that double entendre had us all in giggles and set the tone for the rest of the holiday. Paul also had this habit of continually flicking his long blonde locks with his hand, something we gave him a complex about later in the holiday.

As Judy has stated, on the first morning, all the skippers went out with Paul for a few hours of instruction on how to hoist sails, reef sails, and start the outboard engine, including changing the fuel tank (just a can like the ones some of us keep in our cars) and the correct use of the toilet. This included the threat that if you put toilet paper down the pan and it got blocked, the perpetrator would have to clear it, not them. It was a total 'No-no' to put any paper down the loo, as it was in all the land-based toilets as well.

Very unexpectedly, we did not have to play ducklings all in a row for the first week. Each morning Paul gave us a destination port and a time to arrive by, plus he would point out any navigational hazards to be aware of. On day one, the main one being, 'On no account approach the island of Scorpios (at the time, home of Aristotle Onassis) because the security guards will not hesitate to shoot.' Yikes! Also, he gave us a weather forecast every day, and not once was it anywhere near correct. He claimed it came from the Greek Met Office.

On day one, we were the last boat to arrive at the port, and we very slowly manoeuvred to park up, throwing out the stern anchor as we drifted towards Paul, who was standing on the shore. Judy was ready in the pulpit to jump ashore and use her newfound skills to tie us up. Christ, who am I kidding? When you have a fit, tanned, scantily clad, bleach-haired supermodel standing in the bow with the rope and a 'helpless woman' smile on her face, there will always be a smitten male who is only too willing to take the rope and tie it off for her. That day it was Paul, and then she had a different victim every day. When Paul congratulated us on our skilful parking, we confessed that it had not been difficult, especially as the water was like a mill pond.

'Oh, you'll be surprised,' he answered.

For the rest of the first week, we made a point of trying to be the first boat in. Then, with vodka in hand, we would watch all the mishaps, e.g. some approached the quay too fast, some threw the stern anchor out too early (causing the boat to stop short of the quay). On one evening, we even had the privilege, if that's the right term, of watching a large American boat first demolish the wooden quay to the beach before running into several Dutch boats as he tried to moor up alongside them.

It proved to be good entertainment; thank you for the advice, Paul.

Judith:

When Phil stated his intention to take his new waterproof ghetto blaster with him on holiday, I thought he had totally lost it. However, I have to say that on reflection, it was a masterstroke, and every morning we became the centre of attention (and him the so-called 'wallflower'). This was because each morning, as we left port, we played a suitable tune on the ghetto blaster at such a volume that the whole flotilla got to share it with us. Tunes included 'Howard's Way,' 'The Onedin Line,' Phil Collins 'Another Day In Paradise' (our favourite), 'The Ride of the Valkyries' and Prokofiev's 'Montagues and Capulets,' plus several dance songs.

Philip:

We did very little sailing on this 'sailing holiday,' only doing so when it was necessary to get somewhere. We spent our days anchored in small, deserted coves whiling away the hours sunbathing, reading and swimming, with an odd bonk thrown in for good measure.

We visited some fantastic places (the Ionian Islands is a magical place) and met and got drunk with many other sailors and holidaymakers. Yet the overriding memory was the happiness of the locals, so obviously poor compared to the visiting Westerners; it really got to us and made us think very seriously about our lifestyle.

Our holiday started on Sunday 5th May; on Saturday 12th Manchester United (our team) were playing Crystal Palace in the FA Cup Final. We had established that the only bar in the area that had a TV was the one at the home base of Sivota, and as the 12th was the first day of 'free' sailing, we made the decision to go back to watch the match (it was a 5 pm KO local time). On the morning of the match, we were in Port Kioni on the island of Ithaca, approximately fourteen miles away. Doesn't sound much? Believe me, in a boat; it is a long way. Paul had one final weather forecast for us; the wind was due to be force five to six – in other words, marginal – and Paul urged caution about leaving the harbour. He was no footy fan; did he think a bit of wind was going to stop us from watching the final? As it 'appened guv, there was no fucking wind at all, and we had to motor the whole way; for six hours.

Judith:

When we arrived, there were no berths available to tie up along the quayside. Therefore, we had to learn a new skill; picking up a mooring buoy – we succeeded – and rowed ashore in the little rubber dinghy. We reached the bar with ten minutes to go; we had not eaten since breakfast, but all the bar had was crisps, nuts and beer! The noise and smell of petrol had left us feeling a bit nauseated but getting drunk solved that one. We settled down to watch the match with a bunch of Aussies. The system at the home bar was self-service, and the bar owner would tot up the number of empties on your table before you left. The match went into extra time and ended in a 3-3 draw. We were rat-arsed. After the match, I wanted to take advantage of being at the home port to telephone home to make sure the boys were okay. But where was the telephone kiosk? We followed the signs; the 'public' phone was located in the living room of one of the residents! The boys were a bit shocked to hear from me, and they were obviously drunk, too. Virtually the whole Camborne Town football team were at our house watching the game, and Shaun put most of them on the phone to speak to me!

Philip:

To this day, Judy and I have absolutely no recollection of rowing back to the boat, but we apparently provided lots of laughs to the watching Aussies; they were keeping a motherly eye on us.

We didn't watch the replay because it was a UK evening kick-off. It was also the last day of 'free' sailing, and a get-together beach BBQ had been arranged. We had spent the day moored up in a little bay just by the entrance to the chosen bay for the BBQ. It meant we could see when the other members of our flotilla arrived. As we were showering to prepare for the evening, Judy gave me one of her looks whilst asking me why her thighs and fanny were yellow, green and red. She already knew the answer but had not noticed earlier. I, of course, was wearing coloured sunblock on my nose and face.

Arriving in the bay, we noticed others had dropped

anchor quite a distance from the shore and then rowed to the beach. We were cute; we backed in as close as we could to the beach and ran the stern anchor ashore, just like the lead boat had. The logic was that it would be easier to get back on board when pissed, as all one had to do was find the stern anchor rope on the beach and follow it back to the boat. It worked a treat.

We had been asked to make a cocktail in a water bottle and prepare a sketch to entertain the host crew and the rest of our flotilla. Well, we went OTT (over the top) in taking the piss out of Paul's first briefing and exaggerated his mannerisms to the point of making him paranoid about them. We won the vote for best entertainment and also won 'best cocktail' (us, competitive? Never!). As we keep stating, we know how to throw a party. Then it was back to Port Spigelia for our last night before returning to the home base the following morning, then flying home to the UK. We did not want to leave, but there was no choice.

After landing back at Gatwick, Jude rang home to give the boys an eta for our arrival home and a chance for them to clean up before we got there.

'Everything was fine,' the boys said. 'Brendon's here with his carpet shampooer.'

Judy did not want to ask why a carpet shampooer was required!

Judith:

So, unfortunately, it was back to reality; thank god we

lived in a beautiful part of the country. Having said that, even spending days on the lovely Cornish beaches couldn't stop me from wanting to sail away, but I couldn't, so I had to count my blessings and get on with it. I often wonder if I hadn't got the boys, would I have taken a different path, sold up and 'fucked off?' I like to think I would have, but I will never know the answer.

Philip:

The Greece holiday definitely had an unsettling effect on us; it took over a year to shake the feeling off. We had shared a piece of paradise with some very lovely locals who, whilst being obviously poor, were extremely kind and came across as very happy and content with their lives. Was this not something we could learn from? As I say, it caused us to question our lives, but regardless of all these questions, the mundanities of life continued.

Judith:

In August of 1990, Rebecca (aka David) had her fortieth birthday and was having a party to celebrate. I had told her that it was literally her 'birth' day as 'David was now officially Rebecca.' On the day before her birthday, Phil, Antony and I made the long trip up to Rushton (Northants). It was a very hot, humid day, and we were a bit pissed off to reach Rebecca's house to be met by a note stating she was at a birthday party at one of her friends and that we were welcome to join her; it was only five minutes away. In for a penny, in for a pound, as they say.

Pulling up outside the friend's house – it was just after midnight – we could hear loud music, and people were milling about in the street. We heard someone ask after the whereabouts of someone else, and when we heard the answer 'they are in the pool,' three hot, sweaty bodies literally ran through the house, ready to strip off and dive into the pool. Let me state that the house, large and detached, certainly looked the type that would have a pool. Unfortunately, the Cornish trio were to be disappointed for the second time that night; the 'pool' was a kiddies' paddling pool: only one thing for it, get pissed.

I have previously told you how funny my Antony is, and that night, he was in fine form. He was wearing a pair of glasses without lenses that people, especially one particular married woman, found hilarious, so much so that she was 'hitting' on him. Whilst at first he was enjoying all the attention, this woman was becoming obsessive, and it became fun for us to watch him trying to fend off her advances. He ended up staying glued to us to avoid her.

By two in the morning, we were back at Rebecca's, who stated that she had an appointment (hair and nails) in the morning. A large marquee was being delivered to be put up in her garden, but another friend would be there to look after it if we didn't want to be. We didn't and made plans to escape when we got up.

Philip:

I put paid to those plans because when we got up, I couldn't find the car keys. We looked everywhere, and when I came to put my shoes on to help when the marquee arrived, I discovered the keys tucked in my shoe. Bollocks! Was I in the doghouse? You bet I was! My mistake meant we ended up doing a lot of the preparation work, including taking doors off their hinges, removing furniture, bringing tons of drink in after it was delivered and putting up decorations. All the while, the birthday girl had conveniently been away from home being pampered.

The party was a huge success, and in the early hours of the morning, people slowly started drifting away. Around 2 am, Rebecca said she was just seeing off a couple of her friends, the last guests to leave. This left Jude, Ant and me sitting out in the marquee with Jude and me drinking coffee and staring around at the mess. It was like a bomb had gone off – there would be a lot of cleaning to do in the morning. In fact, because we had drunk at the friend's party the previous night, Judy and I could not face a drink at this party, so we had been on water and coffee all night. When, after half an hour, there was no sign of Rebecca, we thought we had better go and see where she was. We discovered her passed out, fully clothed, on her bed. Pulling her door closed, we returned to the marquee where, finishing our coffees, Jude and I looked at each other.

I said, 'We can't, can we?'

To which she answered, 'Oh yes, we can.'

'What's that?' Ant asked.

'Go home,' we answered in unison.

There was a risk, as the car was nearly empty (of petrol) and, not knowing the area, we did not know if any petrol stations would be open at this hour. We decided to take the chance. As we had not been drinking, we decided to load up as much booze as we could – there were stacks of it piled up all over the place – though, having only a small car, space was limited, and we couldn't nick too much. We had to creep back upstairs and pack our bags, trying, in vain, to zip them up quietly and then sneak back down the stairs and load the car. Fortunately, all this noise and our constant giggling did not wake Rebecca up; I'm not sure that the end of the world would have woken her up! Being the Sagittarian that I am, I found a pen and paper and wrote a note, leaving it in a coffee cup on her mug tree – I thought she would find it there when she made herself a drink in the morning. Closing the front door behind us, we headed home; it had just gone 3 am.

The local petrol station was indeed open, and we had a good run home, arriving back just after 9:30 am. It was straight to bed. When I got up five hours later, I thought I had better ring Rebecca to check she was okay and fill her in on why we had left. Several partygoers, including my eldest brother and his wife (they had stayed at a local hotel), had returned in the morning to help clean and tidy up. Because our bedroom door was shut, everyone thought we were in bed asleep so, bless them, they did not disturb us, and no one discovered the note until they stopped for lunch; no one made the connection that our car was gone. Rebecca was a bit put out that we left her flaked out with the house insecure. Anyone climbing over the rear wall could have just walked into the house, as all the doors had been taken off for the party. She said they could have attacked her; I replied that she wasn't that lucky.

Judith:

Time had flown by, and before we could blink, it was soon autumn 1990; we had been together for over two and a half wonderful years. Shaun was twenty-one and working 'Up North' on the new Manchester Airport terminal, and Antony was eighteen, still lifeguarding 'Down South' until he could join the Met police. Phil had suggested on several occasions that we should buy a new home together. We had survived nearly three years; perhaps it was time to cement the relationship and plan for the future.

Philip:

I had been pleased but surprised at Judy's decision to move into my home with the boys, a house I had bought because it was cheap and within walking distance of my work (which meant I could keep costs down). It was not really suitable for two adults, two strapping teenagers and three large dogs, but her reasons were sound, and without a doubt, she was right (she normally is) about it giving me a better chance with them. My home was smaller than hers had been and only had a north-facing rear yard (not good for sun worshippers), which, in effect, was no more than a dog toilet. Therefore, I made noises on several occasions about perhaps selling up and buying a bigger house that would be a home for all four of us, but she was never keen. I'm not sure we could have afforded it anyway, but it seemed to me to be the right thing to do.

Judith:

In the autumn of 1990, we finally decided to sell up. In the eighties, Peter de Savary, an entrepreneur, had invested heavily in Cornwall; he had purchased the Land's End Hotel and had big plans to redevelop Hayle Harbour. We had seen an advert in the local rag for a new development just behind Hayle Harbour and, thinking it may be an opportunity for a good investment (how wrong were we to be), we went for a look-see. Looking around a couple of show houses, we chatted to a sales rep, and a deal was put on the table that included the developer buying our house. We decided to go home and sleep on it before making a decision.

Driving down the hill from the sales office, we spotted another, smaller sales office, so we stopped to have a look. It turned out to be another, smaller developer on a neighbouring site. Entering the Portakabin, we came face to face with Bob, the chap Phil had bought the Osprey dinghy from; Phil had not known he built houses. Bob said he had something we may be interested in, so we jumped in his car. He took us up another hill to a pair of detached bungalows, the first of ten properties he was building in this cul-de-sac (he eventually constructed over a hundred properties on the adjacent hill site that we had just come up). There was one other large bungalow at the top of the cul-de-sac that apparently was self-built by the owner – he had just bought the plot from Bob. We had not been looking for a bungalow, but it was south-facing, had a drive with space to store the dinghy over winter and could be enclosed to keep the dogs safe. Plus, because the council sheltered housing bungalows to the rear were down the hill, the rear garden would not be overlooked. On the downside, the bungalow was not very big, but at the time, we believed the boys had left home for good (you know what thought did). Bob offered us the same deal as the national developer had, so we had some serious thinking to do.

Philip:

We went for 'Bob the builder's' bungalow and got Rebecca, my sister, to arrange a mortgage for us. She was a financial advisor, after all, and family to boot; surely she would sort out a good deal for us? Dream on. She came up with a 'deferred' mortgage which she did not explain the consequences of very well, and in hindsight, we did not ask enough questions. The bottom line was that it (the mortgage) was to cost us £509 a month which meant we could afford it, or, at least, so we thought. A 'normal' repayment mortgage would have been £610 a month.

The day before we were due to move in, we received a call from our (Rebecca's) solicitor stating there was a problem with the mortgage; basically, the offer had been withdrawn. Fuck! Contracts had been exchanged, so we were committed. Double fuck! It was a complicated mortgage that apparently worked on fixed parameter percentages of the price of the property, not its value. It seemed the builder's secretary had given the mortgage company the higher advertised price rather than our agreed purchasing price, which put us outside of the qualifying parameters for the mortgage. To her due, Rebecca did manage to sweet talk the mortgage company, and we were good to go.

Judith:

On reflection, our time at Tolvaddon surpassed all my expectations. We were young, carefree, very much in love and 'living it large.' I might have had rose-tinted glasses on, but all my memories are ones of love, laughter and happiness. Was it the 'honeymoon' period of our life together? 'Maybe'. If so, I was living my best life; I would have been happy to stay there 'forever.' Yes, it was a tiny two-bedroomed end terrace, but it was our tiny two-bedroomed end terrace, and it was full of love. We could take that love anywhere, and I was finally ready to show some commitment. The boys had fled the nest, so it was time to take a step up the ladder and choose somewhere 'we' wanted to live: somewhere that could become our forever home, somewhere we could grow old together. Hello 'Gwel Tek,' are you ready for us? We won't be the usual sixty-year-old retirees living the quiet life. We are only in our mid-thirties, still living a full, exciting life, and we intend to fill you with energy, laughter and love.

Fun in the surf at Perran
Sands (Perranporth Beach)

Jackie and Judy give the
soldiers their 'Ready, Steady,
Go!' countdown as they
begin their four mile return
run along the beach to
Perranporth town and back

Happy days at Le Cap
d'Agde, our first holiday
together – credit card
not required!

Judy, with niece, looking hot on Marazion beach

Riding the whale at Marazion beach

Phil with Judy's niece at Marazion: this is one of Phil's favourite photographs

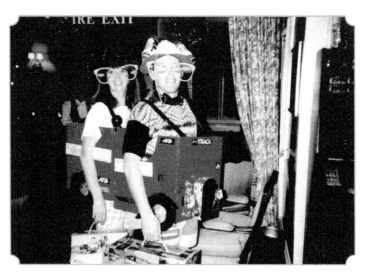

Our worst nightmare – Fancy Dress – at our first 'PISCO'

Flotilla holiday in the Ionian Islands. Captain Phil being colourful in the sun (but watch out where that sun block goes!)

Stress free times: Judy writing her diary on the flotilla holiday – her happy place.

Chapter 10

Busman's Holiday

Philip:

Gwel Tek (Cornish for Fair View) was the start of a new chapter for us – our first home bought together as a couple. At the time of moving, both boys were living away and not really expected back anytime soon, if at all, apart from occasional home visits. Note to self: don't have delusional expectations.

Although just a small characterless modern bungalow, it ticked a lot of boxes on our requirement list. It was a perfect home for retirees – oops, that's one box we could not tick! It had excellent outside space with a south-facing rear garden and a large drive, both of which could be made secure for the dogs, and to boot, the boat could be securely stored over winter. The expansive Hayle (sand) dunes were a two-minute walk away (well, at least they would be until the main development was finished, but it took five years for the developer to reach that point), perfect for giving our dogs (and us) lots of exercise. Plus, it was just a fifteen-minute walk across the dunes to gain access to the three miles of Hayle/Gwithian beach.

Judith:

I had never moved to a brand new home in my life. The bungalow was small but perfectly formed, and as Phil has just stated, it was a stone's throw away from the sand dunes. Its location was ideal for us, slap bang in the middle (distance wise) for work and the sailing club plus, equally important, close to where a new marina was due to be built; so from a financial point of view, a good investment for our future. It was 'the commitment buy'; we chose it instead of marriage to cement our relationship. For the first time ever, I hadn't bought a wreck, and there was no work to do inside; it was all brand spanking new, yippee!

Philip:

The Camborne/Redruth area is a very poor one, and it was where many ordinary folk, including us, were just trying to eke out a living whilst enjoying the natural beauty of the place. In theory, Hayle was a step up the ladder from Tolvaddon. It was a tourist area, which would prove to be testing at times during peak (holiday) season when the one road through Hayle would become gridlocked, even with the new bypass now open. We definitely encountered a different vibe there compared to Tolvaddon: it was good.

So what did this town of Hayle have to offer us? To begin with, Hayle town centre is unusual in that it is really only one street. However, it is a very long street joining the historic Foundry district to the shops in the

Copperhouse district. Then there are those three miles of golden sand. Hayle has built its reputation as a resort town on its beaches, and in our opinion, it is a deserved reputation. At low tide, there is an uninterrupted stretch of beautiful, fine sand reaching from the estuary mouth all the way to Godrevy Point in the north (as I mentioned in the Tolvaddon chapters). These beaches are very popular with surfers, something I had tried, but it had not 'turned me on.'

One thing Hayle is famous for, very much confirmed by the Lea family, is Cornish pasties. Judy, the boys, and all our visitors would always buy them from the 'Famous' Philps bakery down by the harbour and the Foundry (me, I'm a sausage roll man). Even to this day, whenever they visit Cornwall, a Philps pasty is a must. For others, there was a lesser-known, but some friends would argue, superior pasty available from Hampsons on Chapel Terrace. A place we discovered was Bird Paradise. We visited on many occasions with Jude's sister and her girls. The park dates back to the 1970s when it was set up by former 'Milky Bar kid' Mike Reynolds. A large Victorian house set in extensive grounds, Reynolds thought it was the ideal place for a tropical bird garden. Initially called Bird Paradise, it has expanded much over the years to become one of Cornwall's top tourist attractions. These days, the rebranded Paradise Park now boasts a petting farm, a miniature railway, and an indoor play area. Plus, it still maintains a fine collection of birds. We all loved it, especially the bird of prey flying demonstrations.

However you enter Hayle, it is hard not to be reminded that this was once an important industrial town. At one end, there is the old iron works, and at the other, the derelict bulk of Loggans Mill – we lived at this end. Even the names of Hayle's two districts, Copperhouse and Foundry, reflect this heritage. Hayle's industrial credentials date back over 2,000 years when it is said the Phoenicians came here to trade tin. It is also said that wherever you go in the world, there will be a miner with a lineage back to Hayle. Sadly, the last (Cornish) tin mine, South Crofty, closed in 1998. It had struggled ever since the price of tin collapsed in 1985.

Not our scene, but Hayle is firmly on the twitcher's map, with the Estuary and Copperhouse Creek RSPB reserves providing unique habitats. As the most southerly tidal estuary in Britain, the water never freezes here, and in the winter, it becomes a haven for migrating wildfowl. Throughout the year, any number of birds, from the mundane to the exotic, can be spotted. Curlew, Little Egret, Oystercatchers, Widgeon and the occasional Osprey are all visitors.

As I am 'playing the tourist' here, I will mention the St Erth to St Ives train before moving our story on. It is a scenic ride that skirts some of the most picturesque coastal scenery anywhere in Cornwall. In fact, it has often been described as the most scenic railway in Britain. The highlight of the St Ives Railway is as it hugs the cliffs above Carbis Bay beach, and you get your first glimpse of St Ives as you round Porthminster Point. On the return trip, please take care not to do what we did: unload two pushchairs and bags full of gear one station early (we started to get off at Lelant, instead of Lelant Saltings, and held the train up as we all piled back on!).

Judith:

Whilst the inside of our new home was tickety-boo, the outside was a different matter. It was one of the first properties to be built on the site, and the rest of the plots were a work in progress. On a positive note, there were no neighbours but a lot of dirt and dust, and with two dogs, we needed to make the boundaries secure. God knows why we decided to build a concrete block wall. We spent bloody hours mixing mortar and lugging blocks; it nearly put my lights out over that first winter. Some days I could barely comb my hair because my arms ache so badly. Phil told me it was character building, and, come the start of the sailing season, the 'bastard spinnaker' would be a piece of cake to put up and down as I now had arm muscles like Popeye. Cheeky sod! I think he was probably taking this equality lark one step too far.

Philip:

Admit it, though, come the start of the sailing season, you handled the boat like a pro! Also, by the start of the sailing season, we had completed over 60m of 2m high wall and had erected gates across the drive. From moving in up to the following Easter, the only day we had off from working on the wall was Christmas Day. However, the effort was worth it because now half the drive and the whole back garden were totally secure.

At this point, I will mention two short stories in relation to the wall. Firstly, to build a wall, one needs to buy blocks, sand and cement. Lots of it, and all the while trying to keep the costs down. On several occasions, the builders asked us if we had seen any suspicious vehicles the previous evening/night as bags of cement and quantities of sand had gone missing. Unfortunately, we were never able to help them!

Though one morning – and this is the second story – our little extra-curricular manoeuvres gave me heart palpitations. Before taking the dogs for their walk, and while it was still dark, I 'borrowed' a few wheelbarrows worth of sand from a pile on plot seven. Returning from the dunes with the dogs, the dark was lifting, and I could see three sets of wheelbarrow tracks on the damp road and drive, leading from the pile of sand directly to our gate. '*Shit!*' Panicking, I had to fetch buckets of hot soapy water and a yard brush to try and erase the evidence before the builders turned up for work. It was a close call, but I got away with it.

Judith:

We had been having fun at Tolvaddon, blissfully enjoying life to the full, and moving house (to Hayle) did nothing to curtail that. We continued to enjoy a loving, fulfilling relationship, embracing every opportunity to grab life by the balls. We were sailing three times a week, a love that has never waned, and we watched all the shows that took our fancy at the Minack Theatre. (We were now members, which gave one precedence over the great unwashed when it came to buying tickets. Plus, the members' seating area was built of stone, had backrests and was sheltered from the worst of the prevailing winds.) We continued to attend naturist swims at various venues and regularly spent many hours on naturist beaches. However, because the Perranporth crowd had drifted away and an unsavoury 'bag lady,' complete with half a dozen smelly dogs, had moved into 'our' corner, we also changed location. We made the 'official' naturist beach at Polgaver Bay (St Austell) our haunt of choice. Thanks to payments received for our regular articles published in H&E Naturist magazine, combined with our frugal living, we were able to continue to partake in an annual holiday.

We also continued to hold parties (because nobody else did) and attend various social 'dos' put on at either mine or Phil's work. The unexpected return of the boys to live with us added a further ingredient that led to a variety of incidents of note whilst also curtailing our 'swinging from the chandelier' home-based love life. However, the unbelievable chemistry (aka lust) between us drove Phil and me to become born-again teenagers as we sought to satisfy our passion. Knowledge of hidden beaches and sand dune bunkers became very important. I have to admit that lovemaking outdoors, under the summer sun, is just such a beautiful thing to experience;

much more enjoyable than rummaging in the back seat of the car. Although a close encounter (with members of the public) on Logan's Rock did add some unintentional excitement: we were not as alone as we thought!

Philip:

At Tolvaddon, I could walk to work in fifteen minutes. From Gwel Tek (Hayle), it was a ten-minute drive or forty/forty-five-minute cycle ride (two very long steep hills to go up). The cycle trip home was only twenty-five minutes, as one came down the hills this time. Once, I even burnt out my light generator because I was going too fast for it down the hill! As we now only had one car and I was fit and healthy (if not quite a six-pack god), I often used to cycle to work. When Judy started work at Trafalgar House, I could sometimes take the car, but this would involve first running her to work at St Erth (five miles in the wrong direction). When Antony was home and working at the Post Office, it would mean first driving him to Camborne Sorting Office for 0500hrs, returning home and walking the dogs (over the dunes). Then I would drop Judy off before finally heading to Pool (halfway between Camborne and Redruth) to start my working day at SWEB (South Western Electricity Board). The aim was to get there by 0830hrs. We were supposed to start at 0800hrs but had a sort of flexi-time system operating that allowed me to start later. Of course, I then had to pick Judy up at the end of the day, and on returning home, the first thing to be done was to walk the dogs. On Tuesdays and Fridays, we then went sailing, and tea was often a Mars bar eaten on route to Marazion.

Judith:

Winter turned into spring (my favourite season of the year), and as we prepared the boat ready for the start of the new season, it was also time to think about our future. I decided it was the right moment to go back to college and get some qualifications. My research suggested a financial qualification was perhaps a quick route into a well-paid job. So, I signed up for a basic bookkeeping course, to be followed later in the year with a three-year AAT course (Association of Accounting Technicians; a globally recognised qualification), which would mean attending college one day a week. I was currently working three part-time jobs: the auction, the second-hand furniture shop and as a PA/Secretary to the County Organiser of PHAB (Physically Handicapped and Able Bodied). This last role involved collecting money for the charity, giving talks to schools and organising/attending holidays for the disabled, as well as roping in as many people as possible to care and assist. My boss was an amazing person: he was a wheelchair-bound paraplegic with a wicked sense of humour, and we got on like a house on fire. I loved his attitude to work, especially the fact that after a couple of hours in the office, we always retreated to the pub, where he indulged in his love for vodka (via a straw). We had lots of fun; I loved the disabled people, and the holidays I took them on were as memorable for me as they were for them.

One year I organised a coach holiday to Austria, via France and Germany. We settled into the habit of having after-lunch drinks on the coach whilst watching the scenery go past. This worked extremely well until our late arrival at the hotel in Austria. It was dark, and I had twenty-plus people to check-in. I asked the driver not to unload the cases until the morning, but he chose to ignore me. I had probably had one too many drinks and was actually throwing up in the bushes as I helped to get the cases to their rooms. I was sharing/looking after two ladies, and once I had settled everyone in, I discovered, to my horror, that one of my ladies was missing her case, which contained medical equipment she needed in the morning. Needless to say, I didn't sleep too well and at 5 am, I decided to get up and look for her case. I left the door propped open and headed outside to the car park. No, not there, so I checked all the floors in the hotel, but no sign of the missing case. It was too early to disturb the rest of the gang in their rooms, so I headed back to my ladies only to find that the door to the room had automatically shut itself. What the hell! How had that happened? Abject panic hit me; I had inadvertently locked two ladies who couldn't get out of bed without help in a room on their own. I headed to the reception for help; of course, no one was there, as it was far too early for staff, so I just had to wait until they came on duty. I was horrified; it was the longest ninety minutes of my life, but all's well that ends well. They never woke up whilst I was absent, and the case was found in another person's room and reunited with its owner, so no one ever knew what a 'balls up' I had made. They all still loved me, and I loved them.

Having made plans to start studying that year, it made sense to look for a position in Hayle as opposed to Camborne, so I applied for a job that was for four full days a week with a company called Trafalgar House. They had been awarded the contract for the design, build and commissioning of a new sewage treatment plant to ensure clean water, as opposed to raw sewage, was dispatched into the sea off West Cornwall. I applied for the role of document controller, with no idea what that was, but hey-ho. I somehow got offered an interview, so I turned up in a suit and high heels to what could only be described as Portakabin city. As I entered the reception cabin, my heel caught in the thick matting. I catapulted into the reception foyer, doing a double somersault and ending up in a heap on the floor under the reception window. As I gasped for breath, all these men appeared from nowhere to help me up.

I just laughed and said, 'That must be 5.5 for artistic impression,' attempting to hide my embarrassment.

To be honest, the interview was all a blur. I had no idea what the guy was on about, and I just wanted to flee.

Later that day, I got a phone call offering me the job; how amazing was that? I subsequently learned that the guy interviewing me just thought I would fit in, and he was so right. It turned out to be the best job I have ever had in my life, and the initial six months turned into two years.

There were parties most weeks, and with a ratio of eight ladies to eighty men, we ladies were treated like princesses. I worked with a young girl called Kayleigh, who was always game for a laugh. One day, coming into work after a heavy snowfall, we hid behind a cabin and threw snowballs at the men as they went into the canteen for breakfast. They got us back a few days later as we were going in for our breakfast; they pelted us with a load of rotting fruit - you would never be allowed to do that nowadays. It was Kayleigh's first-ever job, and I remember saying to her she would never get another job like it. I often wonder what became of her.

The personnel changed continuously; they came from as far away as South Africa, India, Malaysia, Australia, as well as Europe - places I could only ever dream of visiting. I did various roles; every shift, I went in not knowing what I would be doing that day. It could be picking up pasties, delivering wellies, or trying to get hold of my boss at the golf club because I needed to get his credit card in order to buy something urgent, e.g. netting to stop the sewage foam from blowing from the site onto the A30 dual carriageway! The public were not happy that day, believe me. I was a sort of 'girl Jane'; I was asked to do anything and everything. I felt very privileged to be part of a great team cleaning up the beaches of Mount's Bay, St Ives Bay and the surrounding area. I had been sorry to give notice on the Camborne jobs, but the move to Trafalgar House proved to be one of my better decisions. I was gutted when it came to an end.

Philip:

What a couple of years! Judy loved going to work (at the sewage project), and we had an improved social life because of it. All the personnel working on the scheme, whether from the UK, or the far reaches of the world, worked extremely hard, regularly working very long days, but then they played just as hard. There were organised and impromptu parties, (free) formal dinners, pub piss-ups, and karting events and of course, I took many of them for rides in the Osprey. Of all these socials, one stands head and shoulders above the rest: the first bonfire party.

The new sewage works were located between St Erth railway station and the A30 Hayle bypass. Access was down a single-track lane by the side of the railway station. Whilst clearing an area of trees ready for the new construction works, someone had the idea to build a huge bonfire in the middle of the cleared field, ready for a party on November 5th. This bonfire was literally compiled of felled trees, pallets and any other burnable crap found on the site. For the bonfire party, several marquees (food tent, bar tent, safety tent and DJ tent) had been erected, with a wooden dance floor laid in front of the DJ tent. The tents were definitely required as this was Cornwall in the autumn, i.e. expect rain, and it did indeed rain, very heavily, all day.

The party was well underway, with drinks flowing and the BBQs kept busy, as we all chatted and caught up with the latest gossip when it was time to light the (extremely large) bonfire. The safety officer ushered us all into the bar and food tents before taking his two-metre-long fire lighter towards the bonfire. Imagine the field as a clock with the bonfire in the middle. The food and bar tent was at six o'clock, the DJ tent and dance floor at two, the safety tent at four and St Erth Rail Station at nine o'clock. The safety officer was standing at three o'clock to light it. Because the bonfire was large and wet, the safety officer had doused it with petrol, but when he offered up the lit end of his pole to the bonfire, it did not light. Instead, the petrol fumes exploded in a very impressive flash and explosion, about twenty metres down the field in the three o'clock position, fortunately for us at six o'clock. How we all laughed as the embarrassed safety officer struggled to get the bonfire to light; he did manage to eventually, and the party continued.

That is until after about ten minutes, whereupon we could hear sirens and see lots of blue lights on the bypass.

'Wonder where they are going,' someone commented; they soon had their answer.

A convoy of four fire engines, five police cars and two ambulances came charging down the lane to our party. A member of the public had heard the explosion and seen the flames. As it still been during times of IRA bombings, they had reported that they believed a bomb had been let off at St Erth railway station. Oh dear!

The safety officer had to explain to the emergency service crews what had happened, and the fire chief was not amused when he and the crews were offered a burger. That wasn't the end of the story, though. Only being a single-width track, all the vehicles had to reverse back along it to get out. There was not enough room in the temporary car park for them to turn around as it was crammed full of our cars. The party resumed, the rain stopped, and we had great fun, including dancing on the outside dance floor to music that sped up and slowed down. A generator was being used to power the DJ's equipment, and it kept surging, making his turntables spin from 33rpm to 100+rpm, causing the band/singer to sound like 'The Chipmunks.' It all added to the fun of the evening; one never to be repeated, nor ever forgotten.

Judith:

By the summer of '91, David was now Rebecca. He'd had his bits chopped off, new silicone boobs created, and a nose job done to complete the transformation. He hadn't been a particularly attractive bloke, so despite a mountain of facial make-up, he/she didn't actually become a stunning woman. She invited us to go on holiday with her to Spain. A client of hers who owed her money had offered her his villa near Valencia. Having moved house, it seemed a cheap way for us to have a holiday. The plan was to drive there in her car and stay in the free villa. She had also invited a new friend of hers called Sarah

Jane who, by the end of the holiday, we re-named 'Sarah Jane is a pain.' It would be the first time I had been on a catamaran ferry across the channel, the first time I had driven an automatic car, the first time I had driven on the 'wrong' side of the road and the first time I had visited Spain.

Philip:

It was typical of Rebecca that she rang me at work with a short notice offer to join her on holiday to a villa in Spain. Fortunately, I had an obliging boss who bent the rules to allow me to go and luckily, Judy was able to get the time off too.

The plan was for us to drive up to her home in Rushton (Northants - nothing like going three hundred odd miles in the wrong direction to start your holiday) and then jump in her brand new Audi 80 for the trip to Spain. Knowing that an Audi 80 had a small boot, we turned up with just a couple of small bags. We were met by Rebecca and her new friend, Sarah Jane, who seemed to have their whole wardrobe, plus the kitchen sink, ready to load into the car. Then Rebecca added the pièce de résitance; she wanted to take her sunbed too. What Rebecca wants, Rebecca gets. It was okay, though, because she had bought a roof rack and an 'octopus' elastic bungee. No, it was not okay because the bungee would not be up to the job of securing the luggage, including the sunbed, on the roof rack. Why, oh why had she not mentioned it before we had set off? We had a garage full of strong rope at home - home being the operative word. This was a Sunday evening, and all the shops were shut, so I scoured her house and begged neighbours for any rope or string. I ended up splicing enough pieces together to secure the load, even using a piece of tarpaulin at the front to improve wind resistance – oh, me of many talents.

Rebecca was going to drive down to Dover, including boarding and disembarking the boat, and then Sarah-Jane would take over to Paris. They would be upfront, and the rule was that the driver had the choice of music. Judy and I would be in the back for the first two stints, or at least that was the plan.

Judith:

We left Rushden like Lewis Hamilton starting a Grand Prix, only this being summer in the countryside, there were lots of tractors and combine harvesters ambling along the single carriageway roads. Rebecca seemed intent on killing us all before we even got to the motorway, let alone France. She was taking far too many unnecessary risks – Phil later told me this is part of her DNA – and every obstacle was a challenge.

During one overtake, we all heard a bang.

In answer to the 'What was that?' question, I answered, 'I think something from the roof rack has fallen/broken off.'

However, she was not for stopping to check – all the traffic she had just overtaken would get back past her! When we stopped for fuel outside Dover, Phil confirmed that one of the wheels of her sunbed was missing; that is what we had heard.

Once in France and off the ferry, Rebecca pulled into the first motorway services to change drivers, but Sara Jane said she was too tired to drive. So, Plan B it was.

Phil said, 'Judy, get your arse into the front seat; we can finally have some decent music!'

Phil drove from Calais to Paris and had the joy of driving around Paris on the Boulevard Périphérique to pick up the Autoroute du Soleil (the A6 motorway to the Med).

After a couple of hours at the wheel, he pulled into a service station for a break and afterwards, I took over. As stated earlier, it was my first time driving an automatic car, and it was also my first time driving on 'the wrong' side of the road, but I coped perfectly.

As it got hotter, we all had to learn a new trick if the car started to labour when overtaking up a steep hill: to turn off the air conditioning. This gave us the extra horses to get by or get out of the way of the really fast boys and girls who insisted on flashing their lights at you whilst sitting on your bumper. Phil said that the temptation to 'brake test' them was high, but it was not his car.

The drive there was very long, the villa was very beautiful, but unfortunately, it didn't have a swimming pool. It was very annoying to watch all the neighbours splashing about in their pools, but it did have a roof sun terrace which was good for nude sunbathing if you could stand the forty-degree heat. It also had a couple of rusty

It Started With A Kiss in the magical land of Cornwall

bikes that Phil and I commandeered in order to escape for a bit of privacy and peace during the day. Somehow, wherever we sloped off to, the girls found us. Rebecca had her new boobs, and Sarah Jane, who thought she was a goddess, thought it was okay to sunbathe topless anywhere and everywhere. But no, it wasn't, especially not in this part of Spain (a holiday area used mainly by the Spanish). It was so embarrassing, and that's coming from me, a nudist. They were like a couple of giddy teenagers, loud, proud and very irritating. There were funny moments, though. On the first evening, I opened the bidet and, to my horror, found it was full of stainless steel surgical instruments; apparently, Rebecca had to dilate herself every day!

Philip:

Yes, the journey was indeed very long: it took thirty-one hours from 'door to door,' and, as Judy has stated, whilst the villa was beautiful, it was very disappointing to discover it lacked what it needed: a swimming pool. We had to make do with a hose. The area was beautiful; it was obvious that this was an area where the Spanish holidayed because there was little sign of any foreigners around. This meant that it was also very conservative, especially the town beach, and limited our chances of stripping off. However, we did manage to find a few places where Jude could go topless, and we both wore G-strings (not a pretty sight for me, at least, but it meant we could try to avoid white bits!).

201

Jude has mentioned discovering Rebecca's series of (different sized) stainless steel dildos that she had to use several times a day to 'dilate' her newly constructed vagina. What can I say? What she hasn't mentioned is another of our abiding memories of the holiday: that of the 'clip-clop' sound that announced 'Rebecca's approaching' as she walked heavily on the tiles of the villa in her shoes. No matter what time of day or night one wandered into the kitchen, there was always the clip-clop sound that followed you! Judy, especially, felt like she was being stalked.

Watermelons are another memory. One day, Jude and I had gone exploring on our bikes and were sitting outside a beachside cafe at the end of a long unmade track when the bloody Audi turned up. We started to think they had tracking bugs on the bikes! Anyway, after a couple of drinks, we left them and returned to the villa. They were still not back when we went to bed. When we got up in the morning, the kitchen and living room were covered in watermelons. They had flirted with the bar owner and had ended up going back to his family farm. He had presented them with a truckload of melons – we dread to think why the farmer/bar owner had been so generous. There are only so many melons one can eat, so, even trying to give them away, a lot got trashed.

On another day, we visited a water park; memorable for two reasons. One was Sarah Jane going topless and wearing a tiny yellow G-string – not a pretty sight, and we had to explain that she could not go topless there – the signs said so. The second reason was the high slide. Judy was game to give it a go and went first. She screamed the whole way down (the first big drop occurred under cover), and after hitting the pool at the bottom, she jumped out and ran straight into the toilets (situated by the slide). The poor girl had suffered from a little accident on the way down!

Judith:

We did manage to escape from the girls for one whole day when Phil and I borrowed the car to visit a naturist beach at Valencia, about an hour and a half away. It was an opportunity to visit a new beach and take some photographs and notes in preparation for submitting another article for H&E Naturist magazine. As previously mentioned, the payments for these articles were funding our holidays. Rebecca and Sarah Jane could have come with us, but we had agreed beforehand that we would like a day to ourselves. It was a welcome reprieve.

Philip:

Soon it was time to go home. Working backwards from our early morning ferry time and adding an extra couple of hours for the unexpected, we agreed on a departure time. Packing the boot, Rebecca surprised us by laying out a smart dress on top of everything.

She gave the explanation, 'If we have time, we might be able to detour into Paris.'

There had been no mention of this to the rest of us,

so none of us had prepared easy access to decent clothes; we were in vest tops, shorts and flip-flops for the journey.

Heading up the A6 Autoroute, Jude and I were asleep in the back, and Sarah Jane was driving; it was a beautiful clear, star-studded night. I know this because I was woken, as was Judy, by the car doing a 'wiggle.' We knew immediately what had happened; Sarah Jane had nodded off for a second. Rebecca attempted to talk her into stopping, to at least rest, if not let someone else take over. She had been driving for less than an hour (of her two). She refused, claiming she was okay. Judy and I were now wide awake and looking up at the night sky through the glass sunroof. Within a few minutes, there was a second 'wiggle,' and Rebecca had to grab the wheel to keep us on the road. She ordered Sarah Jane to pull into the next services, where she took over, and a couple of hours later, we pulled into a service station on the outskirts of Paris. Ignoring the 'wiggles,' nothing 'unexpected had happened.' We had a good run, time-wise, so we were well ahead of schedule. Therefore, surprise, surprise, Rebecca changed into her dress, titivated her make-up and off into Paris we went (under my skilful navigation, of course. Maps only in those dark days).

So, there we were, heading up the Avenue des Champs-Élysée, away from the Arc de Triomphe, at two thirty in the morning. Rebecca was interacting with all the locals who shouted and/or pointed at the 'mad Brits' in a heavily laden car with a sunbed on the roof. Then she started to race some of them.

'That's a red light you've just gone through,' I say. 'And that's another. And another.'

'What lights?' she asks, having not noticed that the traffic lights are located at waist level, not high, like in the UK.

It was a good job that traffic was light, or we could have been wiped out. Eventually desisting from her attempts at entente cordiale, we turned around at the Place de la Concorde and headed back, looking for a place where we could get something to eat. We found a restaurant that was still open opposite the Lido, and we were able to park virtually right outside. Wonderful. Trooping into the restaurant, one smartly dressed and sweetly smelling woman, plus two other women and a man, not smartly dressed or sweet-smelling (after all, we had been travelling for the best part of twenty-four hours), the maître d' offered us a table by the front window. Vest tops, shorts and flip-flops do not equate to Paris chic. As the punters from the Lido piled out and into the restaurant, all black tie and gowns to die for, they are shown to the rear of the restaurant, i.e. away from the smelly Brits! Whatever; we order our food. Even all these years later, we still say that the steak we had that morning was the best we have ever tasted. Sarah Jane left half of her meal but still insisted on having a sweet. She was never a friend of ours.

I had the pleasure of driving to Calais, but we were way ahead of schedule. I had to make a mental decision, unable to consult the other three as they were all sleeping.

It seemed pointless to hurry; we would just have a long wait at Calais. Therefore I found a local 'smooth' radio station and proceeded to drive along the motorway at 50 miles an hour (cruise control). It was very calming. Dawn was close to breaking as we neared Calais, so I pulled into a rest area (no shops etc., just toilets and benches). Sarah Jane, who insisted she could not sleep in a car, was away with the fairies in the rear, so we left her in the car as Jude and I wrapped up in the morning chill to sit at a picnic table to have a coffee (we had a flask with us). Rebecca had rescued her make-up bag from the boot and had just finished laying all her 'make me beautiful' powders, creams and instruments out around the (outside) sink when the street and toilet lights went out. Jude and I looked at each other and pissed ourselves laughing whilst trying to hide our faces from Rebecca. The timing was brilliant; the natural light was not yet good enough to see properly to do her make-up, so she gave up and joined us for a coffee, and then we completed the last few miles to the ferry port. There was space on an earlier ferry than the one we were booked on, so we caught that, having first woken Sarah Jane up. 'Can't sleep in a car,' she had told us at the start of the holiday: my arse, she can't.

Judith:

The ferry was a 'fast cat.' It was our first time on one, and it proved tricky to walk around; one step forwards, followed by three steps backwards and to the side. It was a motion that took some getting used to, and it was best just to sit. Arriving at the port, Phil and I decided to go out onto the small outside area (at the stern) as it was docking, giving us a small breather from Rebecca and Sarah Jane before we disembarked and headed back to Rushton. We were leaning on a rail watching the Dockers secure the lines when we both gave a deep sigh. We looked at each other with that helpless shrug of the shoulders Gallic gesture before turning around, as we knew what the approaching 'clip-clop' we could hear meant!

I actually felt emotionally exhausted. I had done my best to be supportive, and I had been a listening ear for all her needs; God, I needed a holiday to get over the holiday. Once we arrived back in the UK, we just wanted to get back to Cornwall as soon as possible, but first, we had to go in the wrong direction to Rebecca's (in Rushton). Getting there, we immediately jumped into our little car, drove a few miles, found a field and parked up. We slept on the grass under glorious sunshine for three hours before heading home. As the saying goes, 'There is no such thing as a free holiday.' How true.

Philip:

What a beautiful sleep that was; shame that we then had to drive six hours back to Cornwall. It had been lovely to be invited to share the holiday, but, 'Rebecca, please do not ask us again.'

Chapter 11

Dangerous Waters

Judith:

I had started my new job, and college loomed. The other ladies on the course were lovely; we were all of similar ages and up for the challenge. We were told that although it was a one-day-a-week course, we would need to do about thirty hours a week self-studying at home; I certainly hadn't bargained on that. The highlight of the day was lunch in the canteen; to start with, it was like having a girly day out. However, we all had full-time jobs, and it wasn't long before the workload caught up with us.

I got on really well with a lady called Carol. She quit after a month but didn't tell her boss and continued to come just for lunch. She became a best friend. I introduced her to the joys of sailing an Osprey, and we had a lot of fun together, on and off the water. She was a single mum with a twelve-year-old daughter whom I looked after now and again to help out. I introduced Carol to a guy at the sailing club who also sailed an Osprey. She ended up secretly marrying him, and then, for some reason, she totally dropped out of my life. To this day, I have no idea why she disappeared. I later found out that she had left her new husband and joined an ex-partner in Germany:

whether this is true or not, I have no idea. It was such a shame because we had become such good friends, and what a week we had when we all went to play at our very first Osprey National Championship. Were we up to it? I had no idea, but we were certainly up for it, and as they say, 'Ignorance is bliss.'

Philip:

The Osprey National Championships. If you are going to race a high-performance sailing dinghy, why wouldn't you go to the National Championships and pit yourself against the best in the country? Why not, indeed? Perhaps because your boat is old, heavy (weight matters in a sailing dinghy), and leaks. Your crew is new to sailing and, in theory, is a foot too short and at least seven stone too light (to be a crew for such a powerful boat). Plus, whilst I love sailing, I am not very good at it. Oh, and at the last minute, a friend at the sailing club, who limps due to childhood polio, announces his crew cannot get the time off work to go. Therefore Judy ('my crew' and always too kind for her own good) offered to sail with John and talked Carol, her new friend from college, who had only been in an Osprey twice, to crew for me. Total madness.

In 1992, the championship was held at Poole in Dorset. We found a lovely B & B to stay in that provided great breakfasts, giving us all the energy we needed to face the daily races. After an uneventful trip towing the boat from Cornwall, we located and booked into the B &

B before returning to the sailing club for a briefing.

Well, they didn't hold back: 101 reasons 'Not' to go sailing. The rather lovely sailing club was located a little bit further up the harbour beyond the Jersey and Cherbourg ferries. National Championships normally take place at least one mile offshore in an attempt to provide clear air, i.e. not influenced by land mass, for the racing. The problem at this venue was that to get out to sea, one first had to sail past the ferry and cargo berths, plus any ferry or large cargo ship entering or leaving the harbour. At this juncture, I need to point out that sailing a dinghy anywhere near a large vessel is disastrous, as they block the wind. This means you have no means of propulsion (to get out of the way), and the ship would not even know it had run you over. Then there were several very shallow sandbanks to be aware of as one sailed around Brownsea Island towards the open sea. The expected wind direction was 'onshore,' meaning one had to beat (zig-zag) up the harbour to reach the sea. Plus, it was forecast to be Force 6 to gale-force all week – borderline weather for novices like us. If you managed to survive this part still upright and alive, you then had the worst obstacle to negotiate: the Sandbanks chain ferry. The warning from the race officer might as well have been provided by the Grim Reaper. He made it abundantly clear that the chain ferry takes no prisoners and will not stop for any sailing dinghy. If you got your timing wrong and found yourself in front of it, it will just run you over! Still alive? Then watch out for one last sandbank just beyond the chain ferry. We came out of the briefing wondering what the hell we were doing there: sailing the Osprey was supposed to be enjoyable!

On day one, Carol and I made it down the obstacle course and started the practice race. As we approached the first (turning) mark – sailing courses are marked by 'turning buoys' – we had to give a wide berth to a capsized boat: Judy and John. On day two, we had a rigging issue on the water immediately before the start of the race, but managed to start and complete it, albeit a long way behind. On day three, we hit the sandbank outside the harbour, smashing our rudder, and had to be towed back to the sailing club.

Whilst the others raced, Carol and I had to make a trip to Southampton, where the only chandlers in the area with a suitable replacement rudder were located. Day four was extremely windy; too windy for John, Judy, Carol and I to sail, so we found a place on Sandbanks beach from where we could watch the brave souls who ventured out attempting to complete the course. Our decision not to sail was vindicated as utter chaos unfolded, with capsizes galore and many breakages. Some poor souls couldn't sail back into the harbour but managed to drift onto our beach, where we all helped them to recover their boats. That evening we went ice skating (less dangerous) before returning to the sailing club.

The club was buzzing; we ordered drinks and sat down with Des (Mount's Bay's best Osprey sailor), who was deep in discussion with his best mate Stubbsy (from Stafford). They were like two old women: gossiping until the cows came home. Out of the blue, this woman walked up behind Stubbsy and poured a full pint over his head.

Not even flinching, Stubbsy said to Des, 'I take it that was my missus?'

Des nodded, and they continued to gossip as if nothing had happened. Later on, we learnt that such behaviour between Stubbsy and his wife was quite the norm!

The wind eased a little for the remaining days, and both John and Judy, Carol and I, managed to complete the remaining races, neither of us bothering those at the front of the fleet. Laurie Smith or Ben Ainslie, we are not, but hey, we had a fantastic time. We vowed to do it again the following year, but this time, Judy and I would race together.

Judith:

What a week we had, the location was terrific, but the sailing was terrifying: that first day I took to the water, I was petrified. I could see the giant ferries, but where were the sandbanks? And the sight of the chain ferry made me feel physically sick. Once in the open water, I was fine. The fear only started again when we had to negotiate all the obstacles to return to our base, the fabulous Poole Yacht Club. OMG! This place was in a different league to Mount's Bay Sailing Club. It was founded in 1852 and had a rich history with strong racing traditions, a diverse membership of Olympians and novices, long-distance cruisers and day skippers, plus recreational sailors. The clubhouse was out of this world, all sleek and modern, with an outdoor patio area, a gun terrace (what the hell?), panoramic views over Poole Harbour, and a yacht haven. I had gone from Sunday league football to the Premier League in the blink of an eye. It was a good thing I had taken some half-decent clothes with me (well, high street labels from the charity shops I frequented). Was the socialising more pleasurable than the sailing? Honestly, for Caroline and I, the answer was a big fat 'Yes!' Perhaps I needed to find myself a rich old man with a giant fuck-off yacht (only joking, Phil).

Philip:

Whilst talking boats, it would be remiss of me not to mention the launch and blessing of the 'Spirit of Gaia,' a Pahi 63 catamaran built by our friend James Wharram (https://www.wharram.com/articles/spirit-of-gaia-renovation). James and his family had become good friends of ours, and we were honoured to be invited to the blessing and launch of their new boat. A High Priest from Polynesia had flown over to perform a blessing, along with the local vicar. The local Morris Men (one of whom was a colleague of mine from my time working in the SWEB Control Room) performed as only they could. After the launch, a meal was held Polynesian style, i.e. we all ate sitting on the floor. It was a very special, mystical day – another day never to be forgotten.

A footnote to the story concerns one of the very few regrets Judy and I have in our lives. The following year, during the boat's maiden voyage, we received a telephone call from Ruth (James's wife) on a Tuesday offering us the chance to join the boat as crew in Vigo, Spain. The intended crew had cried off, and they needed 'hands' to help them with the next leg down into the Mediterranean (I cannot remember to what port) where the boat was going to be based for the summer. The problem for us was that we had to be in Vigo by Saturday. This is where both Jude and I are way too practical, and we allowed our heads to rule our hearts. We thanked Ruth but declined the offer. What? We were both in full-time jobs, the boys were home and still our responsibility, plus there were the two dogs as well. To us then, it was impossible to disappear for at least a month, but we now very much regret that decision.

Judith:

Life, of course, wasn't all sailing and fun. In between, there was work and studying for me, and the first boomerang came back. A bungalow made for two was now a bungalow made for three: Antony had returned. He had applied for the police and RAF and failed on his eyesight and/or a heart issue, so a rethink was needed. After licking his wounds for a few weeks and driving me mad (he developed OCD regarding plumped-up cushions), he made the decision to go to college and do a two-year media course. Then, shortly after his return, Shaun arrived back; we were bursting at the seams again: four adults and two dogs in a bungalow made for two.

Other than pitching a tent in the garden, we were stuffed. We still had my sister and her daughters visiting, plus the uncle, who now came every summer for three months at a time. One year he came twice (note to self: don't be so accommodating). We were forced to board out the loft and chuck a mattress and desk up there. I am not sure who used it most to escape, Phil or Antony. Surprisingly, somehow we all managed to rub along okay: life was busy, hectic, but fun. Both boys had also now acquired girlfriends, and therefore, the house was never quiet. Shaun did bar work for a while, then, after splitting with his girlfriend, saw an advert in the local jobcentre for bulb pickers in Amsterdam. He decided to go off and have an adventure, with the intention of earning big money and winning back the love of his life when he returned.

Antony and I were both desperately short on sleep: me studying before work and him working three part-time jobs. He was at the post office prior to going to college (not to mention poor Phil having to drop him at Camborne for 0500hrs), the garage (overnight), plus lifeguarding at the Riviera Sands holiday park (in Phillack, Hayle) when he could fit a shift in. The poor bugger was trying his best to earn some dosh/play money, but it was taking its toll on him. There was one time we left him at home with a girlfriend for the evening, and upon our return, we found him fast asleep on the sofa with a Post-it note on his forehead. There was no sign of the girlfriend. The note said something along the lines of 'Thanks, but no thanks. I like my boyfriends to be awake.'

Poor Antony, I felt for my hard-working son.

Philip:

We probably contributed to Antony's lack of sleep. One night Judy and I returned home late, from where I cannot remember, but whoever had been driving now started drinking. I had recently bought a CD of good party hits, and I had not realised at the time of purchase why it had been so cheap: it was a karaoke CD, i.e. there were no words! Jude and I hate karaoke, and neither of us can sing, but on this occasion, it seemed like a good idea to put the CD on and have a sing-along. We knew Antony and his girlfriend were in bed, but we didn't care; we were having a whale of a time. An hour or so later, Antony and his girlfriend came through the front door.

'Oh', we said, 'we thought you were in bed!'

They had been, but our attempts at singing had woken them up and driven them out; they had climbed out of the bedroom window to escape. Not only that, but Ant was now in the girlfriend's bad books because, on their drive, he had run over a rabbit which, obviously, was our fault.

There was also a time when I really should have been nicer to Antony. It was another instance of me not controlling my feelings and failing to interact with people in a decent manner. I very definitely still had my 'L' plates on when it came to family living. As Judy has mentioned, when the boys had come home (albeit Shaun's presence was often temporary), and because Jude's sister and uncle were still making their visits, we decided to board out the loft. This was to give us room to lay a mattress up there and create an 'office' space.

A friend of ours, Keith, was a builder, and he was happy to quote and do the job for us. So one day, I came home with Keith having gone and the job completed. Antony was proud to announce that he had been working hard all day, helping Keith to do the work. I went up to inspect the work and was not happy. The boarding was fine, but the 'shelving/tables' had been erected at the wrong height (they were too high to use as a desk). I could see why Keith had put them where he did; some beams made it easy at that height, but I had made it very clear as to the level I needed them to be at. I became very grumpy because I was going to have to alter them. Antony thought I was angry at him, and it probably did come over like that, instead of being grateful for his unpaid assistance. I let my anger with Keith cause me to be short-tempered with everyone around me for a while, making me hell to live with. Tell me again why, later in life, I became a PCSO.

Judith:

Antony successfully completed his college course. For his final assignment, he had written, produced and starred in a thirty-minute video film called 'Bryan Friggs – His Life Story.' (A friend of Ant's uploaded an unedited version to YouTube in 2020 but named it Bryan Friggs – His Life Story). To celebrate this, we held a sort of 'Premiere

BBQ,' inviting the cast and other friends of Antony. His then-girlfriend – she of rabbit fame – was a vegetarian, so I asked Ant what we should buy for her that she could/would eat. The answer was, 'Linda McCartney vegetarian sausages,' and bloody expensive they were too!

Come the night, Phil donned his BBQ chef's hat and cooked all the meat, me having prepared all the salad and savoury stuff, and then everyone crammed into our small living room to watch the film. To our surprise, most people left early, leaving a small group of us outside enjoying the warm summer evening; the drink was still flowing, and we were all stuffed. Phil had cooked the Linda McCartney sausages, but the girlfriend had not touched them, and she didn't want them now. But there was someone who did, namely Bill, the slobbering German Shepherd who was sitting patiently by my side with hopeful eyes. Rather than throw the sausages away, I offered one to him that he eagerly took, but seconds later, he spat it out. If he could talk, you knew he would be saying something like, 'What the fuck was that shit?' We all fell about laughing; even the dog that ate anything didn't like veggie sausages.

Philip:

Antony loved media and films, and his father (the ex-husband) successfully got him some work as an extra on a TV Second World War drama production - I think it was called 'Coming Home.' If I remember correctly, he was paid £50 for each day's work. Returning home after his first day, Ant said they needed more extras, so Ant persuaded Shaun to go as well the next day. They wanted to cut Shaun's hair, but he was reluctant, at least until they offered him an extra £25! Shaun managed to make me very jealous that evening when he told us that one of the stars of the show, Joanna Lumley, was in the make-up room at the same time as him, and she had run her fingers through his new haircut. Lucky Shaun. The punchline of this tale comes when I inform you that they also used the ex-husband's dog (a Rottweiler) in the show, and the dog was paid £125 a day. The boys were rather put out by this.

Judith:

We had some amazing parties in the new bungalow, the first being in March 1992 for my 38th birthday. We had invited the usual naturists, volleyballers, work colleagues, football and sailing friends. A couple of days before the party, Phil had decided to install a patio window lock; God knows why. I was cooking in the kitchen, listening to teeth-grating drilling when suddenly, there was a loud bang, and Phil gave out a huge moaning sound. I ran to the living room, dreading the worst. He had accidentally caught the glass, and the whole thing had exploded. The inner pane had shattered into a million pieces (but stayed put because of the laminated plastic layer). He was moaning in horror; I wanted to kill him! So I had my birthday party with a taped-up window and a claim on the house insurance. However, it was a great party, which also led to a wedding invite later in the year. A friend of mine and a work colleague of Phil's had hooked up at the party, unbeknown to us. We were asked if we would be witnesses at their wedding ceremony, and when we turned up, we were the only people there. We did the ceremony and went for a lovely wedding lunch at Penventon Hotel in Redruth. Then we were press-ganged to go with them as 'back up' to break the news to the bride's parents and children, who had no bloody idea their mother was getting married. Bonkers!

Philip:

I don't talk about the patio door incident. I was attempting to save ten percent on the insurance during times when finances were a struggle. I will, however, talk about Nick and Rachel. They were an unmarried couple whom I worked with at SWEB. Terry was a friend of Judy's from her pre-me doggy days. Rachel and Terry made a connection at the party and started to have an affair. One day, Nick turned up at work with two black eyes. When I asked what had happened, he said 'my friend' had done it. Apparently, he suspected Rachel was seeing someone and had followed her to Redruth rail station, where he confronted Terry when Rachel met up with him. Nick lost the ensuing fight. Oh, the irony! Nick being the driver of the car on the North Cliffs – he of the lunchtime conquest shagging fame, in case you have forgotten.

I thought Terry was onto a loser with Rachel. She had a history of failed relationships, definitely had mental health issues, and whilst not necessarily looking for sugar daddies, she did like money. Nick was an electrical engineer earning a very good salary. Terry was self-employed and had used up all his savings to buy a big townhouse in Redruth that needed lots of work. I think Rachel thought he had more money than he actually had. As Judy has stated, she and I were the witnesses to the wedding and then went to the reception dinner (for four). There we discovered she had packed her three kids off to school that morning and had not told them about the wedding. How cruel is that? Then we got asked to go with them to tell her mum – she hadn't told her either, for fuck's sake! We must have been mad because we went. As suspected, the marriage did not last long because soon, Rachel had ditched Terry and was seeing an accountant. What can I say?

Judith:

Having thoroughly enjoyed the '92 Championships at Poole, we decided to enter the '93 Championships at Tenby, this time sailing together. This championship is engraved in our brains for various reasons. Tenby is a long way from Hayle, so we had decided to set off at 2 am, calling first at our local garage, located at the end of the Hayle bypass, to fill up with petrol. Antony was on shift as the overnight petrol attendant, and the forecourt was chaotic. Every pump was in use with a queue of vehicles waiting their turn. It was the height of the holiday season, and everyone was in an excitable mood, some having an impromptu game of football using the balls (for sale) in a big basket in front of the shop, despite Antony's desperate pleas over the tannoy for them to stop. Antony was working on his own, and there was no access to the shop. One paid for the fuel and any other goods from the shop via the night window. Anthony hated this as customers had a (he believed, often deliberate) tendency to request one item, which, after having fetched from the shop, they then asked for another.

We were the only car with a boat in tow, and we were heading out of Cornwall, not into it, so our journey was easy. However, it appeared to us that the rest of the country was heading into Cornwall. The A30 south was chock-a-block all the way from Hayle to Exeter, with every lay-by totally full of overnighting caravans and motorhomes. Calling into Exeter services for a coffee (it's off the motorway and serves both north and southbound traffic), we could not find anywhere to park, so we had to continue up the M5 to Taunton services (north traffic only, where there was space).

Philip:

The trip is also memorable for the tight-fisted bastard who ran the B&B we had unfortunately booked into. Having been spoilt by our Poole landlady, we were in shock when this miserable specimen of a man produced a full English breakfast consisting of one piece of bacon, one sausage, one egg and a spoonful of baked beans, plus one slice of toast each with barely enough butter to cover half a slice. He nearly burst a blood vessel when we asked for more toast and butter! It was too late to change digs, so we had to supplement breakfast with food from a cafe en route to the harbour; sailing is an energy-sapping business. Then, on our last night, having informed him that we would be leaving in the early hours, he wanted us to leave at teatime so that he could re-let the room. He was told in no uncertain terms what we thought of that suggestion.

Judith:

The weather continued where it left off from Poole a year earlier, i.e. gale-force. On day one, we misjudged the time to get out to the start line; our intention, having decided to give the practice race a miss, was to arrive on the race course just before the start of race one. Unfortunately, because the wind was offshore, we flew out to the course at 'warp' speed and had to sail around for nearly forty-five minutes waiting for the practice race to finish and the first proper race to start. Following several capsizes and beginning to get very cold, we took the decision to return to shore, taking a 'DNS – did not start' for the race. That put an end to our intention of competing for the 'highest placed novice' because you must have a score from every race to be eligible. Oh well, another year, perhaps?

On day two, we left shore with the whole fleet, so there was no issue with starting on time. The race was amazing and terrifying. Sail races start with a beat, i.e. sailing into the wind; therefore, one has to zig-zag up the course to the first mark. Going around that first mark, one then 'reaches,' i.e. the wind is on the side of the boat. This is the fastest point of sailing, and the crew has to put up and then control the spinnaker (a very big sail). There was a huge sea running, i.e. very tall waves, and as we struggled to keep upright along the reach, we could see carnage in front of us at the 'gybe' mark. A gybe is the most dangerous manoeuvre to perform in a sailing boat. The wind is behind the boat, so as the boat is turned, the sail whips across to the new side with incredible force, often causing it to capsize. Phil steered a course away from the mark, not wanting to collide with any of the capsized boats. God knows how, but we managed to complete our gybe safely and set off on the next leg: a run, i.e. with the wind directly behind us. Because the sea (waves) was also running in the same direction, it meant we were surfing the huge waves. However, because we were slower than the waves, the boat would come off the wave and sink into the trough at the bottom until you could pick up the next wave: another dangerous situation. Phil spent the whole leg sitting on the transom (the back of the boat) trying to steer. I couldn't get that far back because I was limited by the length of the rope I had in my hands that controlled the spinnaker. It was thrilling and terrifying in equal proportions as we tried to keep the bow (nose) of the boat out of the water and thus stay upright. We managed to complete the race without capsizing and achieved our best-ever Nationals result: 37th (out of 55 boats). For the rest of the week, the wind eased, and whilst the sailing became easier, we were unable to match our 37th placing.

Philip:

In 1994, we competed in our third and last National Championships, which was held at our home club: Mount's Bay Sailing Club. Between my lack of skill, our old, heavy boat, and light winds, it was a disappointing event for us, especially after the excitement of the previous two years. We were not last, but felt we should have done better. Hey-ho. The best thing about the event (in fact, there are two 'best' things. Shit, I nearly forgot the second!), was that on the final night, Lord St Levan hosted a prize-giving party on St Michael's Mount for all the competitors and volunteers: which was a privilege and not to be missed.

Secondly, about a month after the event, the sailing club hosts a 'thank you' event for all the volunteers that helped during the 'championship week.' Host club competitors are invited as well (the club hosts a National Championship event every year for other classes of boat, and we always volunteer our services for those). On this occasion, we had an offer of a 'taxi' driver, enabling both of us to have a drink: normally, one of us had to abstain). Antony had recently passed his driving test, and we had bought him his first car (he had pleaded with us for it not to be a mini: perhaps there was something he was not telling us?). Antony was now the proud owner of a Vauxhall Astra, and he wanted to thank us (for buying the car) by driving us to the club and back. What he did not know, and we have teased him about it ever since, is that there was a free bar with no limit. He was gutted.

This story does not end here, though, because it will be of no surprise that Judy and I got a wee bit paralytic. Getting home and into the bedroom, Judy sat on the end of the bed, which was about two feet from the wall as it was a small bedroom, and got a fit of uncontrollable giggles.

When I asked her what was so funny, she said, 'I can't get my jeans off,' and promptly fell back onto the bed.

Being the worse for wear myself, it became like a Krypton Factor challenge trying to get her undressed and into bed. Then, the following morning, I was up all bright-eyed and bushy-tailed, had taken the dogs for their walk, prepared breakfast and woken Jude up, chasing her several times to get up and ready for work. She was reluctant, but I was insistent.

Eventually, I got her into the car and was about to drive off when she said, 'I'm going to be sick.'

I replied, 'No, you're not,' as she opened the door and spewed up all over the drive.

I was not in her good books at that point, especially as I still drove her to work.

Chapter 12

Bikes, Royals & Fireworks

Judith:

The Gwel Tek bungalow was to be our forever home, and I loved it; I was happy, in love, and life was just grand. We had a great social life, numerous events with my work lot at Trafalgar House, sailing/drinking at the Mount's Bay Sailing Club and beach parties at Perranporth: happy days. We had also become members of the Minack Theatre.

The Minack is an open-air theatre constructed above a gully with a rocky granite outcrop jutting into the sea, overlooking the spectacular panorama of Porthcurno Bay. A lady called Rowena Cade moved to Cornwall after the First World War, where she built a house for herself and her mother on land at Minack Point. The Minack's story started in 1929 when Rowena got involved with an open-air production of Shakespeare's 'A Midsummer Night's Dream.' It was such a success that the company repeated the production the following year. They then wanted to stage 'The Tempest,' and Rowena offered them the use of her cliff garden for the performance. So she decided to create a practical acting area and somewhere for the audience to sit. Everything you see there today was built by hand. Most of the structures were created from concrete mixed with sand from the beach, which Rowena herself carried up the cliffs in sacks. As she was an artist as well as a builder, she etched complex designs into the wet concrete with an old screwdriver. Many of the seats bear the names and dates of plays performed there. It was her life's work, and she was still working there in her eighties: she died in 1983, a few days before her ninetieth birthday.

What a remarkable woman and what a magical place! Needless to say, we took most of our visitors there to watch a production. With my sister's children only being young, we tended to choose family shows. They loved The Wizard of Oz, especially when we skipped from the car park to the entrance singing 'Follow the Yellow Brick Road.' We will also never forget the spaced-out caterpillar from 'Alice's Adventures in Wonderland.'

We did get it wrong one year when we took them to see 'Sweeney Todd.' We had our usual front row seats bang in the middle of the stage: big mistake! We had no idea the story is about a barber who slits his customer's throats, then gives the corpses to his partner in crime, who bakes their flesh into meat pies: 'Oops!' It was only when he slit his first customer's throat (in the first scene of the show), and red blood gushed out, that we realised our error. This was made even worse when the body vanished over the wall as if it had been thrown into the sea. Not ideal, obviously, but there wasn't a lot we could do under the circumstances other than brush over what was going on. My sister's children, who we called 'Why 1' and 'Why 2,' definitely lived up to their nicknames that day, asking lots of demanding questions.

So if you get the opportunity to see a show at The Minack, and I highly recommend you do, here are my top tips. Do your research, take a homemade picnic and drinks (preferably bottles of wine with crystal glasses), make sure you have lots of layers on and take blankets and cushions. It doesn't matter how hot the day has been; the minute that sun goes down, it gets bloody freezing. Our favourite company was 'The Kneehigh Theatre' group, an off-the-wall motley crew who also did promenade shows as cliff walk productions along the spectacular rugged cliffs of Cornwall, very entertaining for families and adults alike. I think I would have liked to have been an actress. I love escapism, and it must be wonderful to give so much joy to an audience. Unfortunately, I don't think that opportunity will drop in my lap.

Philip:

Mention the Kneehigh, and three things immediately spring to my mind. One, the very first time we saw them was in a production at The Minack, during which they spoke in a gobbledygook made-up language (or so it seemed to us), and it was brilliant. They had us hooked. Give us a Kneehigh production over a Shakespeare one every time. Two, sitting in the twilight in our own camping chairs in a clearing at Tehidy Country Park, awaiting the start of their show, we found ourselves breathing in the unmissable smell of cannabis. There was a rising fog of smoke coming from a screen at the side of the stage. Then, several of the cast appeared from behind the screen, with one flicking a butt end into a brazier. It was (and probably still is) an 'artiste' thing, as we know a lot of the bands we watch also indulge. I must add here the fact that this production, in the middle of the woods, on a balmy summer's night, was yet another instance of Cornwall enthralling us with its magical charm.

Three is a very silly tale that I accept is one of those moments that one really had to be there to appreciate. However, I will never forget it, and I have a smile on my face conjuring up the scene in my head as I type. We were at a local Hayle primary school where they were performing a children's show. Suddenly, when a London to Penzance express train thundered by on the rail line immediately behind them, all the cast members, as one, interrupted their performance. They stood looking at the train whilst swinging their heads from right to left, following the train in a sort of 'diddly-dum, diddly-dum, diddly-dum' motion. The moment the train had gone, they just resumed the play as if nothing had happened. It was hilarious – well, we thought so.

There is one other Minack-related story that needs to be mentioned. During one of their early visits to us, I took the sister and her kids, plus the uncle, down to visit the theatre during the day, and then we went down to the Porthcurno beach for an ice cream and paddle. We were at the water's edge, playing chase and running away from the waves, when I noticed a wave coming that was more powerful than the previous ones (that surfer training: waves come in 'sets'). Not having a child holding my hand at that time, I automatically retreated away from the water, shouting a warning at the others. The sister scooped up the elder of her girls and also ran back. The uncle was late to react and, picking up the younger girl, tried to trot backwards away from the incoming water. In his haste, he tripped over his own feet, and over he went onto his back onto the wet sand with the wave engulfing him. At least he had the foresight to hold the child up out of the water. I always get blamed for the uncle getting soaked and teased because it was alleged I ran away to stop my brand-new trainers from getting wet. They were right; salt water is not good for trainers. In my defence, if I thought the uncle and child were in danger, I would have reacted differently, but hey, they weren't. And truth be known, I was not a fan of the uncle, so was inwardly smiling to myself whilst outwardly helping him up (after the wave had receded, of course).

Judith:

I was at work the day they visited the Porthcurno beach, and my uncle was not a happy bunny when they returned home; he was soaked to the skin. I think we all made matters worse the more we laughed, and I don't think he ever forgave Phil for legging it. The beauty of Porthcurno beach was totally lost on him, and I don't think we ever visited that beach with the family again. We tended to spend more time at Marazion; there was far less chance of rogue waves there, In fact, often, there were no waves at all, so it was much safer for everyone.

We had blow-up rubber boats that we played in the water with. The girls loved being towed in them, even when there was thick fog hanging over the beach (on that day, Phil and I had used the visit [to Marazion] to do some work on our dinghy). The family failed, however, to heed our warning to put on sun cream, and my sister and uncle returned looking like a couple of lobsters. They had to spend the rest of their holiday covered up as they practically had third-degree burns; 'Knowledge is power,' so they say. Phil still laughs when recalling this story, because the uncle was still in pain upon returning home and had to take a week's sick leave.

'Serves the old bugger right,' he said at the time.

Philip:

In 1993 we enjoyed a glorious summer but still felt the need to escape, so we decided to use the funds from our published articles (of our previous holiday) to return to Le Cap d'Agde. We found a good deal for a three-week holiday in September. Although cheaper at that time of year, it was also much quieter, almost too quiet. However, the sun shone, we had a good rest, and met a guy called Neil. He was a fascinating character: a white guy who had spent his early years in the Caribbean and had been a pathologist for a while. He was now living in Del Boy country (Peckham) and running his own high-end Hi-Fi business making very expensive turntables. He had advertised for another male to go on holiday with him, but within twenty-four hours of arriving, he had paid for Andy, the selected male, to be rehoused in another apartment because Neil found he could not abide Andy's habits! Andy was a lovely guy, and the four of us spent many evenings together during the holiday; it was just that Neil found he was unable to share a living space with him. Neil had many entertaining stories about his life and business. One of the best was that on one occasion, having installed a turntable at a client's house, he looked at their record collection and was so appalled he tore the client's cheque up and took the turntable home!

Over winter, we were planning where to holiday the following year, and we fancied a resort in South West France called La Jenny. It looked beautiful, but a bit expensive, and the more affordable accommodation looked like nothing more than semi-detached garden sheds! Research, research, research, plus another fantastic idea from the love of my life: 'Do you think Neil would be interested in sharing a lodge with us?' I had found a private advert in H&E magazine for a six berth lodge, but it was beyond our price range. However, Neil eagerly agreed to Judy's request to join us. The plan was for him to catch a train to Plymouth and join us in our car. After that, we would catch the Plymouth to Roskoff ferry and then drive down to La Jenny. Something to very much look forward to.

In the summer of 1994, everything was organised (this is me we are talking about here), and we were very excited about the trip to La Jenny. On the day before we travelled, Neil rang to say he had a work problem and would not be able to make the train (on Friday). However, he had booked a flight to Bordeaux on Sunday morning, so he asked if we could pick him up from the airport: of course we could. Therefore, when Judy and I set off at midday to make the ninety/minute journey to Plymouth, we were in a very happy, relaxed mood; we were in plenty of time to catch our 3:15 pm ferry. You know it is not going to be that simple, and it wasn't. We got as far as the Bodmin bypass, and the traffic stopped. Something had happened, but with no alternative route to take from our location, we just had to sit it out and hope. We arrived at Plymouth at 3 pm, and fortunately, we were allowed to board the ferry – not sure that would be the case these days – we had made it by the skin of our teeth. Having located our cabin – it was a six-hour trip to Roskoff, and a cabin is a must for (seasick) me – we headed to the back of the boat to have a coffee and chocolate croissant as we sat on the open terrace watching Plymouth in the sun disappear from view. It was another memorable moment in our lives. Simple pleasures.

Judith:

The sail away from Plymouth was definitely another magical moment in our lives. Then we headed down to the cabin for some sleep, having a shower just before the boat docked at Roskoff. The overnight journey down to La Jenny went without a hitch, and early Saturday morning, we booked into our magnificent lodge. The sun was shining, so we decided to take the bikes and head to the beach. The resort is situated in a forest, and following the 'la plage' signs, we headed down the various tracks. We then got confused as the track seemed to be running parallel to the beach. We were passing clothed people, all of whom returned our 'bonjours' and did not seem bothered that we were cycling naked. Hitting a main road, we decided something was wrong, so we retraced our steps. It turned out we had missed a turning in the forest to the sea; I blamed it on lack of sleep, and of course, on Phil. What on earth were we doing? I don't even like cycling, and I was a tiny bit cross, but then we located the magnificent beach which, like Perranporth, opened onto the Atlantic. It was breathtaking, with fantastic Atlantic waves rolling in, and after an hour on the hated bike, I just wanted to throw myself in the water: my happy place.

Philip:

Not in the original plan, but on Sunday, we had to leave the site to go to Bordeaux airport to pick up Neil. We found the airport easily enough, parked up and collected Neil. Then, along with half a dozen French cars, we found we could not get out of the airport car park. It made for a strange convoy as we went from exit barrier to exit barrier and then back to the terminal in our attempts to escape. One of the Frenchmen went to report the problem and came back with the answer. It's commonplace now, but it wasn't back then. One had to take the ticket we got as we entered the car park to a machine in the terminal that then spat out another ticket that would work the exit barriers, hah! This was even though there was a three-hour 'free' time limit. Progress?

The holiday was blissful; the three of us got along famously and had some great experiences. We played archery, tennis and naked golf (there was a three-hole proper course there), having first attended a free lesson where Judy won the putting competition (I finished third and a German second), even though she had spent most of the lesson sitting to one side smoking. She hates golf; it bores her.

The swimming pools were to die for, and during our stay there, the World Cup was televised in the bar. There was a big Dutch contingent at the resort, which, like now for Max Verstappen, turned out in all orange to watch their team. They also adopted the Irish 'olay, olay, olay' sing-along, which created a fabulous atmosphere, especially when the Dutch beat the Irish in the last sixteen. We even played bingo in French over evening drinks; it was a good way to learn French numbers as well as pass some time whilst socialising with other holidaymakers.

The trip home was uneventful until, awaking from being asleep in the back of the car, I was asked by Judy whether she should pull into the services that were approaching to fill up. By the time I cleared my head, we had passed the services.

'We'll call in at the next one,' I said, only there wasn't a next one.

We came off at the next junction. The roads to Roskoff were very rural, and I knew we would be passing close to Rennes, a large town. But could we afford to waste time and petrol driving around Rennes (it was the early hours of the morning), or should we just press on? We recalled there was a petrol station in the middle of nowhere. It was a few miles before a stretch of dual carriageway started, where there was another petrol station, so we decided to take the risk and push on. We made the first station without trouble. It was unmanned, but a card could be used; only both of mine refused to work. It wasn't until we got back home that I realised both my cards had expired: so much for being organised! On to the next station it was, then. Having travelled for many miles with the fuel gauge showing empty, we eventually ran out. I had a full gallon can in the boot (in those days, I never travelled without it) that we put in and hoped it was enough to reach the dual carriageway. Fortunately for us, it was.

Another memory of this trip home was a middle-of-the-night coffee stop at a picnic area in the middle of nowhere. It was very cold, and we were all wrapped up in blankets, but the sky was incredible: magnificent beyond belief. None of us had ever seen so many stars. Even on the clearest night back in the UK, I had never seen, nor ever have since, seen anything to match this. It was during this trip home, whilst tucked up and surrounded by luggage in our little car, Neil informed us that at home, he had a chauffeur-driven Saab that we could have used for the trip. A bit late now, matey: communication is a wonderful thing. The rest of the trip home was uneventful: catching the ferry and dropping Neil off at Plymouth train station before driving back to Hayle.

Judith:

It had been a lovely holiday, my main memories are, of course, cycling naked (ugh), Neil playing a round of golf with Phil – he went to tee off, missed the ball, but the divot flew about fifty yards up the course (right in front of the clubhouse). The sight of him chasing after it stark bollock naked still sets me off in fits of laughter. Me actually beating Phil at something (perhaps I should take up golf), and the stars that night were magnificent. Maybe a trip to see the Northern lights should go on my bucket list.

The holiday was over, but when you live in Cornwall, you are really always on holiday; you just have to fit it in around normal life and work commitments. I think we were very good at doing that, plus we always said 'Yes' if an opportunity presented itself. This amazing county had so many historical festivals and events happening that having to go to work was a bit of a bummer. We needed to win the lottery; we didn't want to work; we just wanted to play.

Philip:

And so to the tale of when I met, albeit very briefly, the man whom I was named after, though it was not planned.

Jude's sister and brother-in-law had decided to visit us with the girls for Easter. A few days before coming down, the brother-in-law had been rear-ended whilst stationary at some traffic lights, writing off his car. Knowing he was due to make the trip to Cornwall, he thought he would do it in style. He hired a (new on the market) Lexus GS300 and gave the bill to the arsehole who had rammed him. As per usual, when the brother-in-law visited, he drank, and I became the chauffeur. What a fabulous car it was; loads of power and beautiful luxury; I loved driving it.

On the Wednesday evening of their stay, the brother-in-law declared that he 'wanted to go to Truro tomorrow.' He needed some new trousers, and he knew from past visits that there was a gentleman's tailor at Truro that he liked. When 'the Lord of the Manor' declared he wanted to do something, we all had to form a queue to jump through the hoop. So, on a very wet Maundy Thursday (31st March 1994), we went to play in Truro with no plan of what we were going to do, other than to window shop, whilst the master was buying his new trousers.

Driving to Truro in the wonderful Lexus, we were whispering along the bypass. I was keeping to the speed limit going down the big hill leading to the Camborne turn-off when an HGV pulled out to overtake me. What?

I admit I was a bit naughty, but there was no way he was going past. I tickled the accelerator just enough to keep him level, and as we hit the bottom of the hill, I floored it and left him for dust. Boy, was this car fast! And silent, too. It was very satisfying, if a bit childish.

Arriving at Truro, we encountered traffic jams and diversions. What the hell was going on? Parking up, we made our way to the gentlemen's tailors and discovered all the city centre shops cordoned off with fencing. Asking around, we were told that the Queen and Prince Philip were in town and were about to do a walkabout. What fabulous timing. Whilst the brother-in-law went and paid silly money for silly clothes, we garnered a spot against the fencing and waited for the procession to arrive. I noticed a flower shop nearby, so I went and bought the girls a bunch of flowers each in the hope they might get a chance to present them to the Queen. And then we waited patiently for the procession to reach us.

The great unwashed public were kept on the pavement behind barriers on either side of the road, running the whole length of Her Majesty's walk along Pydar Street. As the Queen slowly walked along the route, people were offering her bouquets of flowers. However, as she reached our position, she was on the other side of the road, which was a problem because Jude's two nieces were beside themselves with excitement. We had seen a few little girls allowed inside the barriers to present their flowers, so I started to part the barriers to let the girls go across to the Queen. Immediately, a big burly, dour-faced, plain-clothes cop put his hand on the barrier and said they couldn't go.

Then this voice said, 'It's okay, let them go.'

I looked up straight into the eyes of Prince Philip, the man I was named after. 'Thank you, Sir,' I said. 'It's very kind of you.'

He talked to us for the short while it took for the girls to run over to the Queen, present their bouquets and return, whereupon he and his security people moved on. The Duke of Edinburgh has been my hero ever since; may he rest in peace. Meanwhile, the brother-in-law was still in his posh shop choosing his posh pants, totally unaware that his daughters had just met the Queen.

Judith:

Play days come in all shapes and sizes, and on Easter Monday following the trip to Truro, we attended the 'Point to Point' at the Wadebridge showground. My sister's family are a very 'horsey' family – both girls had ponies – so it was right up their street. They are so 'horsey' that once when we went to play pitch and putt at the Hayle mini golf course, the youngest girl asked if she had to walk the course before playing: it's what show-jumping competitors do before they complete the round on their horses. Back at the 'Point to Point,' during our picnic lunch, we noticed people by the rails of the course and could hear horses. That was strange because we had arrived way too early, and the first race was not due for an hour, so we toddled off to investigate. Speaking to the people by the rails, we discovered they were extras for an episode of Wycliffe, the new ITV detective series, and filming was taking place. They were about to shoot (I mean film) the horses coming past them, and the extras had been instructed to cheer as the horses went by. Hell, we could do that, so we did, and jolly good fun it was too! After several 'takes,' a guy from the production company came over and said that scene was in the can, and we now had to go over to the start area. He wasn't happy when we went off in the opposite direction, back to the car and our lunch, so we had to tell him we were not part of his 'extras.' We waited eagerly for the airing of 'our' episode, which we recorded. We wanted to catch our moment of glory when our family was on national TV, even though it was for only two tiny seconds – if that.

Leaving the site to head home, on the narrow winding roads around Wadebridge, Phil, my sister and I were sitting in the back with my two nieces when the youngest suddenly stated she was going to be sick.

She pleaded with her father, 'Daddy, stop, please.'

My brother-in-law, who, on this occasion, had chosen to drive rather than be driven by Phil, ignored her pleas. The next minute, my niece promptly threw up over her mother and me, nice - 'Not!' Phil was out of the firing line, but I could hear him heaving. We were all heaving; not really the perfect way to end a perfect day.

Philip:

With our visitors gone, it was back to the grind of

everyday life, and at work, I needed a new staff member for my team. I think my boss's boss had plans for me, as he took the unusual step of getting me to do the interviews, with him sitting in with me. This was certainly not a role I would want to repeat in a hurry. I had two candidates: one, a young girl who was very enthusiastic, and who I think, with training, would have performed very well. However, my department was being overwhelmed with work. The other candidate, Linda, was a lady of a similar age to me with many years of experience (in SWEB). She could slot into my team without any training. It was a no-brainer, really, but it did not stop me from having regrets about not giving a youngster a deserved break, and I found it very difficult to tell her she hadn't got the job.

An unexpected bonus of appointing Linda became apparent as the next Flora Day (8th May) was approaching. 'What's Flora Day?' you ask. The 'Visit Cornwall' website states the following: 'Flora Day takes place every year on 8th May (except when the date falls on a Sunday or Monday, which is Market Day, when it then takes place on the Saturday before). It is a celebration of the passing of winter and the arrival of spring. It is one of the oldest British customs still practised today and sees massed dances through the streets of the town and the performance of the 'Hal-an-Tow' pageant. The midday dance is perhaps the best known and was traditionally the dance of the gentry of the town. Today the men wear top hats and tails while the women dance in their finest frocks. Traditionally, all dancers wear Lily of the valley, Helston's symbolic flower. The gentlemen wear it on the left, with the flowers pointing upwards, and the ladies wear it upside down on the right.'

For those of us of a certain age, we will never be able to forget DJ Terry Wogan performing a vocal version of the Flora Dance tune on Top of the Pops. It reached number 21 in the UK singles chart.

Returning to 'Visit Cornwall,' 'The origins of this famous celebration dance are more than likely pre-Christian and connected to ancient spring festivals that take place all over Europe. Nowadays, the festival's original purpose of ushering in a prosperous harvest expresses itself in a lively, colourful celebration that involves the whole town. A great family day out. The town is decked out with bluebells, gorse and laurel leaves gathered from the surrounding countryside. Dancing begins at 7.00 am with gentlemen wearing shirts and ties and the ladies in light summer dresses. Not long after the Hal-an-Tow, a boisterous mummers' play featuring scenes of St George slaying the Dragon begins, cheered on by a crowd dressed in Lincoln green and Elizabethan robes. The children of the town dance at 10.00 am wearing flowers and Lily of the valley and at midday, the formal dance of the day begins with men wearing morning dress and the ladies decked out in magnificent ball gowns and hats that could be the envy of Ascot. To round off the day of dancing, the Evening Dance starts from the Guildhall at 5 pm.'

In addition, the 'Helston Flora Day Association'

website states, 'When the big bass drum strikes the first beat of the dance at seven in the morning, the spirit of the day is stirred and the celebrations commence. Couples dance through the streets, entering selected houses and shops to drive out the darkness of winter and bring in the light of spring.'

'What's all this got to do with SWEB and my new team member, Linda?' you may well ask. Well, Linda happened to live in Coinagehall Street in Helston; that's basically the town's High Street and very much on the dance route. Linda invited Jude and me to her house for the day to enjoy the spectacle. It was one of the most fabulous days we have ever experienced, and if you are ever in Cornwall in May, please make the effort to visit Helston for Flora Day.

Judith:

The one downside of living in Cornwall is that as a 'normal worker ant,' you never, ever choose to spend your cash and stay at some up-market luxury hotel; well, we certainly didn't. Imagine our delight when my sister and her husband invited us to spend a night with them (as a thank you for all the years of free holidays they had at our house) at the Idle Rocks Hotel in St Mawes. Over the years, they had built a successful business together, and money was now no object to them. Our ship had finally come in – one night of luxury in a quintessential fishing village on the southern tip of the Roseland Peninsula.

The Edwardian St Mawes hotel is steeped in romance

and history. It was built on the site of the old St Mawes Bakery and opened in 1913; it perches on the harbour wall and has stunning views across the Percuil River. We had never been before, and to get there, we took the Falmouth to St Mawes pedestrian ferry, leaving the car at Falmouth. What a fabulous way to arrive at such a breathtaking location. It was like we had stepped into another world; we could have been in St Tropez. The sun was shining, water gently lapped against the harbour wall, and boats happily bobbed up and down on their anchors: were we dreaming? We were given a sea view room, and my sister, her husband and my nieces were eager to show us around, having been staying there for a few days. This was definitely an upgrade from digging sand castles with them from dawn to dusk. We decided to do the boat trip across the Percuil River to Place Creek and explore the Roseland Peninsula. There, we discovered the Little and Great Molunan beaches, where we dipped our toes and paddled to cool off. It was idyllic in the evening sun, back at the hotel, sitting on the terrace with a cheeky vodka and watching the world go by. I could easily get used to living like this. 'Dream on, girl.'

It had been a very special day, and the evening meal was exquisite. With the heat of the sun, lots of walking, drinks and food, our batteries began to run out. We wanted and needed our bed, and that's when it all went wrong. The brother-in-law wanted to stay up drinking all night. Yes, I know we are usually up for it, but we were exhausted. Even though we apologised profusely, said what an amazing time we had had, and thanked him for treating us, he took the huff and spat his dummy out. Needless to say, the next morning at breakfast, the atmosphere was icy. It was a good job that we had only been invited for one night; it was time to go home.

Well, time and tide wait for no one, and before we could blink, Phil decided he wanted a birthday bash for his 40th (December 1994). I have to say; it was probably the best party we have ever thrown. Our bungalow was bursting at the seams with family and friends. We were so lucky; we had been together for seven wonderful years, I had found my lover and my soulmate, and I wanted him to have the best birthday ever.

Philip:

Ahh, my 40th birthday party. What an event: a party to end all parties! In fact, we have never held another house party since.

All our furniture, including our bed, was moved into number nine's garage. The single beds in the box room were used as food tables, with some dining and patio chairs set up in our otherwise empty bedroom. As per my original Tolvaddon party, sails and blow-up toys were used to decorate the place. I had progressed from making party cassette tapes to making party video tapes (four hours is a long time before one has to worry about changing a tape). This meant, at least in the early part of the evening, when not many guests had arrived, they had sailing videos to look at whilst the quieter music was playing. Then, once it got busy, I would turn the TV off, the music still being played through the Hi-Fi. Lots of food was prepared, and a huge amount of alcohol was purchased. The whirligig washing line was removed, and our car was parked on the extended stone terrace where it lived because it would be the dog's sanctuary from the chaos of the party.

As per usual, invites went out to everyone we knew, including work colleagues (Trafalgar House and SWEB), the football and volleyball teams, the sailing club, our naturist friends, general friends and of course our neighbours. Ahh, our neighbours. The couple at number one were a similar age to us, as was Roy and family at number nine, but all the others were pensioners, including Hannibal Lecter (a nickname the boys had given to the nosey husband at number four). Therefore, we decided that we had better explain to them what we were planning, i.e. there was going to be a very loud party that would go on well into the small hours. We told them they were all welcome to attend and stay for as long or little as they liked. Well, this invite gave Hannibal Lecter the chance he had been waiting for, to poke his nose around our house to see what was going on behind our closed doors – it turned out to be not quite what he was expecting. The eldest neighbours, from number ten, were one of the first to arrive and one of the last to leave at 3 in the morning. The husband actually tried to leave via the cloak cupboard, mistaking it for the front door – he had consumed a bottle of whiskey all by himself!

Jude's brother-in-law was into fireworks in a very big way, buying exhibition fireworks every Christmas and New Year. Therefore it will come as no surprise that my birthday present from him was fireworks; two rockets (£65 each – this is in 1994, remember) and two Roman Candles, each of which was a two-foot by two-foot by two-foot box. They had come to Cornwall with a close friend, Pete, whom Jude also knew: he got the job of chief firework officer that evening. It was Saturday 17th of December, my birthday actually being the 18th, and as per usual for this time of year, it rained all day. In fact, it was about 10:45 pm before it eased enough to allow Pete to go and prepare the fireworks. So, about half an hour later, a house full of drunk party goers braved the outside to watch the fireworks on an adjacent plot of the main development.

The rockets were brilliant, shooting high into the night sky before exploding in a golden cascade and each offshoot exploding a second time in smaller cascades. As amazing as the rockets were, the Roman Candles were in a league of their own. Pete lit the first one, and there was a short delay before this deep thud, followed by a streak of bright flame that went shooting skyward in a shower of sparks with a final explosion about 100' in the air. Then, for five minutes, it was just thud after thud after thud; the noise was unbelievable. Of course, Pete lit the second box before the first had expired. It was like being in the middle of a battlefield. And then silence. Firework display over, it was back into the bungalow to carry on partying.

A short while later, someone rescued me from the dance floor to inform me that the boys in blue were at the door. I somehow managed to remain in a standing position whilst assuring the two fine police officers that there would be no more fireworks. Fortunately, they accepted my explanation that the reason for letting them off so late was the weather.

Without doubt, the complaint to the rozzers had come from the vicar's wife, who lived in the only house so far built on the hill leading up to Gwel Tek. This was confirmed later in the week when the wife (of the whiskey-drinking husband) from number ten told us that when she had attended the church's WI meeting, the vicar's wife was complaining about us to anyone who would listen. Our neighbour said she had to keep quiet about actually being in attendance at the party. She also told us that other attendees at the WI had thought it was the 'maroons' (rockets) for the St Ives lifeboat going off. Oh well, we had given lots of people something to gossip about for a while.

The party went on until 5 am, and for those of us remaining, it was a matter of having a few hours of kip on the floor before having a big fry-up breakfast and putting the house back into shape.

Chapter 13

Darkness Descends

Judith:

We had now been living at Gwel Tek for five glorious years; it was everything I wanted and more. We probably still didn't own a brick, but life is too short to worry about the future. We had our road map: to live, love and laugh. Money was tight, but fresh air, sun and sea cost nothing. Of course, you need the right person by your side, and, fortunately, I had found the right person. Naturally, we had our differences occasionally; after all, we were very different people. Phil was calm and structured, and I was wild and spontaneous. What tied us together was the fact we had similar morals, liked the same things, respected each other and had chemistry to die for. I also think we balanced each other out. He needed me to drag him along, and I needed him to rein me in.

He always tells people that before he met me, he was quite happy sitting having a coffee (more likely an Earl Grey tea) in the motorway service station. Then I came along and dragged him into the fast (outside) lane, and he has never since been able to get back into the inside lane, never mind the service station. He always tells this story with love and affection; deep down, he is as bad as me!

He likes adventures, and we can very easily talk ourselves into trying new things, which has its pluses and minuses. Sometimes he needs a helping hand, and yes, that is a euphemism for 'kick up the arse.' Some things you get right, and some things you don't, but we told ourselves not to have any regrets and always move forward. We were very happy with life.

I had cooked Christmas dinner every year from the age of sixteen, but in December 1995, we were invited to spend Christmas 'Up North' with my sister and her family. It would be the first time in twenty-five years that I hadn't cooked for my family at Christmas. Antony was spending it with the girlfriend's family in Truro, and Shaun was in Amsterdam: they didn't need me anymore. So with presents bought and bags packed, we were just about to leave when Shaun surprisingly rocked up from Amsterdam. He said he didn't want to go with us as he wanted to catch up with his mates, so we left him to it and set off. I didn't know it then, but it would be another twenty-five years before I went away for Christmas, and a lot of water had passed under the bridge during that time. In fact, upon our return home, a tsunami was unknowingly waiting for me, even though we lived on a hill.

Philip:

Yet again, my thoughts were on the wrong planet. When Shaun arrived home unexpectedly, I thought it was going to fuck up our plans for Christmas. If he came with us to

Alsager, it would cost us a small fortune to kennel the dog (Bill, being the only one left now), provided, of course, one could find a kennel with a space at such short notice. There was not enough room in the car for both Shaun and the dog; it was one or t'other. As it happened, he did not want to go with us, so we left him at home whilst we had a very nice Christmas break at Jude's sister's.

Judith:

Having had a nice relaxing Christmas, we returned home to find Shaun's case still dumped in the middle of the lounge and no sign that he had been home whilst we had been away. We didn't really give it a second thought. We assumed he had pulled some girl and was spending time with his mates. He would turn up eventually – he usually did – and I was looking forward to hearing how the work trip to Amsterdam had gone. Although he couldn't tell a story as well as Antony, he did tend to meet some interesting people, and his social skills were top of the class.

Philip:

Shaun's bag being in the exact same place he had left it before we went away did not concern us. He had a habit of staying away and treating home as an occasional place to return to, normally when he needed feeding, clean clothes, or had run out of money.

Judith:

He eventually turned up, but he seemed quite distracted and wasn't making much sense when I tried to engage in conversation with him. I just assumed he was tired when he retreated to his bedroom. Tomorrow was another day with plenty of time to find out how he had got on in his travels. He had always turned the radio on to help him sleep, so that was no surprise when he did, but I thought I heard him laughing and talking during the night. Was I dreaming? Perhaps the pleasure of having my son home was playing on my unconscious mind.

Philip:

This time, when Shaun returned, it was very different. His behaviour was very strange; he talked garbage and nothing he said made sense. Judy knew that something was wrong, but neither of us knew what. We had no idea what we were dealing with; had his drug use got worse whilst he had been in Holland?

Time revealed to us that the answer to the above question was a definite yes. Shaun, the dreamer, had gone to Holland to make his fortune with the intention of coming home to prove to the ex-girlfriend, the love of his life, that he was not useless and that they had a future together. We shall never know exactly what happened in Holland. However, we do know, via a friend of his we met at the Clowance Spa one night (before Shaun returned to the UK), that the conditions out there were terrible, and the workers were not treated well. We also know that Shaun's plans failed, and by his own admission, he did what he does every time life goes tits up for him. He turned to drugs: for him, a sort of self-medication.

Judith:

When, one day, a friend of Shaun's rang me to say Shaun was on the high street of Camborne giving away money to people in cars going by, alarm bells really started to ring. I decided to call the doctor, made an appointment and somehow managed to get Shaun in the car to get him there. At the doctor's, I explained Shaun's bizarre behaviour; he asked Shaun various questions and gave us a prescription. Once we got home, Shaun took off; I looked at the prescription and decided to check what the pills were in a medical book we had. To my horror, they were for psychotic behaviour; I was really worried now, so I rang the surgery and asked if the doctor could ring me back to explain the pills. He rang me back and told me Shaun had the worst case of schizophrenia he had ever seen, and to ensure Shaun took the pills he had prescribed. '*What the fuck?*' How could I give pills to someone who was never home and I didn't know his whereabouts? What did 'schizophrenic' mean? Was it like in the film 'Drop Dead Fred,' i.e. take the green pills until you stop seeing things? This huge wave of worry, despair and sadness engulfed me. I had no idea what to do, how to make it better or what I was dealing with. Thank god for Phil, my anchor in a storm. Little did we know what was to come, and perhaps it was a good job we didn't.

Philip:

It was very upsetting and unsettling, but we didn't know what to think or, more importantly, what to do. However, after the Camborne High Street episode, Judy knew she had to take action, and, god knows how, she managed to get him to go with her to the doctor's.

After Judy returned home and looked up the prescription in the medical drug book, she rang me at work. I had to move to an empty conference room before ringing her back to hear her explain that the prescription was for an antipsychotic drug used to treat, amongst other things, schizophrenia. What a shock. It was hard to take in; schizophrenia was a word everyone knew, and its context was always bad, very bad. Didn't 'schizos' go around killing people?

Judith:

I have to say in those first few weeks, we had no help whatsoever. How I went to work and did the usual day-to-day stuff, I have no idea. I was like a walking zombie. Phil, bless him, did his usual Sagittarian research on schizophrenia, and the prognosis was not good; this was not an illness you got better from. My memories of the early days (of Shaun's illness) are very sketchy. Life at home in our lovely safe bungalow changed: it became a place of horror. To watch your beautiful son turn into a mad, gibbering idiot and become a stranger you didn't know was so hard: all I wanted to do was make him better. The only saving grace was that Antony was at university and didn't have to watch his brother unravel as we did, and we were able to shield Antony from the day-to-day issues. Of course, eventually, you have to deal with the reality of the situation, but at this stage, I hadn't told any of my friends what was happening. The baggage from my teenage years of keeping things to myself had automatically kicked in; we did, however, decide that we needed to tell my family.

It was my brother-in-law's 40th birthday in late February, and we had been invited to his party. Having roped in the useless ex-husband to keep an eye on Shaun whilst we were away, off we trotted. The day after the party, we broke the news to the family. I don't think they had any idea what we were telling them. Before we left for home, we called at the uncle's house to tell him about Shaun's diagnosis and that we were sorry, but we didn't think he would be able to come on his holiday break this year. I had found it very difficult to tell the family; tears ran down my face every time, and once again, my cheeks were wet. I will never forget what he said to me. His words are etched forever in my memory.

He said, 'You need to get him locked up and throw away the key.'

It's a long drive from the North West of England to Cornwall, and I cried the whole way home.

Philip:

What a bastard the uncle was. He could go fuck himself if he ever thought he was going to put upon us in Cornwall ever again. At least he opened his mouth and spoke; most family members put their heads in the sand and pretended to be ostriches. That helped a great deal: not.

Not knowing what to do but wanting to do something, I kept a diary of Shaun's behaviour. I also recorded all contact with the doctor and the various mental health teams because I thought it might be useful in dealing with his illness. What I didn't manage to do very well, and to this day, it is still a problem for me, was to provide enough emotional support for Judy. It's no excuse to say I try, but it does not come naturally to me: I know that is not good enough. Yes, I can do practical, but on many occasions, practical was and is not being asked for. Did I, do I hide my emotional side behind my practical side? Do I even have an emotional side? These are questions that I cannot answer. All I can say is that 'I will keep on trying' and trust that Judy will see an improvement: she deserves that, at the very least.

What I did do, was visit the Camborne library and relieve it of every book I could find about schizophrenia. One book in particular always remains in my memory, although unfortunately, I cannot remember its title or the name of its author. I do remember that the author was an American man of god. What sticks in my mind was that he stated that it was essential to speak honestly with the patient about their illness from the outset and to continually reinforce to them the fact that the 'voices' they were hearing were not real. He also stated that an early diagnosis was essential if there was to be any chance of enabling a recovery back to a 'normal' life.

I also discovered information about several national societies dealing with mental illness. One lunchtime at work, I again retired to the empty conference room and, with great trepidation, rang the helpline for the National Schizophrenia Fellowship. (I note it has now been rebranded to Rethink Mental Illness – I preferred the old title; it stated on the tin what was inside!) I had a long conversation with a lovely lady, but it did not have a helpful outcome. She asked where I lived.

I answered, 'Hayle, Cornwall.'

She replied, 'I am so sorry, my dear. Cornwall has a reputation for sitting on the fence, i.e. delaying making a diagnosis.'

She did, however, send me lots of literature, and I ended up purchasing several books, including a copy of the 1983 Mental Health Act.

With the GP telling Judy that Shaun had the worst case of schizophrenia that he had ever seen, we could not understand why he was not getting any help. To us, Shaun's condition was worsening, even with taking the drugs prescribed, and eventually, after many, many calls for help, a psychiatric nurse from the mental health crisis team turned up. She gave Shaun an injection, spoke to him for a short while, and then buggered off, never to be seen again. This was our first experience of contact with a 'crisis team' and disappointedly proved to be 'par for the course.' Expectations of help are much better if you do not have any.

I have lived under flight paths, next to mainline railway lines and alongside busy main roads. I had never had any problem sleeping, but now I did. The bungalow was small, and the walls thin. It was incredibly upsetting lying in bed alongside the woman you loved and lived for, now a helpless mother, listening to her son talking gibberish to himself and answering his 'voices'. I felt helpless; yes, I was gaining knowledge about the illness, but a fat lot of good that was doing: the prognosis was not good. Help for Shaun was beyond our capabilities, and the medical services seemed not to care. I did not know what to do, and neither did Judy. There was lots and lots of crying. And we still had to get up every morning and go to work.

Judith:

Without Phil by my side, I think I would have crumbled; Shaun's illness was life-changing for him and me. I had not only lost my eldest son, but I had also lost myself. I think the initial trauma of it all changed me forever. It's hard to describe what living with someone who has psychosis is like. It's a bit like living with twenty different people: you don't know which one you are interacting with. When the magic pills kick in after about three months, the manic behaviour spirals into severe depression. Trust me; depression is far worse to watch as a spectator than mania. As a couple who have always fixed problems, we had well and truly met our match; this was not fixable. We had been lucky to have eight superb happy years together; now, we were going to have to find ways to cope and keep our relationship alive.

We were once again at a crossroads in life. As well as Shaun being so ill, our financial situation was pretty desperate. High mortgage interest rates, coupled with the boys returning home, severely impacted our ability to stay afloat. Fortunately, Antony was at university in Farnborough now, so we were able to protect him from the situation with Shaun at home. What I couldn't do was protect myself or, it appeared, help my eldest son recover.

Philip:

Shaun's illness drained us; we were physically and mentally exhausted. We still had to 'put on a face' and go to work every day, trying to distract ourselves with the sailing whilst all the time trying to shield Antony from the real situation at home. Life was taking its toll, and to boot, we were in financial shit. For the first time ever, we did not have enough money to pay the mortgage. We did not know what to do about anything. The obvious thing was to sell the bungalow: easily said. This expensive box we had bought six years ago was not only meant to be our 'forever home,' but it was also intended to be a financial investment. However, the financial crash that occurred just as we were moving in caused the Hayle harbour redevelopment plans to collapse. All of Peter De Savary's investors pulled out, and during our six years there, house prices went down, not up. The housing market was now depressed, and we had bought when it was buoyant. It was not a good time to sell; a loss was guaranteed, but there was no choice. The mortgage lender agreed to a six-month half-payment deal whilst we tried to sell the bungalow. Eventually, it sold for £50,000, £10k less than what we paid for it.

Judith:

So there you have it, the dream was over. Could we have done anything differently? Maybe, maybe not. We had no answers, only questions; life had dealt us a cruel blow. We could fix the financials, but we had no idea how to fix Shaun. All you ever want for your children is to be happy in life. I still hoped that would be possible for Shaun; I just hoped I could be strong enough to ride the wave. I also hoped Phil and I were strong enough to get through whatever we had to face along the road. What we needed was divine intervention (somewhere to rent), and perhaps a guardian angel was looking out for us. A friend of mine rented a property from an old farmer, and he had another one available in a place called Wall. Our choices were not limited; they were non-existent. So, we gratefully took the cottage, sold the bungalow at a loss, and took a deep breath. It was time to start another chapter of our life.

Sailing in Mounts Bay
Above: Approaching the finishing line;St Michaels Mount
harbour wall to the right and Marazion in the background.
Below: Entering Mousehole harbour during the annual
Marazion to Mousehole pub race.

Lost (and naked) in France,
on the hated bike

Anyone for golf?

Chapter 14

We Need Help

Philip:

What on earth was happening? I am not religious (I had it thrown down my throat as a child and, as a result, rejected religion at an early age), but I do wonder about such things as parapsychology, the supernatural, the paranormal, unexplained happenings and fate. We had not gone looking for a rented property; it was purely a chance conversation between Judy and Vyv that enabled us to apply to move into the one this gentleman farmer had available.

Moving into 41 Rosewarne Road, in the village of Wall, in the parish of Gwinear, in November 1996 gave me goosebumps: something supernatural was surely afoot. What remarkable concurrence of events had led to this? Was it just a matter of coincidence? Or was that damn Puppet Master still playing with us? Here I was, just thirty metres down the road from the property where I had begun my Cornish odyssey. You will recall that in May 1976, having dropped out of college, I moved into my then girlfriend's family house, 'Michigan Villa.' It was weird, very weird, but at the same time lovely because Wall was a beautiful place to live.

Earlier in the book, I explained about 'Michigan Villa' and how grand a house it was. Our latest property was not so grand: it was a small semi-detached cottage with a very long garden with farm fields bordering the rear and one side. A five-bar metal gate opened onto a drive that ran alongside the cottage. A side door opened onto a kitchen diner that ran the width of the property; it was just large enough to fit in a small dining table. The rear of the cottage consisted of a small living room with an open coal fire adjacent to the steep, narrow staircase; this led upstairs to two (surprisingly large) double bedrooms and a bathroom. A door from the living room led onto a small grassed, walled-off area that itself led onto the large lawn and equally large vegetable patch. It was a dear little cottage with lots of character. It effused an atmosphere of serenity, and despite all the traumas we were to endure there, it was a happy place to live. It could have become our 'forever home' apart from one significant issue: it was not ours.

Our new home was six miles from my work but further from Judy's; therefore, Judy used the car, and I used my bicycle, regardless of the weather. I got a bit of a reputation at work, i.e. became the butt of many jokes, because when it was raining (which, between October and March, was most days), I often cycled in a cheap oilskin jacket, complete with sou'wester hat, shorts and a pair of wellingtons. But, I am ahead of myself.

As would prove to be normal for Judy and me,

moving house meant hiring a van and doing it ourselves. Santa's little helpers always seemed to be too busy elsewhere to help us. Fortunately, we did not have too much 'stuff' and managed to complete the move in three trips, but that was not the end of our weightlifting for the day. Jude's friend, Vyv, who had given us the heads up over the vacant cottage, had run a little restaurant in a nearby village, but the business had failed, and she was having to vacate the premises. Knowing we had the hire van, she asked us for a favour. Would we use the van to move some paving slabs from the restaurant to her rented cottage in Carnhell Green? Plus, we could take some for ourselves as well, if we wanted. Well, moving them just about put our lights out, and the poor old van's suspension didn't fare much better either. To reduce the number of trips, we very definitely overloaded the poor thing. With the van empty, we just left everything and collapsed into bed, exhausted. The beginning of the next chapter of our lives could wait until tomorrow.

Judith:

New home, new job and a psychotic son: not the best combination to start a new chapter of your life, but that was the reality, and yes, it was very stressful. Fortunately, the old cottage wrapped its arms around me with love, and I needed that. On the positive side, the rent was massively less than the old mortgage, and the cottage was in a beautiful tranquil rural setting. It gave me the space to breathe and reboot from such an emotionally traumatic experience.

I had started a new full-time job at an incubation company on the outskirts of Camborne as an office manager. On my first day, the boss said I could go home at 3 pm as the VAT man was due and, based on his findings, I may not have a job the next day. *'What the hell?'* It turned out to be a very odd place to work, so not surprisingly, I fitted in quite well. We were a motley crew of seven. The boss was having an affair with one of the production ladies; there was an ex-heroin addict on methadone who did or didn't turn up; a guy who incubated and hatched snakes as a sideline in a side room (I hate snakes); a younger guy, who was a right know-it-all, and his mate who licked his boots.

At the time, the big new money-making scheme was in Ostrich meat. As the company already made equipment to hatch poultry eggs, the boss decided to design and build an ostrich incubator. Eggs were duly sourced and incubated, and abracadabra, baby ostriches were born, much to my amazement. They were sweet, pretty little things but grew into large, aggressive birds with eyelashes to die for. They soon outgrew the nursery in the farm building under the office, and the boss persuaded a local friendly farmer to rent him a field. Boy, could those birds run! One nearly decapitated itself in the wire fence and was lovingly named 'Bendy neck' as a result of its injuries. The taller they grew, the more aggressive they became; it was time to sell them on and get rid: after all, we were an incubation company, not farmers. A farmer in Helston took the bait, and with a sigh of relief, we herded them up, loaded them into a trailer - not an easy job - and waved them off.

Surprisingly, we sold incubators all over the world. The boss even went to Sri Lanka to set up a factory there. He was a very clever 'inventor' type of man but was clueless as a businessman, which is perhaps why he employed me. I remember going on a two-week holiday, and upon my return, I discovered he had sacked everyone as he was having a minor meltdown. Daily life there was a yo-yo existence as we lurched from one drama to another. That, coupled with Shaun's deteriorating mental state, certainly kept me on my toes: both work and home life were just bonkers. How I didn't lose the plot, I will never know.

Things with Shaun just got worse and worse. He went through numerous psychotic periods; he would take off to 'save the world' and his disciples from evil. Apparently, Kurt Cobain had taken over his body. If Phil and I didn't get married, he was going to die, and he wanted to be renamed Sinbad. We had been allocated a CPN (Community Psychiatric Nurse) to help Shaun, and I had been offered counselling which I attended twice. I spent the whole time there sobbing my heart out. I couldn't even speak about how I felt, so I ditched it, as, at the time, I felt I needed all my strength just to be able to cope. I thought I cried enough without crying at a weekly counselling session. In hindsight, I perhaps should have persevered, as there's no doubt I still carry a lot of baggage from this episode in my life. The CPN realised how ill Shaun was, and it was arranged to have him sectioned, but I will let Phil tell the story as, even now, it's too painful for me to write.

Philip:

Mike, the CPN (Community Psychiatric Nurse) who had been assigned to Shaun, was a lovely guy and was supposed to spend an hour a week with each of his clients. Working a 40-hour week, and having 60-odd clients on your books, meant this was impossible (especially with so much travelling time in rural Cornwall). He spent many hours talking to Shaun, arranging for his medication and taking him to appointments, but Shaun's condition did not appear to be improving. In fact, to us, it was just the opposite.

There came the time when the camel's back broke; we had reached our wit's end. We had tried everything we could to help Shaun, but he still seemed to be getting worse. He needed more help; we needed divine intervention! We felt that the only place he might get it was in hospital, and it seemed to be the only remaining option, though not one we wanted to take. According to the Mental Health Act book I had purchased, if Shaun would not admit himself willingly (to the psychiatric unit), it would mean us having to get him 'sectioned,' and we felt sick just talking about it.

In UK law, 'being sectioned' means 'having been committed compulsorily to a psychiatric hospital in accordance with a section of a mental health act.' Judy and Mike tried very hard to convince Shaun that it was in his best interest to admit himself into hospital, but he was having none of it. As far as he was concerned, there was nothing wrong with him. We felt we had our backs to the wall, and there was nowhere to go. Naively, we believed that he would get the help he needed in hospital; therefore, we reluctantly asked Mike to arrange an assessment.

On the given day, Judy and I took a day's leave from work. Mike, Shaun's GP, a psychiatric consultant, a social worker and Judy gathered in our small living room to carry out the assessment. I was not allowed to attend. After a couple of hours, I was informed that it was agreed to 'section' Shaun under Section Two of the 1983 Mental Health Act. Although Shaun agreed to go with Judy to the unit, this was not allowed. Once officially 'sectioned,' he had to attend by ambulance, so we had to wait until one arrived and, later in the day, lie to our neighbours as to why it had been there.

Under Section Two of the 1983 Mental Health Act, a person is held (in a secure psychiatric hospital) for 28 days for an assessment to take place. From what we had read, if Shaun's psychosis was drug-induced, this is time enough for the drugs to clear the system and for Shaun to come out of the psychosis. If he did not come out of the psychosis, then it was likely that the damage (to his brain) would be permanent. We were allowed to go to the (psychiatric) unit at Trengweath (Redruth), where

Shaun was being admitted. We were all shown to an interview room whilst he was being processed. The first thing Shaun was told was that he had a 'right to appeal (the section),' which, of course, he immediately asked to do. This led to a problem: the policy at Trengweath was that the consultant psychiatrist would not make any assessment until the appeal had been heard, and the admin staff informed us that appeals often took several months to be heard! FFS! This news both sickened and angered us. What was the point of going through this very painful, emotional sectioning process and effectively holding Shaun as a prisoner if he was not going to be assessed by the consultant? To us, this was the whole point of the exercise. In our mind, one could not attempt to fix anything until one knew what the problem was.

The issues did not end there. Upon returning home, the telephone was ringing as we entered the house. It was the admin from Trengweath.

'Have you seen Shaun?' they asked.

What? Not thirty minutes ago, we had left him in a so-called 'secure unit,' in the care of the psychiatric hospital; now they were asking us if we knew where he was. Unbelievable. We were already traumatised by the whole sectioning process, and now this.

'No, we don't know where he is.'

Apparently, he was given permission to have a smoke in the car park, and he just legged it. Trengweath was situated five minutes from Redruth town centre, a place where drugs were readily available. Shaun did eventually return to the unit - he had nowhere else to go. During his stay there, the consultant also gave him periods of 'one hour leave,' which were permitted under the Mental Health Act. All the trips into Redruth, with the access to drugs, rather negated the premise of 'keeping him clean' for the 28 days: what a fucking shambles.

Millions of people around the world will have experienced situations the same as ours, and I am sure some are far worse than ours, but everything is relevant. When you feel you are standing on the precipice with no hope left, one is left feeling very numb; just waiting for someone to give you that fatal push. Giving up on life was not on our agenda, but it was definitely on Shaun's. We were exhausted, both mentally and physically, with trying to deal with Shaun's illness and also to protect Antony from it, though, in hindsight, I don't think he (Antony) perceived it that way.

Our makeup was 'old school,' i.e. one had to just get on with it. I don't think either of us thought there was any other alternative, so we attempted to deal with each hurdle as it was placed in front of us: there was no plan. Some of those hurdles we cleared, others we just clipped and managed to carry on, but many we crashed into and fell flat onto our faces. It was proving increasingly difficult to pick oneself up to face the next hurdle. Our lifeblood, *joie de vivre*, call it what you like, was quickly being sucked out of us.

Judith:

The facts are as Phil has written. I have no idea what Shaun's thoughts were that day, as we have never spoken about it, and I have no idea if he was frightened, worried or relieved. Madness, like dementia, is an unknown world to those looking on. I truly believed hospitalisation was, at that time, our only hope of helping Shaun. I wanted him to get better, and despite knowing schizophrenia was not an illness that disappeared, deep down, I hoped it would, so that my eldest son could live a happy, full and fulfilling life. I don't think I had really mentally prepared myself for the trauma of that day. I had always coped with what life threw at me; I told myself I could do this, but when I got into the ambulance with Shaun, I felt sick, scared, sad and guilty. You are supposed to look after your family; how the hell had I let this happen? The weeks and months of constant worry, despair, anxiety and helplessness leading up to this day seemed insignificant compared to the trauma of watching your son being sectioned. We were extremely naïve. We thought it would be like getting a broken leg mended, i.e. having it x-rayed, reset and plastered for six weeks followed by bed rest and a bit of physio, and he would come home good as new. If you ever find yourself in this situation, trust me, that's not what happens. The sooner you stop hoping for a miracle, support or empathy, the better you will cope. Sad words, maybe, but if you want to survive, I would suggest that's what you do; you will need all your mental strength just to get through daily life. It's unbelievably hard to face each day when someone you love is there but not really there; all you can do is your best and always be kind.

Philip:

We just seemed to instinctively know that we had to escape the situation occasionally in order for us to retain our sanity. Our pastimes of sailing, beach visits and trips to the Minack had given us many hours of pleasure. Now they became an essential escape from the immense psychological pressure and exhaustion of dealing with Shaun. However, as the situation with Shaun worsened, there was another haunt that rescued us from the madness: our membership of Clowance.

Before Judy and I had got together, the Clowance Estate, located just outside a village called Praze-an-Beeble, had been bought by RCI (Resort Condominiums International), a global timeshare company, with the intention of turning it into a five-star resort holiday. I knew about the Clowance Estate because Mo, the lady who ran West Cornwall women's athletic team, lived there, albeit in the stables (converted into flats). It was a fabulous place to live, with a large lake and acres of woodland to enjoy, plus on three evenings a week, a bar situated in the main house opened up to the public. We had taken Rebecca (my brother/sister) there on a few occasions.

When redevelopment work began, invitations to

attend a two-hour sales presentation, complete with a free gift, landed on the doormat at quite regular intervals. As a local resident, buying a timeshare at the resort carried a bonus: the resort facilities – swimming pool, gym, golf, bar and restaurant, could be used at any time.

Sam (my ex) and I had previously attended three events. We didn't buy any timeshare weeks, but were happy to accept the decanter, glasses, toaster and free return Brittany Ferries tickets from Plymouth to Santander (one was not allowed to disembark in Spain). I later learnt that Judy and her ex-husband had also attended these promotional presentations.

The problem during the early visits was that, although the main house and stables had been redeveloped and further accommodation blocks built, the sports facilities had not yet been started, let alone completed. However, not long after moving into Gwel Tek, Judy and I received another invite, so off we tootled again. By this time, the resort had been completed, including a nine-hole golf course. After a presentation to all attendees, each invitee was assigned an RCI sales rep for a guided tour followed by a return to the room 'to close the deal.' Hah! (Just give us our free gift, and we will be off, thank you very much). Sadly, neither of us can remember our rep's name, so I shall call her Kate. The sports facilities were impressive, with a decent-sized heated pool and spa, attached bar and restaurant, tennis courts, gymnasium, beauty treatments and a croquet lawn in front of the main house. During our tour, Kate was obviously giving us her sales pitch, but we got on with her really well, and by the time we returned to the conference room for the final sales push, we felt like good friends. Just before entering the room, Judy stopped to have a fag.

Kate said, 'I won't waste your time. I know you can't afford the majority of deals on offer, and you're not likely to exchange a timeshare week at Clowance for a holiday elsewhere. But, as locals who would benefit from regular use of the facilities, I think there is a deal that might interest you.'

Basically, it was the cheapest deal on offer: a bi-annual week in January (who wants to holiday in Cornwall in January?). Buying it would give us a 'Gold' membership card, our gateway to enjoying the Clowance Estate.

Were we mugs? Far from it. Leisure facilities in West Cornwall were pathetic, and neither of us enjoyed using the swimming pool at the Carn Brea leisure centre (Camborne). We had to take out a loan (for £2,800) and cut back in other areas to afford it, but it proved to be an investment worth its weight in gold. In the early years of our membership, we visited (Clowance) regularly for pleasure and fitness, facilities being open from 7 am to 11 pm, often taking family and friends there with us. Then once the problems started with Shaun, it became our sanctuary. It was where we retreated to recover from whatever ordeal we had been dealing with, talking endlessly over options and sometimes just wandering in silent contemplation, taking in the peace of the beautiful surroundings before having to return home. It was like having our very own private 'well-being' centre. This alone justified the cost.

Judith:

Clowance was a lifesaver for me, especially when the going got tough. We would go just to walk and talk, have a drink in the bar, as well as late night swims and hottub to help us de-stress. What it gave me most was escapism from the sorrow I felt deep inside. It enabled me to run away for a few hours; I would never again be me. I don't think you can ever find yourself once you lose yourself, but you do have to find a new you. How Phil supported me throughout this period, I will never know. The fun-loving girl only surfaced on rare occasions, but he did stick by me, and for that, I will be forever grateful. He was the only person in the world who had my back; throughout our life together, he has never let me down. He is one in a million, and I am so lucky to have met him; my life would have been very different without him in it. In the main, we mostly kept Clowance just for us, though one time we took Shaun with us (never again). He was sort of between psychotic and depression, and we thought it would be beneficial for him. Phil and I were swimming up and down, both with one eye on Shaun, when he submerged himself underwater for what seemed like an eternity: he eventually popped up. I think we were both holding our breath and counting seconds the whole time he was underwater whilst trying to act as if everything was normal. That was one night I poured myself a large vodka when I got home; we still laugh now about that evening.

Philip:

During one of Shaun's spells with us at Rosewarne, he had a young female social worker visit him, who also had several chats with us. She was very personable and, I believe, quite insightful.

One comment she made was along the lines of, 'Unfortunately, because you obviously love your son and are doing everything you can to help him, the mental health teams will happily leave it to you. The more you do, the less they will.'

We were astounded. Effectively, what she was saying is that for Shaun to get help from the authorities, we should back off and literally abandon him. However, she also believed it was too late to do this because everyone knew just how much we cared and what we were trying to do.

Judith:

I remember the young female social worker. The words, 'You need to let him fall down the hole and prepare yourself that he might not come up,' have stuck in my head for a very long time. I heard what she was saying, and deep down, I knew she was probably right, but was I brave enough to do that, sign my son's death warrant; what mother could do that? Well, this mother couldn't, but I did need to get a better life balance. Once I learnt to accept the situation (as opposed to hoping it would improve), I dug deep within myself, and I did come out at the other end. I tried desperately to engage with the world again, and with Phil's encouragement, I slowly began to take each day as it came, as opposed to worrying about next week or next month. I needed to get back on the horse, go out and play now and again, rebuild my relationship with Phil, save myself and us. We had something so special; I could not lose that, as well as my son. We needed more light and less darkness in our lives, and only we could do something to improve the situation, so that was what we did next.

Chapter 15

Let There Be Light

Judith:

So, time to up the ante. Yes, my life had imploded big time; I still couldn't talk about it to anyone, and I had very definitely lost my *'joie de vivre.'* I could put on the face for short periods, but inside I was still dying. For my own sanity and my lovely Phil, I recognised I needed to start engaging, and of course, alcohol helped. Somehow we settled into a pattern of Phil drinking at home and me drinking when we went out. I think I was too scared to drink at home, as I permanently felt on call. The unplanned system worked really well because a few drinks helped me to relax and play the game. We recognised the need to alleviate the stress, so we looked for things to do to create a diversion in our life. One of the best things we did was to attend an 'Adults Only' event at Butlins, Minehead.

We had the time of our life. My memories are of the girls in the upstairs flat in the block opposite ours, flashing their boobs to the boys passing below whilst singing, 'get your tits out for the boys.' Plus, 'doing statues' to the Blaydon Races song at 4 am outside the amusement arcade, dancing on the tables to Glam Rock tribute bands, screaming at the male strippers 'to get them off,' and laughing till we cried at the comedians. It was just what the doctor ordered: escapism at its best. We went the following year with friends and work colleagues, which was even more fun than going on our own. However, the News of the World reported there were sex orgies at the events and got them banned: bloody shame if you ask me.

Philip:

Alice, Alice, who the fuck is Alice? Two thousand of us, all drunk, dancing on the tables and singing along, having a fabulous time. Jude and I hadn't heard this version of the (Smokey) song but were happy to join in as, boy, the place was buzzing.

It was our first trip to a Minehead Butlins 'Adult Only Weekend.' £29 for room only with entertainment from Friday evening to Sunday night, returning home on Monday morning. There were female strippers, male strippers (they were much better than the girls, as they put on choreographed dance routines as opposed to just standing in one spot and taking their clothes off), many comedians, lots of bands and other general entertainers. The on-site shop was stocked to the ceiling with booze that the bouncers allowed you to take into the main halls. The bars still had ten deep queues at them, so it was a win-win situation for Butlins. Wonderful, and as Judy has stated, playing 'statues' to The Blaydon Races theme in front of one of the outside amusement stalls at four in the morning was one of the highlights of the weekend.

Another, for me, was Stan Boardman. At the start of his show, he spent five minutes walking up and down the stage, looking down at the empty space immediately in front of it. Occasionally, he paused to look up at the audience and say, 'Fucking marvellous,' before eventually stopping and finally stating, 'Fucking marvellous. Not a fucking kid in sight!' This cracked me and the rest of the audience up; he was off to a flying start.

As Judy has mentioned, the following year, we returned, this time as a group of seven: friends Keith and Gladys, Frank from the incubation company and his lover, plus Rihanna, a friend of Judy's (whom we had nicknamed Wonderbra – it lifts and separates, according to the adverts of the day). Keith was desperate to see the female strippers, but they were so boring I left him to it and went to find the girls who were watching the male strippers.

Over the weekend, Gladys and Judy were a sight to behold when it came to nabbing a chair. The slightest inclination that someone was about to vacate a chair and whoosh! They would have their bottoms on the seats the instant they were vacated. If it was an Olympic sport, they would be multiple gold medallists.

One act made a big impression on us: a female artist who combined magic, fire-eating and stripping: she removed an item of clothing after every magic trick. She was brilliant, but beyond question, the highlight of the weekend was Nookie Bear with Roger De Courcey. His slot was late afternoon and Rihanna did not want to go and watch him.

'He's a children's act,' she said, adding, 'anyway, I need to go and wash my hair ready for tonight.'

'Rihanna,' we replied, 'it's an adults-only weekend; it will not be like what you see on the TV.' It wasn't, with knobs on.

Judy was wearing a white lacy body without a bra (very sexy it was too) and jeans. The ultraviolet lights highlighted the white top, making it see-through. I think Roger noticed, as during the show, when he required an assistant from the audience, he, of course, picked Judy. But again, I digress. The show started with Roger, dressed in an immaculate tuxedo, standing at the front of the stage with a box on a table in front of him. There was loud banging coming from the box. Roger enquired if Nookie was all right and whether he would be coming out to join him on stage as the show had started.

Nookie replied, 'Fuck off, I'm having a wank!'

And it went downhill from there, i.e. got funnier and funnier, with, at one time, a big burly guy in the audience having a full-blooded argument with the bear: hilarious.

It was a fabulous weekend, and we were all ready to book for the following year when the News of the fucking World published a front-page story about sex parties and orgies taking place at a Scottish Butlins Adults Only weekend. I think Butlins did not want the negative publicity, so they pulled all the Adult Only weekends. It was a shame. On our two visits, all we saw were about five thousand people having a great time. Most of us were drunk, most of the time, but I do not recall any trouble whatsoever.

Judith:

Of course, nothing ever stays the same. The incubation company I worked for got sold to a company in Falmouth, but they had to take me and Frank (a buy one get one free deal), so at least there were two people who knew what was going on. On the downside, it was now a forty-five-minute each-way commute, which took even longer in the tourist season. Plus, it was miles away from The Countryman pub that we used to relocate to on most days we worked: probably why Frank ended up having to sell the business.

On the positive side, Falmouth is beautiful; it's located on the (river) Fal Estuary, is allegedly the third largest deep water harbour in the world, and has beaches like Swanpool and Gyllyngvase. There is a well-preserved 16th-century fortress on Pendennis Point, and it is near Trebah Garden, which is filled with subtropical plants. More importantly, the main high street in Falmouth has a pub every few hundred yards, as I discovered when invited out by a new work colleague I had become friends with. Ah, the lovely Amelia, she was pretty, articulate and vivacious. Butter wouldn't melt in her mouth – until about two o'clock in the morning. That was when she usually threw up on her shoes as we walked up the hill back to her house. She was a true Cornish maid* and knew everyone in every pub; we sang Karaoke, danced on tables and flirted with boys. A night out with Amelia was just what I needed to help me get back to 'normal.' She didn't know my story even though we were best mates. I think she was instrumental in saving me; she will never know how grateful I was for those Friday night binges, even though I had the hangover from hell on the Saturdays following our excesses. 'No pain, no gain,' I think the saying goes. Thank you, 'bird.'**

**'bird,' like *'maid,' is a Cornish term of endearment, normally, but not exclusively, for a female.

Philip:

In 1996, there was yet another reorganisation at work resulting in huge changes in the way everyone worked. When the Cornwall 'Control Room' finally closed, I was redeployed back to the West Cornwall engineering department (based at Pool). I became a team leader and got involved in the development of a new system for dealing with (electricity) supply outages (failures). It was called FMS (Fault Management System) and is probably the proudest achievement of my working life. These days, it is hard to believe that we did not have computers back then. When people telephoned to report that they had no electricity, all the details were manually recorded on 'T-Cards'. These were approximately 4" wide by 6" high, made of card and had tabs on either side at the top – hence 'T' – which allowed them to be stored in special boxes. We would then have to physically look at huge wall diagrams to work out where each property was 'fed' from, i.e. which substation supplied their electricity, before organising someone to attend the site to locate and fix the fault. Following several severe storms where the system was overwhelmed and the company lambasted for its many failures, a working group was formed to work with a newly appointed computer department to explore different options for dealing with emergencies. My boss invited me to represent the Cornish clerical side.

I will not bore you with the details of the process here, other than to say that after many months of hard work, frustrating meetings and immense pressure from 'above,' a working system evolved. Then came the bombshell: having developed it, the bosses now asked a smaller group of us to instruct all of Western Power's (aka SWEB) staff, including the top dogs, in its use. Fuck! My immediate boss told me I had been chosen because my CV contained three years at Teacher Training college. Plus, he and his immediate boss had been impressed with the way I had been training new employees on how to use all our systems. It was time to put to use everything I had learned and could remember from those college years.

I am pleased to say that the lessons we compiled and delivered were a huge success, and I felt elated at my part in it. There is one incident from the intense teaching schedule that I will mention because it is just another example of the 'normal' life I have led since meeting

Judith. On this particular Thursday, we were completing our last sessions in Plymouth (the depot was based on Elliott Road, would you believe?) and then moving on to Torquay, where a hotel had been booked for the three of us facilitating the lessons. Whilst my colleagues made their way to Torquay, I returned to Hayle (I had permission from my boss to use the work's car for this) to pick up Judy and make our way to Newquay to watch Rick Wakeman in concert at a local holiday park. With its association with Tintagel, Rick's 'King Arthur' album had given him lots of kudos in this part of the world.

After the concert, I took Judy home and then drove to Torquay, checking in at the hotel at 4 am. The alarm went off at 6:30 am (had there been any point in going to bed?), and I met up with my colleagues for breakfast. We had a communication failure before departing for the local depot, where we were due to give a lesson commencing at 8 am (they said it was only fifteen minutes away). I didn't know where I was going, so I would have to follow the other two. They had parked in the underground car park, but I, not knowing that it existed, had parked in the street. I thought we had agreed for them to wait for me at the car park exit. Well, I got there at 7:40 and waited. And waited. At ten to eight, I decided I had missed them and would have to make my own way there. No mobile phones, no sat nav, no clue where to go, and in this case, no map either. Needless to say, I got lost, but I eventually found someone who could direct me. It was nine o'clock as I walked into the classroom, to much mickey taking, just in time to give the final part of the lesson. My colleagues claimed they had waved at me in my little red Fiesta and that I had set off behind them. Really? It had only been when that car didn't follow them into the depot that they realised it had not been me!

Well, that is typical of me, isn't it? I waffled off on a tangent again! I was talking about the 1996 job reorganisation: yet another example of my inability to convey my worth when it mattered. This reorganisation reduced the number of employees from around 21,000 to around 6,500, and productivity improved. Go figure. New engineering teams were formed, each made up of staff with the necessary skills to keep the electricity distribution system running. Each group was to have a team leader, answering to a single middle manager who, in turn, answered directly to the Executive Team. I applied to be a team leader, performed well at the all-day assessment we were sent on, and then totally fucked up my interview, as is normal for me. I was rescued by the young new boss of what was called the 'Cornwall 132kv & Projects Team,' also based at Pool, who offered me the position of clerical assistant in his team. Jim was 32, and he was a lovely guy. He sailed, too, albeit in a cruiser rather than a dinghy (as did one of the other engineers in his team), so that was a bonus.

The reorganisation included the closure of the Pool stores and was replaced with a 'just in time system' for the delivery of materials. All materials were now delivered from the suppliers to Exeter. Then an overnight articulated truck with a trailer transported all requested materials for the next day's work down to Bodmin and Pool depots. This arrangement was fine for the Mid and West Cornwall (Bodmin & Pool) lower voltage teams, but not for my new team that still had materials, including large transformers, delivered directly to Pool. This was an oversight by the bosses because there was now no stores staff available to unload them. Jim's answer to the problem? Send little old me on a course to learn to drive forklift trucks. I was now a clerical assistant, a forklift truck driver and a librarian (you would not believe the number of safety documents the electricity industry produced). It was not long before I was sent on another course so that I could be authorised to enter the 132 & 400kv (132,000 and 400,000 volts) substations. (As 50 volts is enough to kill you, I basically walked around these substations as I do down the china isles of department stores, i.e. keep your distance and don't touch a thing!) In those pre-digital days, each substation had its own library and various drawings on site. It became my job to visit every one of them (in Cornwall) to keep everything updated, and I then gained one more extra job.

On the Roseland Peninsula, there was (and probably still is) what was termed a pocket power station, though we all just called it the Roseland generator. This generator was powered by two Bristol Siddeley Proteus aircraft engines (the generators were run regularly at times of peak demand and when the area suffered power failures on the normal distribution system). They were operated remotely via telephone (by the Control Room engineer with whom I used to work). There were two large fuel tanks on site, and a Western Power (aka SWEB) staff member had to be on-site to oversee the refuelling of the tanks. In the brave new world, there were no spare distribution staff to do this, so it became my job (and a cushy little number it was too).

Judith:

While I went to Falmouth for the odd night out to relieve the stress, I think Phil threw himself into work as a means of survival. Amongst all the home mayhem, his work was being drastically reorganised, and he had to reapply for a job in the new setup. I think most people would have buckled under the pressure, but not Phil. He actively embraced the new challenges in his path, and it paid off. He liked being out of the office, and he was more relaxed because of it. Despite the Shaun chaos, life was settling down, and we were both learning to cope. I think Shaun's abnormal behaviour was becoming more the 'norm' to us, and I think an episode over Xmas shows how far we had come.

Antony had come home from university and was spending a night with us. He had a snotty nose and was sitting with a handkerchief doused in essential oils (Phil swears by them) over his nose to help him breathe. Shaun was lying on the floor in front of a roaring coal fire staring up the stairs at something only he could see.

Antony looked over at us whilst pulling a face and mouthed, 'What's he looking at?'

We shrugged our shoulders and said, 'Who knows?'

This sort of behaviour had become normalised to us, and we just used to ignore it. Shaun then turned to Antony and told him that a spaceship was coming to Gwithian on New Year's Eve. It was going to pick him and his dad up and take them to a new galaxy. Did Antony want to go with them? Poor Antony, I think it was his first experience of Shaun having a psychotic episode, but Phil and I never batted an eyelid.

Antony said, 'I think I'll give it a miss,' which I thought was a very good answer.

Philip

The closure of the Pool stores also affected the number of pallets available for me to take home. When materials were delivered directly to Pool, many of the pallets were non-returnable, and if people like me (and a few others) did not take them home, they were just broken up and thrown away. I used to use our 'A' framed boat trailer to take a load of twelve pallets home at a time, where they were stacked in the garden until I took a week's holiday in September. I spent this week dismantling the pallets: some were dismantled carefully as the timber could be used to build fences and store boxes, whilst others were just sawn up into pieces small enough to burn on the open fire. I started by borrowing a chainsaw from work, much to Jude's concern. However, as I spent more time sharpening the teeth and/or trying to get the thing to start, I soon invested in a handheld electrical circular saw, and I only once cut through the lead! We also had lots of friends of friends who offered us wood, cut down trees and offcuts, so poor old Eric suffered lots of punishment in his wood transportation duties.

'Eric, Eric, who the fuck is Eric?' you ask. Well, Eric was not a who but a what. The Daihatsu had died whilst on a trip up (North) to the funeral of one of Judy's brothers-in-law, who had died young following a heart attack. The replacement was a diesel Citroen BX estate, great for towing the boat and collecting trees, but he turned out to be incontinent. The BX had steering, suspension and brakes powered by a low-pressure hydraulic fluid system, and some of the pipes would come adrift alarmingly often, pissing fluid all over the road. Eric averaged mid-fifties MPG, but one could walk faster away from the traffic lights. He was French and cantankerous; therefore, we named him after our favourite footballer of the time, Eric Cantona.

Judith:

I had a picture of Eric Cantona on my wall at work, and every morning I used to give him a kiss, much to the amusement of everyone in the office. He was my hero (sorry, Phil) for a very long time. Before Shaun became ill, he was one of the main characters in Antony's film that he wrote, filmed and directed. Shaun stole the show with his Eric impersonation, as opposed to Phil and me, who were very wooden. The film Antony made is sadly the only film of Shaun pre-illness, and it's very bittersweet to watch. My handsome, articulate, engaging son, now no more. But this is a chapter focusing on a new start, with new beginnings.

Philip:

Our naturist friend, Jackie, used to live in an ex-holiday rental at Eastern Green, Penzance, with her daughter Kristy. When she met John and moved away, she rented out the flat via a local agency. Then one day, we received a call from her asking for a favour (she was now living in Spain). Her tenant had done a runner. Jackie had rowed with the agency and asked us if we could go and check out the flat and try to find another agent. Like the mugs we are, we agreed. The flat was in a terrible state, and I struggled to find anyone willing to clean it for us. Plus, there was only one agency that would take on rentals in the area – the one Jackie had fallen out with – therefore, I ended up doing both. Jackie did pay me for the cleaning work and my expenses for collecting the rent from the tenants I found. It was more dosh for the holiday fund.

In July of 1997, Jackie and John paid the UK and us a visit giving our hamlets net curtain twitchers something to gossip about. John arrived in a Dutch-registered Renault Megane, and Jackie and Carla came separately in a Spanish-registered Renault Kangoo. Telling the nosey parkers that they were a married couple just added to their confusion. We always remember this day because of the image of this tanned five-year-old with a head of stunning golden hair running up our drive and demanding a cuddle from Judy, even though we had never met. Hello Carla. We would, in time, become her godparents.

Judith:

What a delightful sunny child Carla was; the day they arrived was a breath of fresh air; it was so nice to have visitors. Since Shaun had become ill, visitors, particularly family, had disappeared into a puff of smoke. This visit was another tiny step into normality.

Philip:

Of course, there is another 1997 date etched in everyone's memories: 31st August. As per every Sunday morning, the first thing I did on getting up was to drive the three miles into Camborne to buy the Sunday papers (it was our nearest Sunday paper shop). Eric's radio was playing up. It was normally left on Radio 1, but solemn classical music was playing; in fact, it was playing on every station I tried. It was only on the way back that the music got interrupted by an announcer to state that all normal programmes had been suspended in respect of the death of Lady Diana. What?

During the winter of 1997, Jude's chef friend Vyv won a contract to provide pre-meeting meals for the local Masons, but could not do it on her own, so she and Judy made an agreement to do it together. Preparing meals for thirty-plus people is hard work, especially peeling veg. For the bigger events, I would take a flexi-day off work, spend the whole day peeling veg, and then help Jude and Vyv transport the food to the Masonic Hall, where I left them to it. It was a good earner and helped give us some socialising cash, but Vyv managed to fuck up yet another business, so the income went down again.

Judith:

In 1998 we experienced a moment of awe: meeting some of our sailing heroes. In 1989, whilst we were still living at Tolvaddon, Murdoch had launched his new-fangled Sky Satellite TV, and of course, we had to have it. In the early days, there were not many Sky channels, but one could buy a 'pirate box' to view non-Sky channels being broadcast from the Astra satellite, including Screensport. They showed lots of sailing, including the Sydney harbour 18-foot skiffs. To us, these boats were sensational; they were extremely powerful three-person trapezing boats that provided fantastic racing. We became hooked and watched every single programme. Then, in 1998, Phil came across an article in the local press giving the background for a forthcoming event in Falmouth: the Australian 18' skiffs were coming to Cornwall.

Wow! But were they the real thing? Phil struggled to find out, but in the meantime, he had an idea. Both his boss, Jim, and work colleague Chris, the engineer, had offered to take Phil and me out for a sail on their cruisers whenever we wanted. We wanted now, so he asked which of them fancied taking us out to watch the skiffs. Chris jumped at the chance to take us out for the Saturday of the weekend they were due to be in Falmouth. Chris's boat was kept on a mooring at Mylor, on what is called the Carrick Roads. Therefore, we had set out from home several hours before the event was due to start. It takes time to get to Mylor, paddle the tender from the shore out to the boat, and then prepare the boat before leaving the anchorage. Phew, everything is in the prep, as they say.

Philip:

It was a very wet, misty and windy day, quite miserable, in fact, but our spirits were soon lifted. As we were motoring along towards Falmouth and the open sea, we could hear music coming from Falmouth wharf and then …

And then I screamed, 'It's really them!' almost wetting myself with excitement. 'Look, look!' I said, pointing towards Falmouth wharf. 'That's Prudential's sail, and there's Ella Bache's; ooh and Southern Comforts.'

It looked like all the Australian boats we had been watching on TV were in Falmouth for us to watch in the flesh and from on the water. Fabulous! How lucky were we?

We made our way to the race course, on the open sea, just off Pendennis Point. Locating the 'windward mark' –where all the action takes place as the boats attempt to 'bear away' and hoist spinnakers – we dropped anchor. I did say to Chris that I thought he was a little too close to the mark because skiffs are difficult boats to 'bear away' in, but he was convinced he had left enough room, so it was brew-up and sandwich time.

One by one, the skiffs came out of the Carrick Roads and onto the course. As already stated, there was 'Ella Bache,' 'Prudential,' 'Country Comfort,' plus 'Xerox,' 'Oracle,' 'MSC,' 'DBS,' 'Old El Paso' and a new boat to us, 'The Times.' Having not gone to the launch wharf, we did not have a programme to know who was sailing The Times (the others we knew through watching them on TV). Whoever it was seemed out of their depth, as they kept capsizing even before the racing started. To be fair to the crews, it was blowing a hooley.

Judith:

The (Australian) Grand Prix skiff racing circuit was designed to turn sailing into a more spectator-friendly event; therefore, they held several short races on smallish courses close to land. They also had a helicopter filming the event (the UK events were being broadcast on Sky TV), and the crews took it in turns to wear 'helmet cams,' with our favourite helm being David 'bleep, bleep' Witt.

Philip:

All nine boats made the start of the first race and were soon closing in on us as we waited at the top mark. As the first boat approached and started to bear away, I could see that Chris was becoming a bit nervous. This increased when the second boat went quite far wide round the mark.

It was heading straight at us while attempting frantically to turn the boat to 'bear away' onto the next leg. Did I mention that an 18-foot skiff has a 12' aluminium pole protruding from its nose? I think Chris was having a nightmare about what damage that pole could do to his boat if it spiked us. I don't like to be the one that says, 'I told you so', and on this occasion, thankfully, I didn't have to. As soon as the last boat went past, we upped anchor and moved further away from the mark before the boats came round again. We watched all three races before making our way back to Mylor; Judy and I were as happy as sandboys. It had been a fabulous day, another wonderful memory.

Judith:

On Sunday, we went to watch them again, this time from the cliffs of Pendennis Point. Buying a programme, we learnt the name of the novice helming the, more often than not, upside-down boat, 'The Times.' Oh! It was no novice; in fact, it was the UK's most experienced sailor, none other than Lawrie Smith. And to think we called him an idiot yesterday – an idiot who didn't know what he was doing! There were only two races on this day, but strong winds provided another day of good racing.

We loved watching the skiffs so much that the following week we went to Fowey to watch them again, and the week after that, for the second day's racing on the Saturday in Torquay. In Torquay, we went into the boat park and were able to talk to all our 'heroes', telling them how much we loved watching them on TV. They were all lovely people, and we even got to help Rob Brown (the then-current 18' World champion) and his crew recover their boat, 'Prudential', from the water. The wind was light for the races at Torquay, and 'Witty' was wearing the head cam. There was lots of anger and bleeping (during the racing), and I seem to recall that he got disqualified from one race because of his behaviour. Does it say anything about us if we say that we loved Witty?

Philip:

Hanging around the boat park, we learnt there was going to be a presentation shortly inside the Royal Torbay Yacht Club.

'Could we?'

'Of course we could,' said Judy.

We located the Yacht Club just as Lawrie Smith's party was crossing the road to enter the building.

'Follow me,' hissed Judy.

As we climbed the steps behind Lawrie, a doorman asked Judy who she was with.

She calmly replied, 'Mount's Bay Sailing Club,' and he let us in.

It was the first time in my life that I had gate-crashed anything. We spent a nice couple of hours talking again to our heroes, drinking free bubbles and eating free nibbles. We clapped loudly when Rob and his crew accepted their prize, being the winners of the regatta. Then it was back to Cornwall and the drudgery of life.

Judith:

I never thought we would get the opportunity to see the skiffs and the sailors in the flesh. I had watched them on TV for years, and it was like a dream come true. Thank god I lived in Cornwall, the right place at the right time. For once in our lives, the sailing gods were definitely on our side. Australia to Falmouth, just for us, or so it seemed. I never expected that, and with our financial situation, I didn't see a visit to Australia happening anytime soon. However, in my dreams, I wanted to go and live in Double Bay (Sydney Harbour), the home of the '18-foot skiffs.' Every girl needs dreams; it's another means of escaping reality, and it was beginning to work for me. Baby steps.

Chapter 16

Stoicism

Judith:

Although I told myself I was doing better with the emotional turmoil, deep down, I knew I was really kidding myself. I desperately tried to engage in 'normal' life, and outsiders looking in probably thought I had succeeded. I had just learnt to disguise my pain, despair and internal sadness. Simple things could and did trigger intense sadness; friends just talking about their children was hard to listen to; their world was okay when mine felt destroyed. Yes, I did feel sorry for myself; selfish maybe, but who knows how you will feel until something happens that rocks your world? It makes you question who you are, and I actually didn't know who I was anymore. I think there's a saying, 'You are only as happy as your saddest child'; well, I was sad, very sad. Yes, I was making baby steps, but sometimes it was one foot forward and two steps back. Without Phil by my side, I don't think I could have carried such a burden. I owed him my life, but more than that, I owed it to both of us to get through the darkness; we deserved to be happy together, which meant I had to try harder. Maybe I couldn't change the path Shaun was on, but I could change the path Phil and I were on. I just needed to find the key to the door, open it, and step into the light. I needed to learn how to endure the pain without displaying my feelings and without complaint, which is actually the definition of stoicism, the title of this chapter.

Philip:

I think we had become desensitised to Shaun's behaviour. He was living in his own world, and his actions were often bizarre. We could come downstairs in the morning, and notice ornaments had been moved. As one of us would go to return them to their correct spot, Shaun, if he was there, would scream at us not to touch them as he collapsed on the floor holding his stomach.

'If you move them, I will die!' he would say.

So we would leave them where he had moved them, at least until he went out, and then we would put them back into their proper place – he never noticed.

One day, I returned home from work to see flames shooting out of our chimney; Shaun was burning everything made from paper that he could find in the house: the voices had told him his life depended upon it. Another morning, I got up to go to work and, opening the drive gate, I was presented with all the possessions from Shaun's bedroom littering the front garden, and his bedroom window was wide open. He was nowhere to be seen. Again, the voices had told him to do it. On yet another day, when we got up, the kitchen door was wide open, and Shaun was again missing. When he returned home, he calmly stated that he had been out delivering his writings to his disciples, as if it was quite normal.

For many months, he would often just double up with pain while standing talking to us, and he would say it was Kurt. He told us he was looking after Kurt Cobain's spirit until it could find a new home. When Shaun bought a copy of Oasis' '(What's the Story) Morning Glory?' CD and then lay in bed with the track 'Wonderwall' playing on repeat for hours on end; it was the straw that broke the camel's back. I could take no more. I lost it and told him I'd kill him if he didn't stop playing it, at least while we were in. It was not one of my proudest moments, especially the irony of threatening to kill someone who was constantly threatening to kill themselves.

Shaun would alternate between psychotic (manic) episodes and long bouts of severe depression, during which he threatened suicide on many occasions. Judy returned home from work one day to find him holding a large kitchen knife to his throat. On another occasion, he had a gun (which turned out to be a toy) that he pointed at his head when we entered his bedroom. The morning after this incident, at work, while I was delivering the post around the office, Jim (my soon-to-be new boss) asked me how I was and how things were at home (he knew about Shaun's situation).

'Fine,' I said (why do we say this, because we never mean it?) before adding, 'Shaun was sitting up in bed when we got home last night, pointing a gun to his head.'

His face was a picture, as was the engineers who

was sitting alongside him. Shrugging my shoulders, I continued on my rounds: there was nothing more to say.

Judith:

After his first sectioning and a period of sustained anti-psychotic medication, somehow, Shaun did eventually return to the world of the living, and he decided he wanted to make a new start in Lincoln. He had Cornish friends who lived there, so we bought him his train ticket and helped him to move. To be honest, I would have taken him anywhere he wanted to go; I just wanted some happiness for him, whether it be a week, a month, a year or a lifetime. Like me, he was no longer the person he was prior to his illness. Yes, he was still kind, sensitive and caring, but he had lost his swagger like I had lost my *joie de vivre*.

The quote 'Out of sight out of mind' works as long as you factor in that your first waking thought is of him. Then there are triggers in the day where you wonder if he is okay, and obviously, you say a prayer before you go to sleep, asking God to keep him safe, even though you are not religious: bizarre. So it's not that you don't think about them, more the fact that it's not in your face 24/7, enabling you to have moments when you forget the situation. Having said that, personally, I was never the same happy-go-lucky person as I had been. A part of me had gone missing forever: would that ever change?

What we needed was a holiday – our first in four years. So, despite the desperate state of our finances, we booked a week of winter sun. We had never done a winter holiday, ever, and the cheapest week we could find was the 17th to 24th December, which actually worked well as Phil's birthday was the 18th. Antony was still at Farnborough University (in shared digs), so the plan was to take Xmas to him when we landed at Bristol on Christmas Eve and for Shaun to catch the train down from Lincoln to Farnborough.

It didn't start well. It never snows in Cornwall, but on the 16th, it did, so the decision was made to leg it out of the county ASAP. We hadn't had a holiday for several years, and I was not going to be beaten by the bloody weather.

Philip:

Fate can be cruel. The day before we were due to fly out (from Bristol) on our holiday, I had to attend a meeting with Jim (my boss) in Taunton (a two-hour drive from the Pool depot and just a fifty-minute drive from Bristol airport!). On the return journey, as we were approaching Exeter, it started to snow. By the time we reached Okehampton, it was snowing heavily, only easing as we passed Bodmin. Arriving home, I said to Judy that I thought we needed to get ready and try to get to Bristol as soon as we could because there was a chance Cornwall would be cut off by snow overnight. The radio was forecasting heavy snow in Cornwall after midnight. Our original plan had been to leave at 2 am as our flight was not until 7 am, but we left immediately after having tea.

Judith:

We got to Taunton services at about 10 pm, and it was freezing, with a strong bitter wind blowing. It was hoods up and heads down to battle our way across the bridge for a hot drink (only the Southbound side was open). As we left the services, we decided to top up the fuel to save us a job upon our return: not a chance, the fuel cap was frozen solid. The only positive was that all the Xmas food in the boot certainly would not go off whilst we were away. By the time we got to Bristol airport, it had been snowing steadily for several hours, and it was very definitely settling, but we were there: an overnight stay in the airport lounge was fine.

We woke up to a winter wonderland airport view, and the news was that Cornwall was indeed cut off by snow – thank god we had left when we had. As we boarded the plane, I was a bit concerned to see a man standing on the engine with a (de-icing) spray gun. As we waited in our seats, more vehicles arrived and started spraying the wings of the plane. The captain then announced there was a delay as the runway was being treated with de-icer, and if he got the okay from the control tower, we had one attempt only to take off. It was like the films but in reverse. The captain did get the go-ahead to attempt a takeoff, and as we waited at the end of the runway, he gunned the engines before releasing the brakes. We shot down the runway, and as we majestically lifted off through thick clouds and into beautiful blue skies, the whole plane clapped and cheered. He was my hero. It transpired we were one of only three planes to take off that day, with none landing; the holiday gods were in our favour.

We landed in Fuerteventura in glorious sunshine; why had we never done this before? By day four, I was convinced in my head it was still summer, ice and snow all forgotten. I could feel myself relax for the first time since Shaun's illness, but all too soon, it was time to return home. I needed longer, much longer. I didn't want to get on that plane; I wanted to stay there forever. I wanted to run away from life and live in a happy-ever-after bubble.

Philip:

Why, indeed, had we not had a winter holiday before? On the first morning, we did something we never do: attend the briefing by the holiday rep. It was the first and last time we set eyes upon her. She had nothing to offer us, and for the rest of the holiday, we were leaving the site in the dark at around 8:30 am for the 25-minute walk to the beach, by which time it was light. Being on the island of wind and having done my research, we were always early enough to find an empty 'bunker' that protected us from the wind. Since it was winter, the days were short, so by 4 pm, we were heading back to the apartment in fading light. I sometimes had a dip in the pool, but it was unheated and, therefore, 'quite refreshing.' It was not until our last night, as we explored the bar of the adjacent (German-owned) complex that we discovered they had a heated pool we could have sneaked in and used. *C'est la vie*. For four days, we did nothing but sleep all day long; we were that exhausted, and we just read, swam and sunbathed for the rest of the time.

Judith:

But what you want and what you get are two very different things, so as I got on that plane, my bubble popped and reality set in. The snow and ice had gone, and by some miracle, Shaun had arrived safely at Antony's (sometimes you forget that madness doesn't mean stupidity). The Christmas food was in our car boot, and all was Zen. Well, not quite, as the house that Antony shared with five other students was pretty filthy. Your shoes stuck to the kitchen floor, and I would rather not mention the loo/shower. Fortunately, Phil's OCD to clean up kicked in, which left the boys and me free to hit the alcohol. We stayed up most of the night, playing music and chatting. I remember the song 'The Drugs Don't Work' (by the Verve) being played over and over again. I talked openly to Shaun about his illness, how the medication worked, and that he could have a normal life. At that time, I truly believed that with support and love, and despite the trauma we had been through, as a family, we could conquer the illness and come through the other side. I think that was probably the last time we were all on the same page and united with proper love, affection and hope as a family.

It was no surprise when Shaun declared he was

returning to Cornwall with us; Lincoln hadn't worked out. His mental health had deteriorated, and the roundabout was about to start turning again, only this time it became even faster because street drugs had joined the mix. The days turned into weeks and months, and Shaun was now self-medicating on street drugs – a recipe for disaster. We couldn't keep him locked up in the house, and he would just take off. I don't know what was worse: him being home and off his head, or not knowing whether he was alive or dead. That's how bad it was.

I remember a friend of his fetching him home one day. It was his birthday, and Phil was at work, so we sat in the kitchen together. Shaun was talking to himself and the kitchen wall. I had never felt so sad in my entire life, and the day is etched in my memory forever. To be totally honest, if I hadn't had Phil by my side, I know for a fact that I would have put Shaun in the car with me and driven us both off the cliffs at Hell's Mouth. Death was preferable to life for me that day. I have never disclosed this thought to anyone, ever.

Philip:

Jesus. She is not kidding. I know that writing this book has been cathartic for both of us, but it was only when I read Judy's draft for this chapter that I learnt exactly how she had felt that day. It had never been discussed before, and after the revelation, an evening of tears, alcohol and much discussion continued into the early hours. It left both of us as emotional wrecks, but still with no answers.

Judith:

On a lighter note, there were occasions when if you didn't laugh, you would cry. One evening we went to Plymouth to watch Blood Brothers at the theatre – a musical by Willy Russell. I didn't know the story, but it moved me beyond belief. We were sitting having an after-show cuppa in the theatre's cafe, discussing the show with a couple of strangers, when my phone rang. It was Antony. He said he had received a call from someone who knew Shaun to say he was at a nightclub in Redruth acting bizarrely. We cut short our chat with the strangers and made the ninety-minute drive to the club, parking up outside the entrance, hoping to spot Shaun when he left. I was on the ciggies, Phil was on the wine gums, it was raining, and the wipers were on intermittently so we could see. I have no idea how long we waited, but as Phil popped the last wine gum in his mouth, he crumpled up the empty packet and lobbed it over his head into the back seat.

He then said, 'What the fuck am I going to do now?'

We just laughed and laughed. The reason for being at the club wasn't funny, but the pressure release valve had blown - it's how we dealt with stressful situations, and no, Shaun didn't appear, so we left and went home.

Philip:

Then there was the time when Shaun's medication appeared to be keeping him stable and quite compos mentis, that he offered to help do some gardening whilst we were at work. A good sign, we thought. When I returned from work, I enquired with Judy if Shaun had kept his promise.

She replied, 'Oh yes, I came home to find twelve cannabis plants planted in the veg patch.'

Judith:

One time we certainly didn't laugh was the night we took Shaun to the Mental Health unit at Redruth. He was in a really bad way; he had been missing for days and was off the scale of psychotic. We sat in the waiting room for hours until 'the professionals' called us in, by which time it was 11 pm. I voiced my concerns, and they spoke to Shaun, who was talking utter gibberish; you would have got more sense out of a two-year-old. They asked us to leave whilst they discussed the matter, and when they called us back in, they told me he wouldn't be admitted for treatment. I was very calm, and I told them that Shaun was a threat to himself and that I was leaving him there, regardless of their decision. The consultant asked me if I was blackmailing him, I told him that was up to him to decide, but I was leaving without Shaun. I said that if anything should happen to Shaun and he lost his life, I would sue the hospital and him. With that, I got up, gave Shaun a kiss, told him I loved him and would see him soon and left.

The next day, I rang for an update, and they refused to speak to me, so I had no idea if he had been admitted for treatment or thrown out onto the street.

Philip:

During his last time under section, Shaun had been told that he could voluntarily present himself for admission at any time. However, as Judy has described above, on this occasion, the hospital was proving this promise to be a falsehood. The following day we discovered that they had admitted him to the psychiatric unit at Bodmin, later transferring him back to Trengweath when a bed became available.

We visited Shaun frequently during his multiple stays in Trengweath. At one point, I wrote a letter of complaint to some top dog in the Cornish NHS (it's so long ago I cannot remember whom), and I got an invite to attend a meeting with said person for my troubles. My main concern had been that Trengweath was a 'secure' unit, but on many occasions, we were able to just walk through unlocked doors and up to Shaun's bedroom or into the community room without challenge. Conversely, it was just as easy for patients to walk out of the unit. From their point of view, it was my responsibility to inform a member of staff that we were in attendance. They did not seem to get my point that I should not have been able to get through the doors in the first place!

On one of these visits, we noticed that Shaun had plastered loads of A3 sheets of his 'writings' – he was constantly writing pages, often gibberish – all over the walls of his bedroom. Upon reading them, it became obvious that he was putting all his troubles into words. They started and ended with the stunning blonde, his girlfriend who had been the love of his life: the reason he had gone to Amsterdam to earn money for their future. At the next 'care meeting' (something else I had demanded as our right under the Mental Health Act), I asked the consultant if he, or any of his staff, had read these writings. The answer was no, and he seemed put out when I told him that if he bothered to do so, he might have a better understanding of the reasons behind Shaun's state of mind. It is my understanding that he never did read them. This was the same consultant that, during a previous meeting, I was very frustrated with at the apparent lack of help being given to Shaun. I told him that if I had the power to write prescriptions, I could do a better job than him of looking after Shaun.

Judith:

This was just one story of numerous exchanges we had with Cornwall's mental health authority. We fought so hard to get Shaun the help he needed that it was debilitating both physically and mentally. Phil, being Phil, did a lot of research on schizophrenia, and he discovered that Cornwall had the worst mental health service in the UK; our backs were very definitely against the wall. I never gave up, though, and Phil was amazingly supportive; both Shaun and I owe our lives to him – I'm not sure I would have survived without him by my side. Mental health was very much a taboo subject then, and neither family nor friends ever asked me the most important question: 'Is there anything I can do to help?'

Philip:

It's a very sad, depressing world when the only person who ever asked this question, and showed any empathy towards Judy, was our car mechanic, Dave (sadly now deceased). Like many people Judy encountered, he obviously fancied her, but he genuinely cared and frequently helped us out on the few occasions when we did reach out for help. Most of our family and friends just stuck their heads in the sand and totally avoided the issue. I cannot tell you how much pain this caused Judy.

Yes, me being the OCD Sagittarian that I am, I read anything I could lay my hands on in an attempt to understand what we were dealing with and to try and help us, especially Judy, to deal with the situation. She needed as much help and support as Shaun did. I also attended many support groups (Judy could not face them) in the search for help and information. In most of the groups, I was the only male there. It seemed that it was quite the norm for fathers to run away from mental illness, leaving their wives to deal with the issues affecting their children on their own. I was a bit unique, as Shaun was not my son, and I was, therefore, in theory, emotionally unattached. Yes, I did try to help Shaun, but my main concern was and still is Judy's health and well-being.

Judith:

Poor Phil; he must have been born under a very unlucky star to have ended up with me and Shaun. Thank god he dug in and always had my back; I'm a lucky girl.

Philip:

Some of the meetings I attended were very interesting; one on nutrition is prominent in my memory. Another was a presentation by a medical scientist involved in the research of mental health medicines. She was very articulate and had great empathy with clients and the issues they faced with taking these strong medicines. Many medications had strong side effects that, in turn, required another medicine to be taken to counter the side effects. During coffee after the meeting, it turned out that virtually all of the attendees were clients: yet again, I was an outsider. But, and it is a magnificent 'big but,' they were all talking about the latest episode of some TV programme and asked me if I had watched it. I had not. I had to go home and tell Judy that a bunch of psychiatric patients had told me to watch 'Taking Over the Asylum,' a series about a Scottish psychiatric unit. I readily admit it was a good recommendation. The programme was very funny, and the cast included Ken Stott and David Tenant in his first break on TV (though we first remember David from Casanova, a 2005 TV series).

Judith:

On a lighter note, I can confirm that being on a psychiatric ward is like the film 'One Flew Over the Cuckoo's Nest.' Distinguishing staff from clients is quite difficult unless they are in a white paper overall, having tried to commit suicide in the sea at Penzance. Clients escape on a regular basis. (Shaun's record is fifteen minutes from being admitted; he had again asked to go outside for a cigarette, then legged it, but only after having kicked in the headlights of a BMW in the car park he thought belonged to a staff member.) Clients try to persuade you to fetch them in contraband, and obviously, being in mixed wards means they generate unhealthy relationships. In our case, this meant you sort of end up with a 'bog off' (buy one, get one free) situation where, instead of coping with one ill son, you end up with their psychotic girlfriend as well.

Philip:

During one stay in Trengweath, Shaun had got it together with a lass called Linda, who had her own flat in Redruth, and upon release, he moved in with her. Again, we tried to help support both of them as best we could. For example, Linda had a shit load of tablets to take each day and said she got very confused by it all. Judy devised a box divided into seven sections and each section into three. In each, she wrote a label stating what tablet(s) to take. It was a simple, logical solution and, to us, just another example of how the mental health services were not helping their patients.

I mention Linda because we had bought a new stereo system, and I gave my old one to Shaun and Linda. Their relationship, inevitably, broke down. Shaun ended up back in the psych ward but again 'escaped,' this time ending up at ours, refusing to return. We thought Linda might be able to help persuade him, so I trotted off over to hers to ask her if she would come back with me. When she answered the door, I got a load of verbal abuse, including a statement along the lines of, 'You're not getting your stereo back; you gave it to us, and it's mine now.' After I explained that I wasn't there for the stereo and I was happy for her to keep it, she calmed down and agreed to return home with me.

The idea had been a good one, but it didn't work out as hoped. Linda and Shaun had a fully-blown handbags-at-dawn argument, and we just about managed to stop them from throwing things at each other whilst I stood guard over the knife drawer: yes, it was getting way out of hand. Linda eventually stormed off, and Judy suggested I go after her in the car to take her home as it was a six-mile walk to hers, and we knew she had no money on her. I caught up with her about a mile down the road and drove past her before pulling over and getting out to offer her a lift. She said she didn't want 'a fucking lift,' wished she had never met 'fucking Shaun,' and kicked Eric (our car) before storming off down the road. I returned home with a dented Eric to find that Shaun had also taken off.

What a mess.

Judith:

There are no words, really, to describe what it's truly like to watch your son destroy himself. However, I know 'hope' is the worst word you can use because, eventually, there is no hope. Actually, there never was any, but it takes you years to realise that.

Then sometime over this period of madness, Shaun stopped coming home, and friends stopped fetching him home. He vanished from our life and theirs. He was twenty-nine, a drug addict, schizophrenic and an adult who had lost his way. I was forty-five and an adult who didn't know what to do, so rightly or wrongly, I did nothing. I remember Phil and I going to Truro one day. We went inside the Cathedral to have a look around: for whatever reason, we had never played tourist and done that. It was majestic and very calming inside; people were lighting candles and saying prayers. I felt an overwhelming need to light one for Shaun, and with tears running down my face, I asked God to keep him safe, and if he couldn't keep him safe, to let him go.

Life was never going to return to normal, so we had to create a new normal. For me, that meant only allowing myself to think about my lost son for five minutes every day. Then I had to put that thought in a box, close the lid and not open it again until the next day, so that's what I did. A four-year chapter had temporarily ended, and I needed to start a new chapter of my life somehow.

I found it very hard to re-adjust. In a bizarre way, having lived life on the edge for so long, life actually seemed quite repetitive and boring, sometimes even dull. I had been forced to move jobs and now worked in an office for a local wine importer: good subject matter, but bitchy women. Our social life had dwindled, places had closed, people we knew had moved on, and I was still struggling to get my sparkle back. The best news was that Antony had got his degree; I was so pleased and proud of him. He was the first person in my family that had ever gone to university and obtained a degree. Like many young people from Cornwall, he never returned to work in the county as he found a position near Farnborough. I only recently found out via a family member that at that time of his life, he didn't feel he had a home and thought my only focus in life was Shaun. Perhaps he was right, but being a parent doesn't come with a manual. I didn't know it at the time, but somehow, along life's road, I had managed to lose not one but two sons.

Philip:

Stress was taking its toll. We were both exhausted and drinking too much. Money was an issue again, and sometimes we got irritable with each other, not deliberately because neither of us like confrontation, and we normally went out of our way to avoid it. Still, our life spirit had been chipped away, a little bit each day, until sometimes, the safety valve needed to blow.

Judy started suffering very heavy periods, often

accompanied by severe stomach and back pain. We both dislike going to the doctor, but the pain got so bad there was no choice. (Uterine) Polyps were suspected, and Judy was referred to a specialist who arranged for a 'D&C' (dilation and curettage) operation to be carried out. This is an invasive operation where the contents of the uterus are removed. The specialist even talked about a partial or full hysterectomy. Oh shit, further trips to the library: one needs knowledge to make decisions. The facts became obvious; avoid any form of hysterectomy at any cost. There were even suggestions that the D&C operation was not needed and was an operation from a barbaric era.

The operation went ahead, and when I collected Judy to take her home, she was very weak. For a couple of days, she did not have the strength to get out of bed, which meant lots of visits up the stairs to ensure she was okay. Unfortunately, this was an occasion that I failed her. It was the height of summer and very hot, too hot to stay inside, so I kept busy outside, thus not being able to hear her if she called out. One job I decided to do was to weed her borders. I have never been allowed to weed again; all the pretty flowers I left in situ turned out to be weeds, and yes, you guessed it, all the weeds I pulled up were flowers.

Before moving on with our story, I will take time out to ask, 'Want a story about handling expectations?' Cornwall was buzzing in 1999, leading up to the total eclipse of the sun that was due on August 11th. It was the main subject of local and national news for seven months (and like with Brexit, one gets bored of it). Apparently, Cornwall was the best place in the UK to view the eclipse, and it seemed like the whole world, including Patrick Moore, descended upon us. Western Power and Cornwall Highways had agreed to turn off the power to vast sways of street lights to ensure they would not come on when the eclipse occurred (they automatically turn on when it gets dark). The excitement was huge, the hype even more so, and at 11 am, we were standing out on the road outside work, waiting expectantly.

Unfortunately, there was a problem: the weather. There was heavy cloud cover which meant one could not see the sun. Those that stayed in the office saw more on TV because aeroplanes and helicopters were broadcasting live images above the cloud cover. In the end, Cornwall turned out not to be the place to watch the eclipse. However, I must state that even without being able to see the moon cross the sun, a line of darkness could be seen making its way across the sky and land, and as it approached us, it went eerily silent as the darkness enveloped us. It was all over in a few minutes, and then it was back to work. A bit of a non-event? Sadly, yes.

Judith:

For me, the eclipse was very surreal. Like Phil, I was at work, and we relocated to the car park to witness the event. As the darkness came, the birds stopped singing; it made the hairs on my neck stand up. I found it quite a spiritual experience, and it made me wonder what people thought of it hundreds of years ago. Did they think the end of the world had come? Was it a sign from their gods? Were they scared or excited? I think if I hadn't got the knowledge, I probably would have been very afraid. Nature is such a powerful force; I felt very fortunate to experience the eclipse in Cornwall - the land of sea, wind and wonder. I felt an internal peace and quiet during the event and hoped it was a sign of better things to come (I need to stop using the 'hope' word: such a useless, negative verb).

Chapter 17

Heads or Tails

Judith:

With Shaun gone from our lives (the rumour was he had gone to Plymouth), you would have thought things would improve, but initially, they didn't. I was still struggling to live in the present without being overwhelmed by the thoughts and feelings of the past four years. I still couldn't speak to anyone, even Phil, about how I felt emotionally, as I found it way too distressing. I was very tired, sleep eluded me on many nights, and I was still anxious and worried. '*What sort of state was Shaun in? Was he even alive?*'

I had lots of questions in my head, but no answers, and the guilt I felt was overwhelming at times. I think my biggest mistake was to keep on carrying on as if nothing had happened. I should have taken some 'me time' to process what had happened and come to terms with the changes. I should have opened up more and asked for help, but being me, I didn't. A lifetime of pretending everything is alright (even when it isn't) is a hard habit to break.

We were now in the new 'normal' phase, whatever the hell that meant. Nothing was normal to me anymore;

everything had changed from when Phil and I first met. Apart from losing Shaun, we had lost friends, family, our home, the dogs, and various naturist venues had closed; we were too old to play volleyball, and, being very physical, sailing was becoming harder. What a bloody mess! For once in my life, I had no idea what to do next and no idea how to recover, rebuild or move on in a positive way.

Philip:

At the time, I was unaware of Judy's true feelings. She was trying to protect me, but in doing so, she was causing herself too much pain. Unfortunately and regretfully, I was oblivious, but despite all the travails, our relationship was still solid, and our love for each other was stronger than ever. However, our life had become dull, depressing even. Where once I had enjoyed going to work, it had now become a chore, and Judy was working at a place full of arseholes. Both of us were going through the motions for money, and neither of us could see a way out. The highlight of our social calendar was the ability to make a fiver last a night at the Penmare Hotel in Hayle. They used to have local musicians performing on a Saturday night, and we would nurse a single drink watching them. We had very definitely got ourselves into a rut, and it was proving difficult to see a way out.

Judith:

Time, however, was not on my side. Unbeknown to me, fate had something else up its sleeve. My parents had both divorced and remarried when I was in my teens (surprisingly, I never got the wedding invites; they must have got lost in the post!). My dad had a son (who was three months younger than Shaun) with his new wife, who was a lot younger than him. Out of the blue, he rang me in tears to say his wife had left him. Apparently, the son had passed his PhD - the highest level of academic qualification you can achieve - so 'Her job was done,' and 'She was moving in with a new man.' What a bombshell! By the time I drove from Cornwall to Cheshire, she had the estate agent at the house in order to get it sold.

My dad was sixty-nine, and they had been married for thirty years. He really struggled to come to terms with the situation and wasn't coping at all. I spoke to him every day on the phone, and Phil and I ended up travelling to and fro, from Cornwall up to Cheshire, on a regular basis; it nearly killed us. My dad had retired from work with ill health at fifty, and this situation was pushing him over the edge. I managed to stop any immediate house sale and level off the financial issues, but that didn't stop him from posting a jiffy bag of grass to his ex-wife: his protest regarding who was going to cut the grass.

'*Do I attract madness or what?*' Something had to give. I know life had become a little dull, but I needed this like a hole in the head. Here I was again, out of the frying pan and into the fire. I never expected to be assisting in divorce number two, but for the second time in my life, I unwittingly got the job. Surely parents are supposed to assist their offspring, not the other way round.

Philip:

Driving up to Cheshire every three weeks was such fun; not. Work all week, drive 320 miles on a Friday night, be a therapist for 36 hours, then drive another 320 miles back to Cornwall on a Sunday night, and be bright-eyed and bushy-tailed at work the following morning. Or the same morning, depending upon what time we got home. Travelling back from Cheshire on a Sunday was a nightmare. We tried leaving at midday, two o'clock, three o'clock, four o'clock, five o'clock, six o'clock and seven o'clock. It made no difference; we always got caught in traffic jams. It didn't help that there were three sets of extensive long-term roadworks on the M6 between Knutsford and Birmingham. On a good day, it took six hours to get home, and by trial and error, we discovered that the quickest way to get home was to leave after 8 pm (meaning it would be at least 2 am when we got home, but it was a far more relaxing drive than being stuck in jams).

We became so laid back about the journeys that we still talk about the time, like the earlier wine gum incident, when we got caught in a Friday night jam (on the way up) just before the M5 joined the M6 at Birmingham. We moved ten feet in two hours and were totally non-perplexed by the delay, just chatting away with rain pelting down outside. We were so chilled, it was untrue.

Judith:

I was on auto-pilot; work, plus trips up and down to Cheshire, were mentally, financially and physically killing me. I asked my sister and stepbrother if they would step in and visit dad on a monthly basis, but for whatever reason, this didn't materialise.

'Ask for help,' they would say.

'Don't waste your breath,' would be my reply; very negative, I know, but at the time, I felt bloody negative, as well as exhausted and emotionally drained.

I rang my dad every day to see how he was coping, but his world had collapsed; I think it was worse than if his wife had died. I felt so sorry for him; he had no idea the wife was having an affair, let alone planning to move in with her new man. Watching my dad cry was something I had never ever seen, and my heart broke for him. Now I had two people to worry about; Shaun, who I couldn't help, and my dad, who maybe I could help. I had forgotten about myself, who probably needed the most help.

Philip:

In the autumn of 1999, work started another reorganising process (a phrase that I think just meant they were reducing worker numbers again). Yet again, there were some redundancy packages available, with the caveat that your role had to be taken over by someone who was being redeployed, i.e. their job role had disappeared.

As the majority of redundancies were at the accounting office in Plymouth, it was difficult to imagine someone from there wanting to become an engineering clerical assistant sixty-odd miles away in Redruth. However, I did apply for my 'figures,' there being no obligation. My figures showed that I would be entitled to a reasonable cash payout, and I would be able to draw my pension at age fifty. The problem would be that I would have to find another job. Employment with similar pay and conditions to those I was enjoying at SWEB did not exist (in West Cornwall), so we sort of put it to one side, even though we were rather disillusioned with life at that time.

Judith:

Although put on the back burner, the potential to take early redundancy probably altered everything. I think we both knew we were at a major crossroads in our lives and needed a change of direction. Despite all the trauma, we still loved the bones of each other and Cornwall. What we should have done was take time out (gone on a bloody holiday), discuss what we had lost, and come up with a workable plan for a happy future, but we didn't.

The timing of my dad's crisis, following the Shaun trauma, couldn't have happened at a worse time for any of us. In my exhausted state, all I wanted to do was run away and hide where no one could find me. I think I thought that if I ran away, I would be able to forget; I didn't know at the time that you can never forget. The only thing I did know was that the only person I wanted to run away with was Phil.

Philip:

One option offered by Judy was, 'What if we moved to Cheshire? We could move in with my dad and sort him out, and it would give us the chance to sort ourselves out.' It was an idea we had not previously thought of. When looking at how to change our lives, both of us had made the assumption that we would just remain in Cornwall and 'carry on regardless.'

The other option was to stop being so 'risk averse'; just take the redundancy and go with the flow. At least with this option, we would have some cash in the bank and breathing space to weigh up our work-life balance.

However, the seeds were sown, and after another late night of discussion, we decided that 'Step 1' was to apply for the redundancy package. It was a last-minute decision and entailed me spending all Friday morning at work filling in the necessary forms and then faxing them off to HQ in Bristol in order to make the midday deadline. It was now a waiting game.

As expected, my request for redundancy was declined, but, along with many others, I was put into an 'under review pool.' Final decisions would be made before the end of January. 'Would this be our last Christmas in Cornwall?' We still had no bloody idea what the year 2000 would hold; we were still reeling from 1999.

Judith:

I needed Christmas like a hole in the head. It would be our fourth Christmas at Wall, where every Christmas with Shaun had been disastrous. Somehow all the lovely Christmas memories prior to his illness had been blown away in a puff of smoke. I needed to get my act together. My dad was facing his first Christmas on his own, there were no offers from my sister or step brother to have him over, so of course, we stepped in (don't we always?).

I took the train to Cheshire and then drove him and his two rescue dogs back down to Cornwall for a two-week break. I was hoping a change of scenery would do him good; however, the Cornish weather didn't play ball, and it never stopped raining. One of his dogs ran away one day (see, the dog could do it, why couldn't I?), and he nearly had a heart attack. Other than that, we did actually have a lovely time; we binged on boxes of Quality Street in front of the roaring coal fire, I made sure he ate well, and our snug little cottage did what it did best, wrapping its arms around us all. Hopefully, it was a tiny step on my dad's road to recovery. A bit of kindness and support goes a long way in life: if only some would come my way occasionally.

Philip:

It seems quite funny now, looking back on the events of 1999. The world had been panicking that all computers were going to stop working at midnight on New Year's

Eve, and chaos would ensue. Like Brexit, it was always on the news, and the subject became very boring – also like Brexit. In the end, absolutely nothing happened, but so many experts had been convinced that 'the end was nigh' that the majority also believed it would. Hey-ho! All I remember New Year's Eve for was the fact that it stopped raining enough to let us take Jude's dad down to see the Mousehole harbour lights.

It was the last day of his two-week holiday with us, and it had rained non-stop the whole time; I think every man and his dog were at Mousehole that night to see the lights. It is such a picturesque village, full of old-world charm. Local cottages made of Lamorna granite huddle together around the inner edge of the harbour, and the Christmas lights on the water are very pretty. They get switched on in the middle of December and remain on until the end of the first week of the New Year. They are lit from 5 pm to 11 pm every day, except for one hour. On the anniversary of the 'Penlee lifeboat tragedy,' they are turned off as a mark of respect to the eight crew who died whilst trying to rescue the crew of the 'Union Star' off Lamorna cove on the 19th December 1981. Another date etched in my memory, never to be forgotten.

On a lighter note, The Mousehole Cat is a **children's book** written by Antonia Barber and illustrated by Nicola Bayley. It is based on the legend of Cornish fisherman Tom Bawcock and the stargazy pie; it tells the tale of a cat who goes with its owner on a fishing expedition in rough and stormy seas.

Judith:

Well, somehow, we survived Christmas. My dad was still very lonely and distraught with his life, as he didn't know what the future held. What he didn't know was that Phil and I had no idea what our future held, either. We had done the right thing in having Dad with us for Christmas, and as unexpectedly nice as it was, we had not been able to chat in private about how we were both feeling and what we both wanted going forward. There was no doubt my dad seriously needed me close by. I felt eaten up by guilt that I hadn't saved Shaun: how would I feel if I failed my dad as well? How could I ever forgive myself? On the other side of the coin, Phil and I had been through so much; was it time to spread our wings and fly away, or just stay, give ourselves time to adjust and reboot? As long as we were together, did anything else really matter in the grand scheme of life? I had no idea, I wanted to both run away and stay, but if the redundancy came through, a decision would have to be made; we certainly couldn't stand still.

'Cornwall had been my dream, and I had lived my dream; was it time to give that dream up? Could I give that dream up?'

Philip:

For once in our lives, we were struggling to make a decision, but eventually, we made one; a coin would be used.

'Heads we stay; tails we go,' I said to Judith as I tossed the coin high into the air.